The Wee Ice Mon Cometh

The Wee Ice Mon Cometh

Ben Hogan's 1953 Triple Slam and One of Golf's Greatest Summers

ED GRUVER

Foreword by Trevor Williamson

University of Nebraska Press
LINCOLN

The University of Nebraska Press is part of a land-grant institution
with campuses and programs on the past, present, and future
homelands of the Pawnee, Ponca, Otoe-Missouria, Omaha, Dakota,
Lakota, Kaw, Cheyenne, and Arapaho Peoples, as well as those
of the relocated Ho-Chunk, Sac and Fox, and Iowa Peoples.

Library of Congress Cataloging-in-Publication Data

Names: Gruver, Ed, 1960– author
Title: The wee Ice Mon cometh: Ben Hogan's 1953 Triple Slam and one
of golf's greatest summers / Ed Gruver; foreword by Trevor Williamson.
Description: Lincoln : University of Nebraska Press, [2024]
Identifiers: LCCN 2024011383
ISBN 9781496238986 (hardback; acid-free paper)
ISBN 9781496241627 (epub)
ISBN 9781496241634 (pdf)
Subjects: LCSH: Hogan, Ben, 1912–1997. | Golfers—Rating of. |
Golf—Tournaments. | Masters Golf Tournament—History. |
U.S. Open (Golf tournament)—History. | British Open (Golf
tournament)—History. | BISAC: SPORTS & RECREATION /
Golf | BIOGRAPHY & AUTOBIOGRAPHY / Sports
Classification: LCC GV964.H6 G784 2024 |
DDC 796.352092 [B]—dc23/eng/20240506
LC record available at https://lccn.loc.gov/2024011383

Designed and set in Arno Pro by Scribe Inc.

For Nana and Poppy

CONTENTS

FOREWORD

My Memories of Ben Hogan in 1953

TREVOR WILLIAMSON

When the summer of 1953 arrived, there was a great feeling of excitement in the town of Carnoustie. The Open was coming to town! Golfing heroes from all corners of the globe were about to descend on this small town that was also the home of a very big golf course. It is known to the locals as "The Medal Course" and known to the rest as "The Carnoustie Championship Golf Course."

Carnoustie is also the town that gave so much to the development of golf worldwide. The term the "Carnoustie 300" refers to the young men who left Carnoustie to go all over the world, taking with them the skills in club making, playing, teaching, and working on courses that they had learned in the club maker's workshops in Great Britain.

I am proud to say that my grandfather Robert Simpson played a great part in all of this. The perfect example of the Carnoustie 300 is Alex Smith, who was a foreman in Robert's workshops, and it was Robert's recommendation that took Alex to America, where he won two U.S. Open Championships and became a hero. In the summer of 1953, another hero was crossing the Atlantic Ocean, and this time it was from America to Carnoustie. The hero was from Texas, and his name was Ben Hogan.

I have been brought up in golf and have been in and out of the shops since I was five years old. I have many great memories, have met hundreds of wonderful people, and have made and repaired many golf clubs, so I feel very lucky. While I sometimes worry about getting older, the good thing about that is that I saw firsthand Ben Hogan play Carnoustie and saw how well he did. The course played to seven thousand yards, and Hogan had to use the British size ball (1.62).

There are many stories in Scotland about Hogan. Perhaps he didn't rush to sign autographs, and he certainly would not have enjoyed this era of "selfies." However, to the very knowledgeable Scottish golf spectator, those things did not matter at all, for they judge golfers on their play.

It is well reported that Hogan was surprised by the affection shown to him at this legendary Open, and that was because it was easy for them to know that in that week in July 1953, they had witnessed the best. And perhaps there was a certain amount of pride among Scottish fans, for after all, one of the few people whom Hogan looked up to, and observed keenly, was Macdonald Smith, who learned his craft just two hundred yards from where Ben holed his final put to have his name engraved on the Claret Jug and earn the title "Champion Golfer of the Year."

In Great Britain, Slazenger would make and distribute "Ben Hogan" clubs. My uncle Bob had bought a Ben Hogan Equalizer Wedge to sell in the shop, and he gifted this to me. I loved it; it went everywhere with me and was literally attached to my hands. As British people were always keen on American things—the films, the cars, and so on—American-made golf clubs started to take over. Names like Wilson, Power-Bilt, and MacGregor would take away from the Scottish club-making firms like John Letters, Ben Sayers, Robert Forgen, and so on. Ben Hogan's win at Carnoustie seventy years ago played a part in these changes, and that Open at Carnoustie is still talked about to this day.

I am happy to add this contribution to Ed's book, the first full-length work on Ben Hogan's unprecedented Triple Slam. I know you will enjoy reliving the memories of that historic season, which is still perhaps the greatest summer any golfer ever enjoyed.

The Wee Ice Mon Cometh

Prologue

A Great Champion Meets Defeat

"Defeat," English essayist Havelock Ellis wrote, "ennobles and fortifies." Ben Hogan, golf's greatest champion of the 1950s, had long battled the demon of defeat.

Disadvantaged from the days of his youth when his beloved father, Chester, committed suicide while Ben was in the family home and could hear the sudden and awful gunshot, the young boy, his siblings, and his widowed mother struggled to survive. Taking an interest in golf because caddying paid more than delivering newspapers, Hogan was beaten up by bigger boys in the caddie yards. Forced to fight back or be run off, Hogan fought back.

It would become the central theme of life for this tough, taciturn Texan. The introverted Hogan found enjoyment in the solitary nature of golf. He was not a natural at the game, and haunted by a hook he went years without winning an individual tournament title. Hogan and his wife, Valerie, went bust several times, and he stole oranges to eat—"I know what it's like to be hungry," he would say years later—but he battled and, in his tenth season as a professional earned his first individual victory.

The 5-foot-8.5 140-pound Hogan also earned a moniker from the media, "Bantam Ben." Hogan hated the nickname and hated more the fact that in his first sixteen years as a pro he failed to win a major title. It led to another nickname bestowed upon him by an unforgiving press, "Mr. Runner-up." The proud Hogan liked this even less than being called Bantam. But he persevered and, at age 34, won his first major title, the 1946 PGA Championship. The man *Time* magazine called "Little Ice Water" for his "assembly-line precision" in dismantling even the most difficult courses became golf's little big man, winning another PGA title in 1948 along with the U.S. Open.

The PGA's Player of the Year, golf's smallest giant stood astride the sports world like a goliath. Featured on the cover of *Time*, Hogan personified postwar America—industrious, successful, and at the peak of his powers. Yet he was struck down once more, his slender frame partially crushed in a near-fatal car crash on a fog-shrouded road in West Texas in February 1949.

Told he may never walk again, Hogan believed otherwise. People had always told him what he couldn't do, he would state defiantly. Doubters be damned, Hogan would show them.

Limping on legs encased in elastic bandages to promote the circulation of his blood, he returned to the pro tour in 1950 and won his second U.S. Open in the "Miracle at Merion." Hogan's niece Jacque recalls believing that if anyone could come back from such an injury, it was her uncle. His great-niece, Lisa Scott, says fans respect Mr. Hogan in part because of what he had overcome and what he ultimately accomplished.

Once again named PGA Player of the Year for his heroic comeback, Hogan took his game to new heights the following spring and summer, winning his first Masters title and third U.S. Open, the latter coming in a brutal battle with the ferocious "Monster" of Oakland Hills. It was the most satisfying victory of his career, and he punctuated it with the most famous posttournament quote in major golf history. "I'm glad that I brought this course, this 'monster,' to its knees," he told reporters.

Hogan's historic victories in 1951 gained him his second straight PGA Player of the Year award and third in four years. He began the 1952 season as a seemingly unbeatable machine, a chiseled-from-stone, chain-smoking champion, a conqueror of courses and competitors. A biopic of his life was titled *Follow the Sun*, yet like Melville's Ahab, Hogan would strike the sun if it dared insult him. His fierce competitiveness, stoic demeanor, and dark stare chilled opponents and scared scribes.

Contemporary Bob Brumby thought Hogan's steely squint reminiscent of an old West gunslinger. British golf writer and commentator Henry Longhurst spent considerable time studying Hogan up close, noting that the Bantam was a small man of 140 pounds, with dark hair and a wide mouth that tightened into a thin line when the pressure was on. Longhurst noted that in an age when many of America's golf aces were large men, Bantam

Ben developed an edge through means that were cold and deliberate. The process took years, Longhurst wrote, but Hogan conditioned his mind so that nothing could rattle him.

Hogan became golf's indomitable force. He played the gentleman's game with a ferocity that suggested he had not only brassies in his bag but brass knuckles on both hands. He turned tournaments into back-alley brawls, fighting ferociously to save pars.

Despite the expectations of experts, Dame Fortune did not favor him in 1952. Shooting 70s his first two days at Augusta National in April, Hogan was in second place at the midway mark as he sought to become the Masters' first repeat winner. His 74 in Saturday's third round left him tied with rival Sam Snead heading into Sunday's final round. Wearing his customary muted colors—white shirt, tan pants, white linen cap, and black golf cleats—Hogan struggled to negotiate Augusta's slick greens. Whipping winds and chilly climes conspired against the defending champion, Hogan playing unevenly and shooting 79 to freefall into a tie for seventh place with a 293. Snead's 286 was the highest winning score in Masters history to that point, eclipsing the 285 shared by Horton Smith in 1936 and Henry Picard in '38.

The *Pittsburgh Post-Gazette* headlined its coverage with the declaration "Ben Hogan Blows Up" and stated that Hogan was "one of several players who had a chance to win the windswept tournament on its final day but couldn't make it."

Brawling with the wind, Hogan's approach shots into the gusts were poor, leaving him with long putts, and as the AP reported, "He wasn't sinking them." The die for Hogan's difficult day was cast early, the defending champion three-putting the first and third greens. He made the turn with a 39 and, despite the wind sending shots astray, was able to steady his game early on the back nine and keep in contention. Yet in the closing stretch, when Hogan would typically raise his level of play and drop the hammer on courses and contenders, his disciplined game deserted him. Inaccurate approach shots led him to shoot over par on three of the final five holes, and his reign as Masters champion was over.

Hogan's friend Dan Jenkins, who covered Ben's play for the *Fort Worth Press*, wrote that what happened in that final round was "Bitter Disappointment

No. 1" for Hogan in '52. Ben found balm by returning to his hometown of Fort Worth and winning the Colonial National Invitation. He then began preparing to defend his U.S. Open title at Northwood Club in Dallas, Texas.

Sport magazine's June 1952 issue ran a feature story titled "Can Hogan Make It Four In A Row?" The headline was not entirely accurate. Hogan won the U.S. Open in 1948, '50, and '51 but didn't play in '49 due to his horrific head-on collision with a Greyhound bus. But Bill Rives's story was correct in that Hogan was aiming to win his fourth Open in as many appearances from 1948 to 1952. Hogan was also seeking to join Willie Anderson as the only men to win three straight Open titles in as many years, Anderson accomplishing the feat from 1903 to 1905.

An opportunity to make history whet Hogan's appetite, and Rives told readers, "he wants that fourth straight Open and can be depended upon to go all out for it." As had been the case at the Masters two months prior, Hogan put himself in position to defend his title, taking a two-stroke lead in his home state. Again, extreme weather conditions conspired against the reigning champion. The windswept conditions at Augusta were replaced by 98-degree heat and high humidity at Northwood.

Hogan's consistency was on vivid display in the first two rounds, the champion carding 69s on Thursday and Friday. The AP's coverage stated that the tournament opened "under the whip of its master and grim Ben Hogan seized the midway lead with a record-tying score of 138." Black and white footage showed a smiling Hogan, tanned by the sun and wearing a light-colored, short-sleeved polo and trademark white cap, chatting with fellow golfer Ed "Porky" Oliver, the latter tossing his left arm around Ben's shoulders.

Hogan tied the thirty-six-hole mark set by Snead in 1948 on the Riviera Course in Los Angeles, a tournament that ultimately yielded Hogan's first U.S. Open title. At Northwood, he played the first two rounds like a craftsman, the AP noting that "Hogan, his face a mask of determination, put his shots together like a master mechanic and then, like a master showman, climaxed his [second] round by sinking a 12-foot-birdie putt on the final hole."

It would be the final highlight of the tournament for Hogan. Dealing with debilitating heat and a bothersome head cold, Hogan followed his strong opening rounds with a 74 in Round Three. Wearied and worn down by the weather and illness and hauling his battered body across the scorched grounds of the thirty-six-hole Saturday demanded by the U.S. Open format, golf's precise machine broke apart in the final round. The dogleg par-four sixth hole saw Hogan spray a shot out of bounds—the deciding shot of the tournament, he would say—and card several three-putts to shoot another 74 and place third behind new champion Julius Boros.

"Mr. Hogan won Colonial, but at Northwood in Dallas, the heat got him," Hogan acquaintance Randy Jacobs says. "It was brutally hot. That 36-hole finish in the summertime in that kind of pressure must have been unbelievable. It was a survival contest as much as a golf tournament."

United Press sportswriter Oscar Fraley remarked that no one gave Boros, a comparative unknown, much of a chance when the day began beneath "a blazing Texas sun. . . . For Hogan, the implacable, deadly little fairway killer with the ice water nerves, was booming along two shots in the lead—and four fat strokes ahead of the untested Boros."

But it was the favored Hogan who fell victim to what Fraley called "the nerve-shattering stretch" of a U.S. Open. Hogan's 37-37 in the third round opened the door for Boros, who responded with a 35-33 to take the lead. The Bantam watched "Moose," as the two-hundred-pound Boros was known, beat the heat by employing his strategy to "swing easy, hit hard." Having been dethroned, the exhausted Hogan declared the Moose "a magician."

The *Palm Beach Post* ran a headline stating "Boros Rally Shatters Hogan's Golf Dynasty." A great champion had been defeated, and his future, seemingly certain amid the aromatic azaleas of Augusta in April, was suddenly in deep doubt following his faltering finish on the sunbaked grounds of the Lone Star State. Hogan's losses in the Masters and U.S. Open offered stunning collapses for a man *Time* had lauded as "one of the greatest tournament players" in golf history.

Jenkins called it "Bitter Disappointment No. 2" for Hogan, and he was certain that the losses would make his friend work harder. The '53 season would showcase the former champion's star power and skills in a summer-long soap opera that gripped fans and the rich and famous on both sides of the Atlantic. President Eisenhower, Frank Sinatra, Bing Crosby, Toots Shor, and Jackie Gleason were among those who would follow Hogan as he looked to settle old scores. Sinatra would even travel to Carnoustie in Scotland to watch Hogan compete in the British Open.

Hogan was forty years old in 1952, but his body felt much older. He would need to double down on desire to overcome his physical limitations, deep fields of Hall of Fame–caliber competitors, and three of the toughest courses in the world. "He had such a competitive fire," says Robert Stennett, CEO of the Ben Hogan Foundation. "I knew him in his later years, but I could tell you of instances where you could still see the fire."

Bruce Devlin was a friend, practice partner, and playing partner of Hogan. The '52 season, he says, fueled Hogan's fire in '53. "Nothing Ben Hogan ever achieved was anything but hard work," Devlin says. "He knew where he wanted to go and how to get there." Where Hogan wanted to go was back to the pinnacle of his profession. And he knew that to reach it he would have to overcome his failures from '52.

"He was really motivated because of two uncharacteristic flops for him the previous year in the Masters and in the U.S. Open," says John Boyette, former sports editor of the *Augusta Chronicle*. "He was very motivated in '53 to right the record."

Ellis would write, "It is on our failures that we base a new and different and better success." Hogan would base on his failures in '52 a success in '53 that would be not only new and different and better than anything he had done but arguably better than any golfer has ever done, including Bobby Jones in 1930 and Tiger Woods in 2000 and 2001. It is a season so great it has become known as the Hogan Slam.

Augusta

The buds burst forth in brilliance every spring, azaleas and honeysuckles, dogwoods and oaks, forsythia, tulips, and magnolias, more than 350 varieties of plants and trees in all, providing a fragrant flowering of warm colors on seventy acres of lush land in Augusta, Georgia.

The pageantry of color is further intensified by tradition. Caddies wear white coveralls; winners don green jackets. Marshals and trash squads are similarly dressed in standardized uniforms. The brown water in the hazards is transformed into a more optically pleasing bright blue, courtesy of calcozine dye. A sudden spring rain casts what *Sports Illustrated* once called "a mellow patina" over brightly colored umbrellas hastily raised over the heads of fans dampened by a downpour. Spectators, thousands strong, stand among the purple frieze as players ponder putts amid pine-lined grounds.

Augusta is a spectacle of sport. It is a ritual; it is tradition. It is a former indigo plantation being transformed in 1857 into a nursery by the new owner of the land, Louis Berckmans, a baron of Belgian descent. A native of the small town of Lierre, Louis was born in October of 1801 into a family of proprietors and estate owners in Belgium. The Belgian Revolution in 1830–31 was contested over the Berckmans' land, and in 1851 Louis and his family came to the New World and took up residence in Plainfield, New Jersey. Louis and his son Prosper began a nursery boasting wide varieties of pears and additional fruit trees. The nobleman moved with his family to Augusta in 1857, buying the 365-acre indigo plantation and converting it into Fruitland Nurseries.

Emphasizing plant life, Louis and Prosper imported plants and trees from other countries. Prosper is said to have favored the azaleas that populate

Augusta, with more than thirty varieties of the colorful, sweet-smelling plant blooming in brilliant colors for two to three weeks between March and May.

When Bobby Jones arrived in Augusta seeking a plot of land upon which to build the golfing champion's dream course, he was stunned by the beauty of the property. "Perfect!" Jones reportedly exclaimed upon his first viewing of Fruitland Nurseries. This ground, he said, had been waiting years for someone to place a golf course on it.

Augusta's ground is historic, playing critical roles in the Revolutionary War and Civil War. Inhabited in the early 1700s by Cherokee, Chickasaw, Creek, and Yuchi Indians, it was used by Indigenous Americans as a place to cross the Savannah River, named after the Savano Indians. Augusta's first English settlement came in 1736, with British general James Oglethorpe naming the colony in honor of Princess Augusta, the wife of the Prince of Wales, Frederick Louis.

Augusta would become known as the second city of Georgia, as it was considered the second capital of the state. It served as the capital during the Revolutionary War following the fall of Savannah to the British. Augusta then fell to Lt. Col. Archibald Campbell in January 1779, but the British withdrew not long after as American troops gathered on the shores of the Savannah. Augusta again became the capital city of Georgia but fell again to the British during the war.

The city of Augusta hosts the lone structure built and completed by the Confederate States of America, the Confederate Powder Works. It entailed twenty-six buildings along a two-mile stretch and produced 2.75 million pounds of gunpowder, making Augusta the centerpiece of the Confederacy's production of firepower. The Augusta Canal, constructed in 1845, allowed Augusta to become the second-biggest inland cotton market in the world. Unlike its role in the Revolutionary War, Augusta was mostly unscarred by battle in the Civil War. It served as a major rail center for Confederates, the most notable being in September 1863 when the rebel troops of Lt. Gen. James Longstreet traveled from Virginia to Chickamauga via Augusta. It became a hospital center to accommodate mounting casualties, with funds for the sick and wounded being raised by many of Augusta's leading citizens, including the Rev. Dr. Joseph R. Wilson, the father of future U.S. president Woodrow Wilson.

On his historic March to the Sea late in 1864, Maj. Gen. William Tecumseh Sherman bypassed Augusta. Despite Sherman's assertion that he decided not to attack Augusta due to the large concentration of Confederate troops in the city, local folklore states that Sherman had been secretly ordered by U.S. president Abraham Lincoln not to destroy Augusta because the First Lady's sister owned large stores of cotton in the city.

A century later Bobby Jones, a man called by essayist Herbert Warren Wind the most favored son of the South since Robert E. Lee, made sports history in 1930 by winning the Grand Slam of golf. Described by the Associated Press as having a "short, stocky figure" and being golf's "Napoleon" who strode over rolling battlegrounds, Jones nonetheless was a weary warrior at the still-young age of twenty-eight. Having achieved a feat for the ages, he retired from competitive golf. Jones's announcement shocked the sports world, but physically and mentally he had paid a price, dealing with the pressure of high-level competition and the stress of being the favorite in every tournament he played in. He longed to play the game in a more relaxed atmosphere, to enjoy it with friends.

Jones met Clifford Roberts in the autumn of 1930, the young champion having been invited by the middle-aged Wall Street investment banker to view a tract of land they believed fit with Bobby's plans to build a course that reflected his love for the sport. Jones and Roberts proved as different as two people could be. Jones was a southern gentleman, Roberts a native midwesterner who had moved from Chicago to New York. Jones was sensitive, Roberts relentless. Traveling from Atlanta to Augusta, Jones met with Roberts, and Cliff drove Bobby down the double row of magnolias that led to Fruitland Manor, which dated to the antebellum era. Fruitland Manor would later be converted into the Augusta National Clubhouse.

Jones stood in front of the manor and viewed the vast expanse of land before him. He said later he knew instantly it was the terrain he had always hoped to find. He once told *Sports Illustrated* he was overwhelmed by the "possibilities of the golf course that could be built in such a setting."

The course would serve as the grounds for an annual tournament for Jones and his friends, and as Bobby and Cliff shared the same passion for a private club, they set about raising money. That they did this during the Great Depression, a time when most golf courses were closing, made for a great challenge.

Jones and Roberts paid $70,000 to purchase Fruitland Nurseries and worked with the third generation of Berckmans associated with Augusta, Prosper's sons, Prosper Jr. and Louis Alphonse. It was Louis who advised on the placement of the many trees and plants. Jones teamed with Scottish architect Alister MacKenzie to create a course that Herbert Warren Wind in 1955 called "very probably the most appealing inland course ever built anywhere."

The *Augusta Chronicle* on July 15, 1931, announced the news with the headline "Bobby Jones to Build His Ideal Golf Course on Berckmans' Place." Course construction took less than two years to complete, a remarkably quick process aided no doubt by the fact that, as golf historian John Boyette wrote in 2016, Jones and MacKenzie were two men of one mind when it came to Augusta National. Jones chose MacKenzie over more famous course architects, Donald Ross among them, and the history behind the friendship between Jones and MacKenzie is somewhat shrouded.

"The mystery of how Bobby Jones and Alister MacKenzie first met—and how Jones arrived at picking MacKenzie to design Augusta National Golf Club—has never been fully explained," Boyette wrote. The mystery involves the Old and New Worlds, yet as Boyette notes, golf historians have never been able to state definitively when the lives of these two legends first intersected.

Their initial encounter may have come at St. Andrews, the birthplace of golf. Jones was a teenager when he first played St. Andrews's Old Course in the 1921 British Open, and it was in the early 1920s that MacKenzie, a civil surgeon in the British Army and veteran of two wars, became a consultant for St. Andrews, designing a system for the locations of flagsticks in championship tournaments. Jones returned to the Old Course in 1926 for the Walker Cup Matches, and Boyette states that this was when MacKenzie watched Bobby play for the first time. MacKenzie next saw Jones three weeks later at Royal Lytham & St. Annes, Bobby winning his first British Open. MacKenzie and Jones were back at St. Andrews in 1927, Bobby shooting a record 285 and successfully defending his championship.

Boyette wrote that according to *The Life and Work of Dr. Alister MacKenzie*, St. Andrews in 1927 is when the architect first met Jones. Seven years earlier, MacKenzie had written a small book outlining his thirteen principles of course architecture and sent a signed copy to Jones in 1927. Bobby agreed with Alister that the best golf course should represent an interesting challenge to golfers regardless of their abilities. Strategy and skill should be equally emphasized and the land's natural beauty preserved.

It was one thing for Jones to read MacKenzie's principles on paper; it was another to experience them firsthand. As Jones dominated golf in the Roaring Twenties, MacKenzie was building a brand as an architect. He moved to California in 1926 and was commissioned by Samuel Morse and Marion Hollins to design Cypress Point, a club in Pebble Beach. With an eye toward bringing the U.S. Amateur to Pebble Beach in 1929, Morse commissioned MacKenzie to redesign the greens on numbers eight and thirteen. Hollins created the breathtaking sixteenth hole at Cypress Point and a new club—Pasatiempo—in Santa Cruz. Pasatiempo has been ranked as one of the greatest courses in the country.

Seeking a record third-straight U.S. Amateur title, Jones prepped for Pebble Beach by playing courses across California. One of those was MacKenzie's Cypress Point, and on August 30, 1929, Jones's first outing on a MacKenzie course resulted in a 71 on a course that his biographer Charles Price stated Bobby "fell head over heels in love with."

Price said Jones found the design "almost perfect." Jones would return to Cypress Point, and this time he met MacKenzie and had what golf historians believe were their first detailed discussions concerning course architecture. Price wrote that as the two men talked, Jones grew increasingly impressed with MacKenzie's theories. Price added that while neither Jones nor MacKenzie realized it, their conversations gave birth to Augusta National and the Masters.

Jones's reading of MacKenzie's book, their subsequent talks and concurrence on the qualities that made for a great course, and Bobby's rounds at Cypress Point and then at Pasatiempo convinced him of Alister's abilities and that he would be the ideal architect for his course. Had Jones and MacKenzie not had their talk on the West Coast in 1929, it seems safe to say, as Price wrote, "that Augusta National would not be the Augusta National we know today."

Following their meeting, MacKenzie traveled east to New York and on July 10 met with the Augusta National Golf Club committee in the Vanderbilt Hotel. Boyette suggests that it was then that MacKenzie was probably offered the opportunity to design Jones's "dream course."

Jones and MacKenzie headed to Long Island and played Bayside, a course the latter had recently designed. On July 14, MacKenzie was in Augusta for a three-day stay, and he and Jones were photographed for the *Augusta Chronicle* inspecting drawings and checking the grounds for their future course. MacKenzie returned to Augusta in October and joined with Jones to start routing the course. In March 1932, MacKenzie headed back to Augusta and worked to shape the greens. After the land was cleared of stumps and the holes placed, MacKenzie took notes as Jones hit a variety of shots.

Jones told writer O. B. Keeler in 1932 that the ideas of he and MacKenzie were "synonymous." Jones and MacKenzie were in complete agreement when it came to Augusta, and because they were, the construction of their course was swift. MacKenzie so valued the opinion of Hollins—a trailblazer among women of her era, as she was a champion golfer, race car driver, polo player, horsewoman, and advocate for suffrage—that he asked her to critique the course. The course was seeded in late May 1932, and seven months later Augusta National opened for limited play. It was formally opened in January 1933, with *Time* magazine reporting the following in its January 23 issue: "Robert Tyre Jones II, for whom Georgia has killed a great many fatted calves, last week opened a new golf course of his own planning, the Augusta National. The course—6,700 yd. from the back tees—was designed by Golf Architect Allister MacKenzie, with Jones's help. Intended to be the 'ideal course' for both experts and dubs, it contained only 22 traps. Its appearance—rolling ground in a pleasant valley edged by pine trees—suggested that another Bobby Jones, Stage Designer Robert Edmond Jones, had done the settings." *Time* noted that Augusta National was planned along the lines of the National Golf Links of America in Long Island's Shinnecock Hills and was backed by Fielding Wallace, an Augusta businessman. Wallace and his friends formed the holding company to buy a tract of 364 acres, 192 of which were used by the club. Ed Dudley of Savannah would serve as the club's first pro.

The vast Augusta meadowland had been transformed into eighteen risk-reward holes that replicated what Jones considered to be the essence of the great courses he had played in the United States and the United Kingdom rather than duplicates of existing topography. Each hole at Augusta is the product of the natural contours of the land, and each would be named for the flower, tree, or shrub featured most prominently in the areas of the greens or serving as a decorative border on the fairways.

MacKenzie called Augusta the "World's Wonder Inland Golf Course," but he never saw the final product. He left for England in May 1932 and did not return to Georgia, passing away in January 1934 at his home in Pasatiempo two months prior to Augusta's inaugural tournament. Roberts said later that MacKenzie often called Augusta his best work. It was a pity, Roberts wrote, that MacKenzie did not live long enough to see his course in all its majesty.

While MacKenzie and Roberts disagreed at times, primarily over money matters, MacKenzie maintained a kinship with Jones. Writing of Augusta, MacKenzie stated that Jones rendered him assistance of "incalculable value." He considered Jones a student of golf and golf courses. MacKenzie was amazed at Jones's sharp knowledge and recollection of the famous golf holes in England, Scotland, and America. Jones repaid the praise. He thought MacKenzie deserved credit as the architect and he, Jones, was simply his advisor and consultant.

As the club was suffering financial difficulties early, there was talk of holding the U.S. Open at Augusta. The idea of Augusta hosting the American championship at the height of the South's steamy summer months cooled that notion. Jones and Roberts decided to host an invitation-only tournament. When Augusta National held its first Masters in 1934, the tournament was considered, according to Herbert Warren Wind, "just a notable competition."

The Masters' rapid rise to prominence rated, in Wind's words, as "one of the relative miracles in modern American sports." At the time of Wind's writing on the Masters in 1955, the tournament's prestige and prominence were such that it stood with the World Series and Kentucky Derby as an American sports classic.

The Masters took its place as the first summit on a spring-to-summer journey involving the four peaks of golfing prestige in the United States and UK. That it moved to the forefront so quickly was due in part to the age of information but also because, as Wind noted, the Masters was everything one could ask for in a golf tournament.

While the U.S. Open remained the most coveted title among American golfers, because the Open was competed on a different course every year, the tournament did not have what Wind described as "the especial patina that seems to affix itself to those events which have the advantage of taking place year-after-year in the same, ever-more familiar locale."

Great golf tournaments have the same essential elements, and by 1953, many competitors considered Augusta to be the best and fairest test of major championship golf in the U.S. It annually boasted a field of topflight competitors, inspired and inventive leadership, and a history of high drama. *SI* has called the Masters an "idyllic test of golf," and heading into the 1953 season, its list of winners offered a gallery of greats—Gene Sarazen, Byron Nelson, Jimmy Demaret, Sam Snead, and Ben Hogan.

Jones and Roberts nursed the Masters from its infancy, the 1934 Augusta National Invitation Tournament having daily updates broadcast on CBS Radio by former U.S. Golf Association president Herbert H. Ramsay. On March 22, 1934, Jones stood on what is now the tenth hole of the Masters and at 10:35 a.m. delivered the first official tee shot in the history of the tournament.

There had been speculation about whether Jones would play at all. Though he had shot a course practice record 65 several weeks before the tournament and a one-under 71 in a practice round, he preferred to act as host. Roberts would write that it wasn't until he had persuaded Jones to play that the former champion agreed to come out of retirement. Roberts's argument was that Jones could not invite his golfing friends to play on his course and then decline to play with them.

Jones's appearance stirred the masses. The *Chronicle* ran a headline declaring, "It's the Field against Bobby." Renowned sportswriter Grantland Rice previewed Jones's playing in the Masters by remarking that Bobby would be returning to pressure golf for the first time in four years. "No one can say in advance how the nerve strain will affect him, what his mental attitude will be against the keen blades of so many stars, all after his scalp," Rice wrote.

The unique opportunity to see Jones up close drew spectators from thirty-eight states and Canada. Bobby played well off the tee, but his short game suffered. That he was no longer the indomitable champion of 1930 was evident in his requiring thirty-five putts in the first round, including three from seven feet on eleven.

Horton Smith, meanwhile, shared or owned first place from wire to wire and showed a flair for the dramatic amid raw, bitterly cold climes by sinking a ten-foot birdie hole on number seventeen to finish one stroke ahead of Craig Wood. The AP heralded Smith's victory: "Picking up in Georgia where he left off four years ago as the last man to whip Bob Jones in open golf competition, lanky Horton Smith of Chicago paced the professionals to a smashing triumph over the former world champion today in the final round of the $5,000 Masters invitation tournament."

Jones shot 294 to finish ten strokes behind Smith and tied for thirteenth. The AP noted that competitors handled their former nemesis and did so on a course he had designed. *Time* stated at the time that the full meaning of Augusta is that it's a monument to one of the "finest sportsmen and sporting careers ever known."

What this first Masters represented, *Time* added, was an opportunity for his game's greatest idol, golf's answer to fellow Roaring Twenties sports heroes—baseball's Babe Ruth, boxing's Jack Dempsey, football's Red Grange, and tennis's Big Bill Tilden—to prove that he had been active in retirement. Jones gave his sport what *Time* called "a new golfing institution and a new competition, rivaling even the U.S. Open in importance, far surpassing it in atmosphere."

True to his character, Jones insisted that his hosting duties did not impact his performance. Paired with "Little Poison" Paul Runyan, the tour's leading money winner in 1934, Jones displayed little of his former championship putting. His 76 and 74 in the first two rounds left him struggling to stay in contention. Jones improved his game in Round Three, shooting 72, but he was two off the pace set by his partner and past-time rival, Walter Hagen. "Jones Surrenders Final Chance" was the headline in the *Chronicle*, and he wrapped up his comeback tournament with another even-par round of 72. Jones's tie for thirteenth place would prove to be his best finish in his twelve Masters Tournaments.

This initial tournament provided the color and drama that has marked the Masters since its inception. There was Smith, the eventual champion, described by *Time* as "lanky and wavy-haired" and ultimately, "the Master of Them All." *Time* noted the presence of Wood, "the game's handsomest exponent, and the short, dogged Runyan," who needed a 69 in his final round to win but had to settle for a 71. There, too, was the "aging" Emmet French, who started fast before fading, and Billy Burke, "clenching his cigar and straining for distance" and being betrayed by three long putts that led to an unlucky 73 in his final round. And there was Ed Dudley, the "long-legged, drawling home professional," driving his ball into the creek on number four to end his hopes.

What would become a history of fantastic finishes kicked into high gear the following year. With Wood leading at six under par, Sarazen studied the 235-yard fairway drive to the fifteenth green on the hole titled "Firethorn." Gripping a four-wood, "The Squire," as the Connecticut farmer was called, found the cup on the par-five hole. Immortalized in golf legend as the "shot heard 'round the world," the first double-eagle in Masters history helped Sarazen seize momentum, and he caught Wood that Sunday afternoon to force a historic thirty-six-hole playoff.

Grantland Rice was at Augusta that April 7 and, in a story headlined "Miracle Blow Wipes Out Lead," wrote that "millions of stars and duffers have played billions of golf shots in the 500-year history of the ancient game. But Gene Sarazen played one in the final round of the Masters' tournament at Augusta that holds all records for all time."

Writer Richard Leivenberg in 2014 ranked the 1935 finish as the third best in Masters history, stating that Sarazen's shot was "one of the greatest ways to finish a sports competition ever." It was because of this finish that the second annual Augusta National Invitation Tournament came to be regarded as "The Masters."

The Monday playoff proved anticlimactic as Sarazen, playing a cold-blooded game that seemed suited for the semifrosty temperature, defeated Wood by five strokes. Smith won his second Masters in three years in 1936, playing amid downpours and once again taking advantage of an event on number seventeen to win by the barest of margins. This time, however, it was "Lighthorse" Harry Cooper's bogey that was the difference-maker in a tournament plagued by heavy rains that postponed the first and final rounds and prompted a player's protest that was filed by tournament manager Robert Harlow with the Augusta National Golf Club executive committee but was promptly rejected. The AP wrote that Smith "staged a sub-par finish on the flooded links to overhaul 'Lighthorse Harry' Cooper of Chicago and win by a single stroke."

Nelson stepped to the fore the following spring, winning the first of his five majors. Once again, the script seemed almost fictional. Starting with a six-under 66 amid near-perfect weather, Nelson fell four strokes back following a 75 in the third round. He stormed the course in the final back nine, carding a birdie and eagle on twelve and thirteen, respectively, and gaining six shots on front-runner Ralph Guldahl. In 1958, the Nelson Bridge on thirteen was dedicated in honor of Byron's blitz.

Nicknamed "Bashful Byron" by the press, Nelson became a favorite of reporters, Rice included. He wrote admiringly of Nelson during the tournament, describing him as "big-handed, stout-hearted Byron Nelson . . . with a pair of hands that could throttle a gorilla." The AP likewise praised Nelson. "Blazing over the home stretch with a spectacular 32, Byron Nelson, gangling Irishman from Reading, PA, clamped a 'Full Nelson' on the field today to win the fourth Augusta national golf tournament featuring the return to competition of Bobby Jones," the AP wrote.

Adverse weather returned to force postponements in the '38 Masters, but the angular Henry Picard persevered with a precision short game and won his lone Masters by two strokes over Cooper and Guldahl. Picard, the Pennsylvania pro whose "Hershey Hurricane" moniker was particularly fitting for the elements, was methodical and consistent, carding rounds of 71, 72, 72, and 70 for a 285. "No one was more certain that Henry Picard would win the all-star Augusta National golf show than the 'Hershey Hurricane' himself," wrote the AP.

Following consecutive years as runner-up, Guldahl broke through in '39. That he carded a Masters record nine-under 279, which was three strokes better than the 1935 mark set by Sarazen and Wood, was even more impressive considering the field was forced to deal with wind, rain, and hail. It was the third major title for Guldahl in as many years, with Ralph finishing first in the 1937 and '38 U.S. Open.

The AP reported that the Texan "shattered the tourney record in winning the sixth annual event with a 72-hole total of 279. Guldahl . . . pronounced he was tired of finishing second in the Augusta 'masters' classic and intended to win." Guldahl won by flipping the script from the previous year. The back nine that Nelson had ravaged the year before to pick up six strokes and snatch what seemed certain victory from Guldahl saw Ralph post a 33 to secure the win.

The 1940 Masters didn't come down to the final round, but it didn't lack for drama. Lloyd Mangrum opened with a course record 64 that would stand for forty-six years, but it was Demaret, battling an illness that nearly caused him to withdraw, who delivered a four-stroke victory over Mangrum that was a record margin at the time. "Give him fair weather or foul, sickness or health—little Jimmy Demaret is the hottest thing in golf today," wrote United Press sports editor Harry Ferguson.

Another record was set the following year, the hard-hitting Wood becoming the first wire-to-wire winner in Masters history. He led early but was tied in the final round by a surging Nelson. Staring at a scenario that might see him lose yet another championship in excruciating fashion—he had lost a playoff in each of the four majors—Wood steadied and shot two under on the back nine to place three strokes ahead of Nelson.

The United Press played up Wood's recent run of tough luck and his breakthrough victory: "Fickle Lady Luck finally smiled on 40-year-old Craig Wood today and helped him win the Masters' golf championship. . . . Dame luck had turned her back on Wood many times and almost gave him the cold shoulder today to take a stroll with Byron Nelson, but she decided Wood's time as a rugged campaigner was running out and that there were plenty of years to court the dashing Nelson."

Hogan's history at Augusta would prove at times to be as frustrating as Wood's and as checkered as the early years of Ben's pro career. Making his Masters debut in 1938, Hogan tied for twenty-fifth. He placed ninth the following year, tied for tenth in 1940, and finished fourth in '41 after being tied for second following the first round.

Three consecutive top ten placements, capped by a top four, served notice that Hogan could contend at Augusta. In 1942, with the U.S. in World War II, Hogan was barely in the tournament mix early, posting a 73 in the opening round and a 70 in Round Two that tied him for sixth but was still eight strokes back of his boyhood rival from the Texas caddie yards, Nelson.

Hogan blistered Augusta in Saturday's third round with a five-under 67 that moved him into second place three shots behind Nelson. The UP wrote, "Looming large in the final round picture for today was slender Ben Hogan, a great finisher, who toured the long and picturesque Augusta National course yesterday in 67, five under par and the best score of the day."

Successfully battling the winds that wreaked havoc with many others in the field, Hogan made the turn in 34 and then birdied the eleventh, thirteenth, fifteenth, and sixteenth on the back nine. A three-putt on fourteen led to a bogey five and cost Hogan a chance for a 66. "Hogan, with a 54-hole total of 210, thus picked up five strokes on Nelson and set the stage for a great stretch duel," the UP wrote. "The struggle for the title between Nelson and Hogan is a fitting climax to the winter tour on which Hogan, for the second year, has been the leading money winner, with Nelson not far behind."

Sunday's final round saw Hogan live up to the UP's label as "the long driv-ing Texan" as he got great distance out of his woods. His iron play was only average, evidenced on the seventh when he was short to the green with his iron and sent his ball into a sand trap. Hogan hammered out and set himself up two feet from the hole. His putt went long, and he bogeyed the hole. Playing three rounds ahead of Nelson, Hogan putted for birdies on the back nine but got them on thirteen and eighteen only. Black and white footage showed Hogan dressed in a light-colored outfit consisting of a long-sleeve shirt, slacks, and linen cap, framed by a large gallery as he sank his putt on eighteen. Hogan's short game was slightly off, otherwise he might have won the Masters on Sunday. Fast greens forced a half-dozen of his birdie putts to miss the cup by inches, and he was close to shooting 67 or even 66.

AP writer Gayle Talbot called Hogan "the little man who never quits," and as Ben proved that yet again with a birdie three on eighteen for a two-under 70, Nelson produced what Talbot described as "a spectacular birdie" on fifteen. Though he was struggling through his worst round of the tournament— he took a bogey on number four and again on number six—Nelson appeared to have the tournament won. Hogan believed the same as he trudged toward the clubhouse at the climax of his round.

"I don't see how Nelson can miss now," Hogan told reporters. Nelson was two shots up on Hogan and needed only a pair of par fours on seventeen and eighteen for his second Masters crown. According to the UP account, the pressure was building on Byron. His trapped second shot on seventeen led to another bogey, dropping him into a tie with Hogan. Nelson could have played safe on seventeen to protect his lead. The hole was a comparatively easy one, with just a single shallow trap between him and the flag. A wide stretch of open green yawned to the left, and Nelson might have opted for the regulation two putts rather than go for the pin. Instead, he went for the pin. "I can't help it," Nelson told reporters. "I'll always go for the pin."

Nelson's eight-iron sent the ball sky-high and spinning toward the flag. To the dismay of his fans, Byron's shot settled deep in the sand, a yard short of the green. His next shot skittered past the hole, and two putts were required to end his nightmare on seventeen. Nelson, Talbot wrote, "transformed from an almost sure winner into a shaken young man."

Nelson still had a chance to win on eighteen, and he got to the green in two. But even that took great effort, Byron making a tremendous recovery to the green following a shot slashed into the woods. A twelve- to fifteen-foot putt (accounts varied) separated him from victory or a playoff with Hogan. Nelson's putt for a par three and the title curled to the left, stopping five inches from the cup, and he settled for par and a 280 that paved the path to the playoff.

Talbot previewed the playoff as a match between "slender Ben Hogan and towering Byron Nelson, two of golf's crack professionals." Hogan and

Nelson had met in playoffs before, Byron winning the Texas Open by one stroke. Years before that, Hogan had lost by one shot to Nelson in the Glen Garden Country Club caddie championship.

The AP reminded readers that Hogan's comeback to force the extra round was typical of Ben. "One week ago, he started out on the last round in the Land of Sky tournament at Asheville, three strokes behind Lawson Little but breezed home four under par to win by a stroke," the AP wrote.

The eighteen-hole duel, set for 2:30 p.m. Monday, stirred fans and media. "The play-off between these two iron-nerved competitors, who have been battling each other ever since they were caddies, was a corker," wrote Talbot. "They are among the best shot makers in the world today, and their private duel for the Masters' was worthy of their abilities."

It would be a manic Monday for Hogan, Nelson, and the gallery. Nelson appeared to be still feeling the effects of the previous day when he lost a late lead and certain victory. Byron was also feeling the pains of a nervous stomach. As was often the case, Nelson spent the night before the playoff and the morning of the match being physically ill. Hogan was a hard case when it came to competition, but he was moved enough by Nelson's sickly condition that he politely offered to postpone the playoff. Nelson just as politely declined.

There may have been more to Hogan's generous offer than genuine concern. He saw Byron's wife, Louise, in a corridor of the Bon-Air Hotel the morning of the playoff. She told Ben that Byron was sick. "Uh-oh," Hogan recalled thinking, "I don't want to play him today," the reason being that Ben had seen many golfers play their best when ill.

Byron's opening series of shots was problematic. His drive sailed into the woods on the right of the first green and rested at the base of a tree. His second shot was backhanded from the woods; his third cleared the green. He was fortunate to card only a double-bogey 6.

Nelson trailed by two strokes heading to number two and was behind by three after the fourth hole. He recovered, and the "slim, red-faced sharpshooter," as Talbot described him, took the lead with an eagle on eight. He made the turn with a 35, one stroke ahead of Hogan. The crowd, reported by the UP to be 2,500 and including virtually every golfer in the tournament who had stayed to watch just the second playoff in the brief history of the Masters, witnessed Hogan and Nelson battling on the back nine amid ideal weather conditions. From numbers six through thirteen, Hogan played at even par; still, Nelson gained six strokes and sprinted into the lead courtesy of three birdies, three pars, and an eagle. The latter came on number eight, Nelson's second shot stopping eight feet from the hole and Byron banging in the putt.

Hogan had bogeyed number six and number ten, and Nelson charged ahead with birdies on eleven, twelve, and thirteen. Back came Hogan with birdies on fourteen and fifteen to cut his deficit to one stroke with three rounds remaining. If this "epic match," as Talbot called it, turned on one hole, it was the short sixteenth. Hogan underclubbed, his shot from the tee caught a bunker, and he carded a four to Nelson's par three.

"That did it," wrote Talbot. Nelson's six-under-par surge over eleven holes, and his five under on the final thirteen allowed him to survive a bogey on eighteen and shoot 69, one stroke ahead of Hogan. Ben had five birdies in the playoff, and fans had been fortunate to be a part of one of the great showdowns in major golf history. Writing for the *Chronicle* in 2017, Martin Davis called it "arguably the most exciting head-to-head 18 holes of all time." Joining Horton Smith as the second two-time Masters champion, Nelson said that apart from the first hole, it was the finest round of golf he had ever shot. "It easily could have been a 66 or 67," he stated.

Augusta's sixteenth hole had proved to be something less than a sweet sixteen for Hogan, just as it would for Herman Barron eight years later, Jack Nicklaus in '64, Charles Coody in '69, Gene Littler in '70, and Johnny Miller in '71. Hogan and Nelson were filmed afterward smiling and shaking hands as a crowd that included U.S. servicemen in uniform looked on.

Due to World War II, the Masters was not contested from 1943 to 1945. Hogan again came in second in 1946, reinforcing the "Mister Runner-up" reputation from six years earlier, this despite the fact that he was the tour's money leader in '46. He then tied for fourth at the Masters in '47 and for sixth in '48. His accident the following February prevented him from competing in '49, but he made a dramatic return in '50 and tied for fourth.

In the '46 Masters, Hogan was in second place after three rounds but five shots off the pace set by Herman Keiser, a quiet and efficient competitor whose serious demeanor led to his "Missouri Mortician" moniker. Extremely deliberate, and with his eyes shaded by a white sun visor, Keiser three-putted on eighteen for a final-round 74 that dropped him into a tie with the hard-charging Hogan. Film shows Hogan in his white flat cap and white golf cleats and performing to his pre-war capabilities. Playing behind Keiser, Ben could win with a birdie or force a playoff with a two-putt par. Instead, he missed a two-foot putt and three-putted, giving Keiser his lone career win in a major.

Keiser believed Augusta members tried to prevent him from beating Hogan in the '46 Masters. He said his third-round tee time was changed without his being informed, his caddie was changed to a thirteen-year-old who had difficulty carrying his golf bag, he was warned to play faster or call a penalty on himself, Augusta patrons sought to rattle him in the final round with death-ray stares, and that fans were allowed to invade the fairways just as he was about to swing.

Keiser was aided in the fourth round, he said, by having Nelson as his playing partner. The classy former champion encouraged Keiser throughout, and he hung on to win. Hogan found balm for his latest disappointment by finally winning his first major four months later, defeating Ed "Porky" Oliver in the PGA Championship at Portland Golf Club.

"Mister Runner-up" was now a major champion, the thirty-four-year-old Hogan having finally broken through. He added his second and third majors two years later, winning the U.S. Open at Riviera Country Club in Pacific Palisades, California, and the PGA Championship at Norwood Hills Country Club in St. Louis. The crushing car accident in 1949 left him in the hospital for fifty-nine days, and while doctors said he might never walk again, Hogan's determination and willpower led him to his fourth major, this coming in 1950 in a playoff at Merion Golf Club in Ardmore, Pennsylvania. When Hogan went to Augusta in the spring of 1951, it was with a drive to win number five.

Seemingly strapped together by baling wire and bandages beneath his tan sweater and slacks, Hogan opened at a two-under 70 and was fourth behind leader George Fazio, with Lloyd Mangrum and Snead tied for second. A second-round 72 served to move Hogan up into a tie for second with

Fazio and Lew Worsham at 142. The fifty-four-hole lead of 211 was shared by Snead and Skee Riegel, with Hogan one back after matching his first-round 70. The veteran Snead fell from contention in the final round with an 80, but the young Skiegel hung tough, posting a 71 for a six-under 282.

Dressed in his familiar flat white linen cap, long-sleeve sweater, and white buck golf cleats, Hogan started with birdies on the second and third holes. The AP reported that the "wee champion played meticulously slow, measuring every difficult assignment for minutes and taking no unnecessary chances."

Bruce Devlin recalls Hogan's meticulous play as being true to his nature. "It fits in with his personality," says Devlin. "He was a hard worker and worked just as hard at finding his way around the golf course. The first time I played Augusta I played a practice round with Mr. Hogan and it was interesting to watch him in that practice round, chipping from different areas. He probably knew where the pins were basically going to be, and he practiced from where he thought might be the best way to miss a shot into that green. That tells a lot right there. 'If the flag's over here and I'm going to miss it, I'm going to miss it over there so I might as well hit a chip to where I think the flag is going to be on Thursday or Sunday.' He had it plotted out pretty good."

As Hogan was playing a couple of hours behind Riegel, he heard of Skee's finish as he was heading to the eighth tee. Another birdie on number eight, and Hogan was on his way to a three-under 33 for the front nine. Aware that he owned a one-stroke lead over Riegel, Hogan had only to shoot par the rest of the way to earn his first Masters championship. Still, he took no chances. On number eleven he examined a four-foot putt from every angle before sinking it. Studying the par-five, 480-yard thirteenth, Hogan at first reached for a wood to get to the green. Thinking better of it, he went with an iron, left his shot short of the green, and followed with a putt from eight feet.

Hogan's birdie on thirteen highlighted his back nine and, playing close to the vest, he shot par for a 68 that tied Riegel, Snead, and Fazio for the best round of the tournament; his 280 was one stroke off the record shared by Guldahl (1939) and Claude Harmon (1948). Hogan recorded fourteen pars and four birdies, and his only five came on the 485-yard fifteenth when he again played conservatively. As the soft afternoon sunshine filtered through the stately pines at day's end, Hogan was two strokes better than Riegel, and he had avoided the disasters that dogged many of his competitors. Black and white film of the '51 Masters called Hogan "golf's indestructible man" and said his victory "adds new laurels to one of the sports world's greatest careers." Footage showed Hogan pitching to the green on eighteen and holing a short putt before being enveloped by onrushing fans.

Snead, Mangrum, Cary Middlecoff, and Dave Douglas all fell victim to what the field called "heartbreak highway," a short stretch on the back nine comprising holes ten, eleven, and twelve. Snead sank two shots into the water on the par four eleventh and posted an eight. Mangrum absorbed a five on the par-three, water-protected twelfth. Demaret, the defending champion and three-time Masters winner, shot 71 to finish with a 299 that was sixteen strokes off his winning total from the year before.

Demaret turned his title over to his longtime playing partner, who lived up to his nickname "Little Ice Water." The AP began its report on Hogan's victory by noting that whatever ran in Ben's blood wasn't warm. "Icicle-nerved Ben Hogan added a sensational flourish to one of the greatest comeback sagas in sports today when he won his first Masters golf championship with a near-record 280," wrote the AP. "The gristly little man from Texas subdued Augusta National's treacherous acres with a grim and meticulous last round 68, four under par golf that burned off all opposition."

Grim and meticulous were traits Hogan displayed throughout his life. Even decades later, retired from competitive golf, he was still showing himself to be serious and meticulous every time he stepped on a golf course. In 1973, Randy Jacobs was a member of a Texas high school golf team when he got a job shagging golf balls for Mr. Hogan.

Being able to observe him was very valuable. . . . Summer of '73, he was 61. He was dealing with the aftereffects of the automobile accident and the infirmities that left him with. But he hit the ball better than anyone I've ever seen. Even at 61, dealing with pain and the results of those injuries, he was amazing.

We were not friends. I was an employee of the club, but he never failed to be polite to me. He was not real talkative; he was focused on what he was trying to do. It wasn't just killing time; he was trying to hit quality shots. There wasn't a lot of chit chat. He didn't small talk. Golf was his business, and he was very serious about it.

When you headed out to shag, he exchanged pleasantries and pretty quickly got into his mode mentally when he was about to hit golf balls and give his best effort. It was a pretty quiet ride out and then he might talk a little bit afterward, but he was still pretty much in game mode.

It was the absolute easiest work you could do, but you tried not to get hit because those balls were coming right at you. If you didn't pay attention, you could get hit, because he was that accurate.

Hogan's accuracy in the 1951 Masters allowed him to complete his career slam of major American golf championships, and he headed to Augusta in 1952 seeking to extend his reign. The '52 tournament earned the tag of the "mystery" Masters due to a strike of Western Union telegraphers; writers had to phone their newspapers and dictate their stories.

For the second straight year Hogan started with a 70 and was tied for third one stroke behind co-leaders Ray Gafford and Johnny Palmer, both of whom opened with a 69 amid a warm sun and slight breeze. Another 70 on Friday put Hogan alone in second place and three shots behind Snead, "Slammin' Sam" shooting a 67 that tied Jack Burke Jr. for best round of the day.

Hogan and Snead struggled on Saturday, shooting 74 and 77, respectively, but they maintained their front-running status and were tied for the lead heading into the final round. Chilly, windswept conditions didn't stop a crowd of up to twenty thousand from turning out to see the expected duel between Hogan and Snead. Writer Dan Jenkins thought the course played more windy and tougher than it had in years.

Hogan played unsteadily, particularly around the greens, and his final round 79 left him at 293 and sent him staggering into a tie for seventh. Snead played what the AP called "sound, conservative golf" and won his second Masters title with a 286. Hogan had lost his chance to repeat as champion, but he would return in 1953 seeking to master Augusta again.

2

Georgia on Their Minds

The roads led the golfers to a familiar destination, drawn as they were by the sweet siren song of the South. They were a formidable field, masters of their sport, and in Augusta National they would be facing a formidable course.

Defending champion Sam Snead joined Jimmy Demaret, Claude Harmon, Byron Nelson, Henry Picard, Gene Sarazen, Horton Smith, and Craig Wood in an impressive list of Masters winners. U.S. Open champs Julius Boros, Billy Burke, Olin Dutra, Chick Evans, Lloyd Mangrum, Fred McLeod, Cary Middlecoff, Sam Parks Jr., and Lew Worsham added to the distinguished field. So too did PGA first-place finishers Jim Ferrier, Vic Ghezzi, Bob Hamilton, Chandler Harper, Johnny Revolta, and Jim Turnesa. Past amateur champions from the U.S. included Dick Chapman, Charles Coe, Skee Riegel, Jess Sweetser, and Jack Westland, and there were British Open champions Jock Hutchison and Denny Shute and British Amateur champs Frank Stranahan, Robert Sweeny Jr., and Harvie Ward.

And then there was Ben Hogan. He remembered well the indignities of the previous year, when he had won but one tournament, his hometown Colonial National Invitational. He would turn forty-one in the coming August and knew the limitations the accident had placed on his body. His injuries no longer allowed him to play in the PGA Championship, its format being match play, and he had never traveled abroad to compete in the British Open.

John Boyette recalls Dan Jenkins telling him that Hogan was "driven to get even" in 1953. Of the bitter losses Hogan endured in failing to retain his Masters and U.S. Open titles in '52, Jenkins told Boyette that the disappointments of '52 made Hogan work even harder in '53.

In January '53, Hogan prepared for the Masters by playing in pro-ams, among them the fifty-four-hole Plymouth Pro-Am in Palm Springs in January. He finished two strokes behind Demaret and two months later headed to Seminole Golf Club in Florida. Hogan was said to have practiced eight hours a day and, starting with his pitching wedge and working his way through to his driver, would hit a bag of balls with every club. Several times each week Hogan would play a game with Harmon or friends. "I play with friends," Hogan once stated, "but we don't play friendly games."

Honing his game, Hogan tied for second place in the thirty-six-hole Seminole Pro-Am and then headed to Aiken, South Carolina, for an eighteen-hole pro-am. Hogan arrived early at Augusta to practice, and on the Sunday prior to Thursday's opening round, writer Randy Russell reminded *Augusta Chronicle* readers about Hogan's intense preparation. The former champion had spent weeks tuning up for the tournament. "Watch out for him," Russell wrote.

Hogan was quietly confident. He told writer Gene Gregston that he had practiced every day that winter at Palm Springs, and by the time he went to Augusta in '53 he was hitting the ball better than ever. The long hours on the course served also to tone his muscles for the Masters.

"Mr. Hogan was a really fit guy," Robert Stennett says. "You see pictures of his backswing and you could see his muscles; he was ripped. He was a strong guy."

Randy Jacobs says Hogan was "golf strong." "His grip was like a vise," says Jacobs, recalling the times he shook hands with Mr. Hogan:

People work out now for golf, and there are golf-specific workouts you can do. Mr. Hogan was what I call "golf strong." There's a certain strength you obtain in your hands specifically by hitting a lot of golf balls that I don't think you can duplicate any other way. His hands were incredibly tough and very, very strong.

Ray Coleman worked for the Hogan Company for a long time, and he told me a story that Mr. Hogan walked into his office holding a set of iron heads and dumped them on Ray's desk and said, "These are not ground properly." Ray reached over and picked one up and it was as hot as it could be, and he couldn't hold it in his hand. But Mr. Hogan had carried the whole set of the heads from somewhere in the back of the plant up to Ray's office in his bare hands. That will tell you how tough Mr. Hogan's hands were from all those golf balls he hit. There's a golf strength you can only get by hitting thousands of golf balls.

On the eve of the Masters, it was another Texan who was also capturing the attention of the media. Mangrum's nine-under 63 in a practice round bettered by one stroke the course mark he recorded in 1940. Lloyd was riding his sport's hottest winning streak. He had claimed five consecutive tournament victories in the U.S. and Australia, in the process pocketing the sum of eleven thousand dollars in prize money from November 1952 to January 1953.

Four months prior to the 1953 Masters, *Time* magazine featured the thirty-eight-year-old Mangrum in an article titled "Money Player." Mangrum stated in the article that the reason he was better under pressure than most golfers was because he was a ham at heart. He also had a gambler's nerve, and because it was always better to be a winner, he would take a chance rather than play it safe.

Time stated that Mangrum's looks—"lean, tanned, well-tailored, and sporting a trim mustache"—were consistent with his being the gambler he claimed to be. The magazine noted that Mangrum's inability to win majors caused him to be eclipsed by that era's Big Three of Hogan, Snead, and Nelson. Yet Mangrum was a plugger, with what *Time* called "the gambler's instinct for the law of averages." He reportedly traveled forty thousand miles a year by car and another forty thousand by air. *Time* stated that Lloyd played in more tournaments and won more money than his fellow pros. Mangrum said that figuring his winnings, exhibitions, and bonuses, he had earned three hundred thousand dollars from his golfing talents over the previous five years.

Mangrum may be the best golfer time has overlooked. At the 1996 Masters, Nelson asked three young pros if they had ever heard of Mangrum. Not one of them had. Nelson shook his head. Lloyd was the best player who's been forgotten, said Nelson. Famed *Los Angeles Times* sports columnist Jim Murray called Mangrum "the forgotten man of golf."

Mangrum and Hogan shared much in common. Both were natives of Texas, Mangrum being born in Trenton, a city in Fannin County that sits fifty-seven miles south of Dallas. Both began their golfing lives as caddies, both served in the U.S. military during World War II, and both worked numerous odd jobs before becoming successful touring pros.

Hogan and Mangrum both went broke on the tour, and both studied the styles of others before becoming champions themselves. Never receiving an official golf lesson, Mangrum believed the best way for him to learn was to watch the top players. Believing Horton Smith to be the best putter, Mangrum studied Smith's every movement on the green. Mangrum admired Revolta; Lloyd felt Johnny owned golf's best short game and would practice Revolta's short game technique. When Lloyd first saw Sam Snead, he knew the swing of the celebrated "Slammer" was the sweetest he'd ever witnessed. Thus, Mangrum copied Snead.

Golf, Mangrum said, was "a mimicking proposition." Hogan and Mangrum unconsciously mimicked one another in that they were fierce competitors, chain-smokers, and clipped in their verbiage. Fiery combatants both, Hogan and Mangrum shared similar monikers complimenting their coolness under pressure. Hogan was "Little Ice Water" and the "Wee Ice Man," Mangrum "Mr. Icicle." Both battled back from serious injuries—Hogan following his car accident in '49, Mangrum on multiple occasions in World War II. Both defied doubters who believed they would never recover enough physically to again play pro golf.

Like a young Hogan, Mangrum initially found life on the pro tour frustrating and difficult. Seeking to follow in the footsteps of his older brother, Ray, who finished fourth in the 1935 U.S. Open, Lloyd turned pro at age fifteen. The early years of his career found Mangrum scratching for money. He stayed in cheap hotels, skipped meals, and rejoiced when he earned as much as fifty dollars in a match, as he did when he placed sixth in the 1936 Southern California Open. He earned money working as a bouncer, caddying, driving a taxi, parking cars, and singing in clubs.

Playing a full tournament schedule in 1937 broke him financially. With little money in his pocket following the season-ending St. Paul Open, Mangrum asked tour radio announcer Scotty Chisholm what one does when he has no money and he's two thousand miles from home? Chisholm, nearly busted himself, told Mangrum he could drive him to Los Angeles. Lloyd accepted, and to save what little money they had, the two drove nearly nonstop. By the time they arrived at Mangrum's place in Monterey Park, they had a combined $1.90 to their names.

Knowing he was better under pressure than most golfers, Mangrum began padding his pockets by outplaying competitors in local matches. On-the-job training suited Mangrum well. It wasn't until 1940 that Mangrum, then age twenty-five, finally got his big break—an invitation to play in the Masters. Lloyd seized the moment. He opened with a 64, a major-tournament record at the time and still a Masters record on the eve of the 1953 tourney. Years of hustling golf had helped lead to his rousing record at Augusta and eventual second-place finish. He followed by tying for fifth with Hogan, Nelson, and Ralph Guldahl at that year's U.S. Open at Canterbury Golf Club outside of Cleveland, Ohio. Six years later, Mangrum returned to Canterbury for his greatest golf triumph and lone major championship.

Mangrum's first pro victory came later in 1940 at the Thomasville Open in Georgia, and there was something about the South that appealed to this native Texan. He would finish in the top eight at the Masters every year from 1947 to '56.

One year after Mangrum's record-setting performance at Augusta, America entered the Second World War. He landed at Omaha Beach just after D-Day and saw action serving as a reconnaissance corporal in General Patton's Third Army. Mangrum earned two Purple Hearts and four battle stars (two Silver Stars and two Bronze Stars) as the Third Army rolled across Europe. A Jeep accident, however, left Mangrum with a broken arm and severely damaged shoulder.

Wartime experiences in France, Germany, and Czechoslovakia gave Mangrum a sense of perspective when it came to the pressures of sport. Golf, he would say, was a cinch compared to what he went through in the war.

In his first U.S. Open following his return from service, at the 1946 championship at Canterbury, Mangrum shot a 70 on Friday to remain in contention in a field fronted by Hogan and Ghezzi, with Nelson, Lawson Little, and Ed "Porky" Oliver a stroke back. In the third round on Saturday,

Nelson carded a 69 in the morning round to move one shot ahead of Mangrum, who shot a 68, and Ghezzi. Lloyd holed a 75-foot putt in the afternoon round and then dueled Nelson and Ghezzi in an eighteen-hole playoff the following day. All three posted a 72 in Sunday's morning round to force a second eighteen-hole playoff that afternoon. The excruciating tension was exacerbated when inclement weather invaded the course. Mangrum was used to invasions and chaos, and the storm seemed to invigorate him. Trailing Ghezzi by three shots and Nelson by two with six holes to go, Mangrum began making up lost ground amid rain, lightning, and thunder. While Ghezzi and Nelson were thought to have been distracted by the conditions, Mangrum welcomed them.

United Press sportswriter Oscar Fraley wrote that Mangrum morphed into the battle-hardened soldier he had been in Europe. "His cream-colored sports shirt seemed to turn to khaki and to him it no longer was a golf course," wrote Fraley. "That rumble was all too familiar, and it meant trouble. And that's when Mangrum looked up at the flashes, laughed, and really started to play."

As lightning crashed, a rain-drenched Mangrum made up his deficit and birdied three of the final six rain-soaked holes to finish with another par 72. It was one stroke better than Ghezzi and Nelson and proved so impressive that Amateur champion Bud Ward was moved to call Mangrum's performance the greatest demonstration of courage he had ever seen on a golf course. Noting that the new champion had been a decided underdog, Ward said Lloyd successfully negotiated a dicey seven-foot putt on a storm-soaked green to win. "He didn't even hesitate," Ward marveled. "Just stepped up like nothing was at stake and banged it in."

Mangrum's putting would come to be considered the finest in golf. Nelson called him an excellent putter. Bing Crosby, an avid golfer and host of the famous Crosby Clambake tournament, wrote the foreword for Mangrum's first instructional book and stated that Lloyd had what most considered the "finest putting touch in the game."

Mangrum's putting technique relied on solid balance and consistent tempo of the stroke. Success in the short game translated into trophies, Mangrum winning seven times in 1948. His hardware collection increased with four victories in '49, five in '50, four more in '51, and an additional four in '53.

One of his wins in '53 was notable, as it came in the Los Angeles Open in Riviera on a course sportswriters claimed was "Hogan's Alley." Following Mangrum's victory in '53, Charles Curtis wrote in the *Los Angeles Times* that Riviera should be renamed from "Hogan's Alley" to "Mangrum's Meadows."

By the '53 Masters, Mangrum was attributing his recent victory streak to a new driver that had been made specifically for him. Mangrum was also benefitting from a style based on Snead's swing, Revolta's short game, and the putting of Smith and Harry Cooper.

In January 1953 Mangrum started the ten thousand dollar San Diego Open with a 68, but by tournament's end he had fallen to fourth place and an $840 purse. Finishing first was Tommy Bolt, a relative unknown just two years before and one of the young guns Mangrum had mentioned. Still, despite the presence of surging up-and-comers, Mangrum remained, in the estimation of *Time*, "the man to beat in any tournament he enters."

That included the 1953 Masters. Certainly, golf fans were looking forward to watching the movie-star handsome Mangrum work his magic on the Masters' tricky greens. It was said that Mangrum could go weeks without three-putting. A Vardon Trophy winner in 1951 for lowest scoring average, he would win it again in '53.

Mangrum's harrowing war experiences contributed to his cool response to pressure golf. Like Hogan, Mangrum rarely put his emotions on display. When he did, he struck fear in fellow golfers. Some members of the tour weren't sure Mangrum was quite right mentally due to what he went through in the war.

What Mangrum went through was such that only he and one other man from his original platoon survived the war. He joined the U.S. Army following Japan's bombing of Pearl Harbor on December 7, 1941, and could have taken a comparatively cushy job as a pro at one of the many military bases. Mangrum was offered a position as a club pro while training at Fort Meade in Maryland, but he refused. He broke his arm in two places when his Jeep turned over following the D-Day landings. Mangrum was sent to England to recuperate and told by medical personnel he may never play golf again. He stated later that not even the thrill of winning a U.S. Open could match the one he had when he was finally able to lift his broken arm following rehab.

Returning to action, Mangrum was on reconnaissance when he earned his first Purple Heart, taking a sniper's bullet in his knee while attempting to save a wounded soldier. Mangrum's second Purple Heart came courtesy of shrapnel he took in his chin in the Battle of the Bulge.

The icy-nerved Mangrum could be cold to acquaintances. When a woman objected to his cigarette smoking and told him, "Athletes shouldn't smoke," Mangrum snapped, "I'm no athlete lady. I'm a golfer!" A similar reply would be issued decades later by Philadelphia Phillies first baseman John Kruk, a long-haired, barrel-shaped member of the club's raucous "Macho Row."

One person Mangrum did listen to was his wife, Elita. Lloyd was twenty years old, and she was a widowed mother of three small children when they wed in 1934 in California. Lloyd called his new bride "Maw" and *Time* noted that she was his traveling companion, secretary, and business manager. The couple remained together until Lloyd's death from a heart attack at age fifty-nine in 1973.

While Mangrum was renowned for his putting, Melvin "Chick" Harbert earned notoriety for his distance off the tee. Along with Mangrum, Harbert was one of the leading challengers to Hogan's plan to regain his title, and he brought to the Masters a record that included six PGA Tour victories to that point—he added number seven the following year in the PGA Championship, his only major title—and three top-ten finishes in the Masters. The Ohio native and future member of the Michigan Golf Hall of Fame served in the U.S. Army in World War II and also battled many of golf's greatest players in a career that included two runner-up finishes in the PGA Championship and a four-stroke playoff victory over Hogan (72-76) in the 1942 Texas Open.

Harbert claimed six Michigan PGA Professional Championship victories and four Michigan Open crowns. In the latter, his twenty-three-under 265 in 1948 at Tam O'Shanter Country Club is a record that has been equaled only once, in 2012 by Barrett Kelpin at The Orchards.

The son of PGA Tour pro E. W. "Pop" Harbert, Melvin's moniker was an homage to Chick Evans, an outstanding golfer who, one year after Melvin's birth in 1915, became the first to win the U.S. Amateur and U.S. Open in the same year. Winning the 1954 PGA Championship made Harbert the first son of a PGA pro to win the title. Harbert's victory came over defending champ Walter Burkemo, a fellow future member of the Michigan Golf Hall of Fame. Their thirty-six-hole match was a dramatic one. Burkemo won three of the first four holes, but Harbert rallied to claim nineteen of the next twenty. On holes nineteen and twenty Harbert wedged his shots within the shadow of the cup. He maintained his three-up lead the rest of the match. It was a big victory for Harbert, who had lost in the finals in 1947 and '52.

Harbert's three title appearances in the PGA Championship's match play era stood second only to Nelson, Snead, Sarazen, Walter Hagen, and Jim Barnes. Harbert holds the tournament mark for the longest match scheduled for eighteen holes; he needed twenty-six holes in the second round of the 1948 PGA Championship to beat Eddie Burke.

Chick was just a young boy when *Golfers Magazine* put his name in print. "Among the golfing marvels of quite the youngest generation is Melvin (Chick) Harbert, 6-year-old son of E. W. Harbert, professional for the Marion, Indiana, Country Club. Young 'Chick' has a perfect stance, plays naturally and gracefully and seldom makes a mistake on the links, either in judgment or execution." *Golfers Magazine* noted that the boy learned from his father, studying his swing to the point that he was soon hitting drives that traveled seventy-five to one hundred yards. Before long, *Golfers Magazine* predicted, Chick would "challenge anyone his size or age."

Harbert grew up with the game of golf. His father was a club pro at several stops in the Midwest before residing in Michigan. While "Pop" Harbert served as pro at Battle Creek Country Club, Chick's mother was the club manager.

Harbert was twenty-two when he shot a then-record 268 to win the 1937 Michigan Open. A year later he was a finalist in the Michigan State Amateur and in '39 claimed the Trans-Mississippi Amateur. Harbert turned pro the following year and joined the PGA Tour in '41. He earned his first Tour victory that year, winning the Beaumont Open, then followed with his playoff win over Hogan in the 1942 Texas Open. He placed second to Snead in the St. Petersburg Open, then served in the U.S. Army Air Force in the Second World War.

Returning to the PGA Tour, Harbert finished first in the 1948 Jacksonville Open and Charlotte Open and added a pair of runner-up finishes as well. In 1949 he teamed with Bob Hamilton to win the Inverness Invitational

Four-Ball, and one year later he lost to Harry Ransom in a playoff in the World Championship of Golf.

In 1953 Harbert would win the Michigan Open and Michigan PGA Championship, and he arrived at Augusta with a history at the tournament that included a third-place finish in the 1948 Masters and top-ten finishes in 1942 when he tied for tenth and in '46 when he tied for seventh. In '38 Harbert had shared the Masters' low amateur honors.

Just as Mangrum was known for his short game and Harbert for his drives off the tee, Bolt was considered by his competitors to be one of the best strikers of the ball. His sweet swing, however, was sometimes overshadowed by a sour temper that resulted in tantrums and far-flung golf clubs.

A future member of the World Golf Hall of Fame, Bolt would finish first fifteen times from 1950 to 1965 while competing against fields that included Hogan and Snead. Bolt had the most notable jutting jaw in pro sports prior to pro football head coach Don Shula. The *New York Times* noted once that Bolt boasted a "country manner, an impeccable wardrobe and one of golf's most envied strokes." Yet Bolt was notorious for his nuclear rage. His dressing down of golf officials and heaving his clubs caused Bolt to be hit with warnings, reprimands, fines, and ultimately suspensions. He became known as "Terrible-Tempered Tommy," "Tempestuous Tommy," and "Thunder Bolt."

Bolt sometimes threw multiple clubs over the course of a round, and sensational stories soon became associated with his volcanic temper. It was said his caddie once offered him a two-iron for a particular shot, even though it was too powerful for the lie. The reason it was offered, the caddie explained, was because Terrible-Tempered Tommy had tossed from his bag all of his other irons. Another story stated that Bolt heaved a club into a canal in Miami with such fury that even divers failed to extract it.

Bolt's club-tossing revealed certain truths. He advised a young Arnold Palmer and other protégés that if they were going to throw their clubs, to always throw them forward. The idea, Bolt said, was not to waste energy by going back to pick up the clubs. Bolt said the irony of throwing clubs is that the driver went the shortest distance, the putter the farthest, followed by the sand wedge. Additional irony was found in Bolt authoring a book titled *How to Keep Your Temper on the Golf Course.*

Bolt would tell *Golf Digest* in 2002 that his rage was orchestrated for the enjoyment of galleries. He figured weekend duffers enjoyed seeing pros suffer. That's why he threw clubs so often, Bolt said, because fans loved to see golf get the better of Tour members. After a while, he added, it became showmanship.

At the same time, Bolt recognized that his violent displays of temper hurt his reputation as a shotmaker, particularly in comparison to Hogan and Snead. "I think I can hit a shot as well as the next man," Bolt told the *Saturday Evening Post* following his U.S. Open victory in 1958. "But do people come out to watch me hit golf shots, the way they do Ben Hogan and Sam Snead? No. They come out for one reason, and one reason only. To watch me blow my top."

Hogan once opined that Bolt would have won more tournaments had he been able to control his emotions. "If we could've screwed another head on his shoulders," Hogan stated, "Tommy Bolt could've been the greatest who ever played."

Bolt credited Hogan with helping save his career. Suffering from a hook that became more pronounced under pressure, Bolt sought out Hogan, who had dealt with a similar dilemma. Bolt went to Hogan and all but begged for help. Ben's response was to invite his fellow competitor to practice with him in the offseason. Hogan worked with Bolt to change his grip, cure his hook, and helped turn around Tommy's career.

Born March 31, 1916, in Haworth, Oklahoma, Tommy was two years old when his mother passed away and he and his family moved to Shreveport, Louisiana, to accommodate his father Walker's construction job. Like many members of his era, Tommy's introduction to golf came via caddying as a youth. Bolt began caddying at age thirteen, and his life changed forever when Al Espinosa arrived at his club. Espinosa had lost a U.S. Open playoff to Bobby Jones in 1929 at Winged Foot, and his manner and dress so impressed the teenage Bolt that he determined at that point to become a golf pro.

Bolt joined the U.S. Army and served four years in World War II, spending 1945 as a golf instructor at an elite officer's club in liberated Rome, Italy. Upon arriving home, he split time between golf and construction work. Lack of money prevented Bolt from being able to concentrate solely on golf. According to the World Golf Hall of Fame, Bolt was thirty-four when he joined the PGA Tour fulltime in 1950. He earned his first victory in 1951, claiming the North & South Open Championship.

The World Golf Hall of Fame states that the fact that Bolt's golf career was sidetracked several times before he became a success made his accomplishments more extraordinary. It speaks to Bolt's determination, which serves as a more accurate legacy than his temper. Despite being opposites personality-wise, the emotive Bolt and restrained Hogan became friends. Hogan's high regard for Bolt's talent was shared by other golfers, many of whom turned to Tommy for advice.

Remembering his own tough climb to reach the tour, Bolt counseled golfers and did so away from the spotlight. He offered both instruction and financial assistance to younger pros and later provided equipment and sponsored tournaments to support local golfers and Native American student golfers. Entering the 1953 Masters, Bolt was seeking to build on the third-place tie he had engineered the year before amid the Georgia pines.

Providing a colorful contrast to Thunder Bolt was Al "Bessie" Besselink. Tall and athletic, Besselink was gregarious, blessed with good looks and a go-for-broke playing style. If Bolt was one of the tour's perceived bad boys, Bessie was its glamour boy.

Born in Merchantville, New Jersey, Al learned golf as a caddie at the Merchantville Country Club. Al's athleticism extended to several sports, but it was golf that he worked at to make a living. Planning on playing college golf following high school, Al dropped out of school and enlisted in the U.S. Army, serving three years in World War II as an Army Air Corps radio operator. His pleasant personality and considerable golf skills endeared him to officers, and following the war Al took these traits to the University of Miami in Florida.

Establishing himself as the Hurricanes' most prominent player, Besselink was a varsity golfer from 1947 to 1949 and was Miami's first national champion golfer. He twice won the prestigious Southern Invitational Championship, at that time one of the major amateur championships. He fine-tuned his skills competing in pro-ams and taking on south Florida's country club elites. Bessie also played with golf hustlers, making thousands of dollars while maintaining amateur status.

Besselink turned pro in 1949 and finished twelfth at the 1950 U.S. Open at Merion that marked Hogan's famous comeback. One year later, Besselink was among those who took on arguably the greatest challenge in golf history, Robert Trent Jones's Monster of Oakland Hills. Bessie did his best, but like every other golfer in the 1951 U.S. Open's tortured field, save Hogan, he was bested by the beast.

Besselink's first PGA Tour triumph came in 1952 when his final round 64 enabled him to win the Sioux City Open in Iowa and collect three thousand dollars. His breakthrough in '52 continued with a victory in the Colombian Open in Bogata, one of several winter events he would play in South America. Besselink also teamed in '52 with legendary women's champion Babe Didrikson Zaharias at her request, and the pair won the International Mixed Two Ball Open in Orlando. A highlight of his '52 season was his play at Augusta, a third-place tie with Bolt and Jim Ferrier.

As Bessie honed his game for the Masters, he was also looking ahead to the inaugural Tournament of Champions, a twenty-man field consisting of event winners from the prior twelve months. This new addition to the PGA Tour was held at the Las Vegas Desert Inn Country Club. The purse was a hefty thirty-five thousand dollars, this at a time when the Masters' purse of twenty-six thousand dollars was the largest of any major tournament on the PGA Tour. Prior to the tournament, Bessie bet on himself with a Vegas bookie—plunking down five hundred dollars at 25-to-1 odds.

Besselink recorded rounds of 72, 68, and 68 to take a one-stroke lead into Sunday. Final round birdies on sixteen and seventeen allowed Bessie to carry his single-shot lead to the eighteenth. Before a crowd of five thousand spectators, Besselink sank a six-foot putt to save par. Under pressure, Bessie's eight-under 280 beat Chandler Harper by one stroke. Black and white photos show a smiling Besselink accepting a wheelbarrow of silver dollars totaling ten thousand dollars. Bessie's bet paid off another $12,500. Having just learned that his former playing partner, Zaharias, had been diagnosed with colon cancer, Besselink donated half his official earnings to the Damon Runyon Cancer Fund. Some say Bessie gambled away the remainder of his winnings on the Vegas strip.

Besselink was accustomed to betting on himself. He reportedly earned a golf scholarship to Miami by duping the university president. Arriving at the university president's home early on a Sunday morning, Bessie lined up four golf balls in the president's yard, which sat adjacent to a football stadium. He then teed off on each ball and accompanied the president into the stadium, where they found the balls sitting some 275 yards away and within proximity of one another. The president, who had initially told Besselink to see the athletic director for scholarship information, reportedly offered the scholarship on the spot.

Bessie is said to have sneaked into the stadium earlier and placed the balls in their locations. Besselink may have hustled the university president, but he didn't see himself as a hustler. His best game was playing hustlers, playing the guys who cheated and tried to take advantage of others. Bessie preferred to play them or millionaires. He never tried to beat anybody, he once said, who didn't have money.

Besselink stated once that he spent one hundred thousand dollars a year despite making ten thousand or less on the pro tour. The rest of his income, Bessie claimed, came from money games on the side.

Besselink would bring his renowned wedge play to Augusta. He had to try ten wedges before he found the right one. It's not known if Bessie arrived at the 1953 Masters sharpening the sole and grinding the edge of his wedge by dragging it along the road from a moving car. In later years Arnold Palmer enjoyed speaking about seeing sparks flying from Al's wedge on one occasion.

Bessie followed in the mold of Ky Laffoon, a Depression-era Arkansas golfer known for his antics. Laffoon was part Bessie, part Bolt. Like Bolt, Laffoon's temper led him to break golf clubs as he tossed them into trees or down fairways. Similar to Bessie, Laffoon was a gambler. He teamed with golf shark Titanic Thompson, with one of their hustles having Laffoon serve as caddie while Thompson taunted opponents that his caddie could beat them. Once the enraged mark took the dare, Laffoon would win the match, and he and Thompson would split their winnings.

Laffoon taking down unsuspecting opponents wasn't surprising, since he was the owner of ten Tour wins and eight top-ten finishes in majors. Laffoon's golf swing was held in high regard by peers, and his teachings helped both Hogan and Nelson.

Like Laffoon, Bob Hamilton was considered by competitors a superior wedge player. His success on the tour included a victory in the 1944 PGA Championship at Manito Golf and Country Club in Spokane, Washington, as well as wins in the 1944 North and South Open, 1946 Charlotte Open, 1948 New Orleans Open, and 1949 Inverness Invitational Four-Ball, in which he partnered with Harbert. A Hoosier, Hamilton also claimed several first-place finishes in his native Indiana, including the 1936 Indiana Amateur. Two years later he won the Indiana Open, and then won the Indiana PGA Championship in 1943 and '44.

Hamilton would become associated with golf in Evansville, the pro at Helfrich Hills Golf Course claiming five straight men's city tournaments from 1932 to 1936. His first major was the 1941 U.S. Open, which saw him place forty-fifth at Colonial Country Club in Fort Worth, Texas. His victory three years later in Spokane came via a one-up score over Nelson in the championship match. Due to World War II, many leading pros did not play in the PGA Championship, the lone major held in '44. Because Hamilton was serving at Fort Lewis in Washington state, he was able to participate in the tournament. Hamilton advanced to the championship against Nelson by defeating Gene Kunes, Harry Bassler, Jug McSpaden, and George Schneiter. In the final, Hamilton and Nelson were tied through eighteen holes before Hamilton went two-up after twenty-nine. Nelson tied it again after thirty-three holes, but Hamilton regained the lead for good on thirty-four.

Previously at the Masters, Hamilton had placed third in 1946. It was the first Masters held in three years due to the war and was won by Herman Keiser, who held off a surging Hogan in the final round to finish first with a 282.

Among those who had competed against Hamilton in the 1941 U.S. Open in Fort Worth was Ted Kroll. The native New Yorker got to Texas by hitch-hiking. Called "Lippy" because he was a talkative, friendly person who helped fellow pros with their game, Kroll was also known as a solid striker of a golf ball. Leading up to the 1953 Masters, Kroll earned wins in the 1952 San Diego Open and Insurance City Open. He also partnered with Worsham to win the 1952 Miami Beach International Four-Ball, normally a PGA Tour event but not in '52. Kroll would also win the National Celebrities Open at Woodmont Country Club in Rockville, Maryland, in September 1953.

Kroll grew up playing golf with hickory shaft clubs he built. He served in the war, where he was awarded three Purple Heart medals for being wounded in combat. Following his service, Kroll became club pro at Philmont Country Club in Huntingdon, Pennsylvania. He became a member of the PGA Tour in 1949 and three years later defeated Demaret by three shots in the San Diego Open. Kroll enjoyed a successful year in 1952, winning twice and on fifteen occasions ranking among the top ten.

In 1953, Kroll continued his successful ways, winning once and earning fourteen top-ten places. He would also play for the first time on the U.S. Ryder Cup team.

Like many of his contemporaries, Ed Oliver went from caddying to being one of the top Tour pros of his era. Also, like several of his peers, Oliver had a colorful moniker. In Oliver's case he was called "Porky" for his prodigious frame. He said the name was bestowed upon him by Snead, who took note of Oliver's 5-foot-9 height and 240 pounds. As a youth, Oliver was nicknamed "Snowball" for his ability to toss icy missiles. He was just as accurate hurling baseballs, averaging fourteen strikeouts a game while helping pitch his high school team to a title.

Staked by a trio of country club members who recognized his athletic ability, the Wilmington, Delaware, native joined the pro golf circuit during the Great Depression. In 1936 he won the Central Pennsylvania Open, the following year the Wood Memorial. In 1938 Oliver again earned the Central Pennsylvania Open championship and also claimed the South Jersey Open. He won the Buffalo Open in 1939 and '40, the latter year seeing him finish first in the Mid-South Better-Ball Championship with Clayton Haefner as well as earn his first PGA Tour victories in the Bing Crosby Pro-Am, Phoenix Open, and St. Paul Open.

Oliver added another PGA Tour win in '41, the Western Open. Oliver served four and a half years in the U.S. Armed services, longer than many of his fellow golf pros, and he then came back to win the San Antonio Texas Open in 1947 and the Tacoma Open Invitational the following year. In 1953, he finished first in the Kansas City Open. Oliver was a winner, and he was also a player with a flair for high drama. He tied for first with Sarazen and Little in the 1940 U.S. Open at Canterbury Golf Club in Beachwood, Ohio, but was disqualified for teeing off half an hour early due to concerns about inclement weather. Bobby Jones called it the most unfortunate golfing occasion he had ever heard.

In 1946 Oliver defeated Nelson in their PGA Championship quarterfinal, and a year later he set a new scoring record in the Canadian Open before bowing to Bobby Locke in a playoff. In 1952 he placed second behind Boros in the U.S. Open at Northwood Club in Dallas, Texas. Driving across the country to support his family of six, Oliver drew large galleries and became one of the most beloved figures on the tour. He was called by Ken Venturi golf's "greatest ambassador" ever.

Golf's greatest ambassador was familiar with golf's greatest player, Oliver and Hogan having a history together. Oliver defeated Hogan in 1940 in San Francisco and Phoenix and again the following year in the Western Open. In 1945 Oliver beat Hogan once more, this time at the Durham Jaycee Open, before falling to Hogan in the 1946 PGA Championship at Portland Golf Club outside Portland, Oregon, Ben winning the match play final 6 and 4. It was the first of Hogan's major championship victories. In the '52 U.S. Open, Hogan was vying to become the second man to claim three consecutive victories in the Open. He was a native Texan who had grown up in nearby Fort Worth, and he started strong with rounds of 69 and 69. But the Bantam, faltering in the ninety-eight-degree heat on Open Saturday, shot 74-74. Oliver, who shot 71-72 his first two rounds, surged past the defending champion with a 70-72 to take over second place behind the eventual champ, Boros.

Oliver's play that Saturday on the sun-washed turf was praised by many, Fraley among them. "Oliver breathed on Hogan's neck throughout the day but made his greatest progress on the backside, which he played each round in under 34, one under par," Fraley wrote. "The crowd lined from tee to green when he laid an iron shot 30 feet from the pin and sank his second putt for the second-place money."

Oliver and others would again be breathing down Hogan's neck as the field gathered in Augusta for the '53 Masters. Having sized up the competitors and the course, Hogan turned his focus to reclaiming his title. The former champion would tee off in Thursday's opening round with, as Jenkins later wrote, "revenge somewhere in his mind."

3

"Best Golf of My Life"

Ben Hogan began his preparation for the Masters in Augusta in what had become a pretournament ritual following his near fatal car-bus collision on U.S. highway 80, twenty-nine miles east of Van Horn, Texas, on February 2, 1949.

Ben and his wife, Valerie, were in room 217 of the El Capitan Hotel in Van Horn, a tiny West Texas town that lay between their departure from Phoenix to Fort Worth, where they would be settling in their first new home in fourteen years of marriage. Checking out of the El Capitan that winter morning, Ben and Valerie bid farewell to desk clerk Dorothy Evans and climbed into their Cadillac sedan. Ben then nosed the car west onto Route 80.

Hogan at this time stood firmly atop the golfing world. The previous year had seen him win ten tournaments, including the U.S. Open and PGA Championship, the first to win those two titles in the same year since Gene Sarazen. Hogan also claimed his sport's money title and accompanying Vardon Trophy. He had started 1949 in much the same fashion, picking up where he had left off, winning two tournaments in January and barely missing a third when he lost a playoff in the Phoenix Open to his old pal, the colorful Jimmy Demaret.

Eighty miles east, Alvin Logan stepped up the stairs of Greyhound bus number 548 in Pecos, Texas, and settled in behind the wheel. A substitute driver for the Greyhound Bus Company, the twenty-seven-year-old Logan lived in Pecos and drove the 210-mile, three-to-four-hour trip from Pecos to El Paso three times a week. Seated behind Logan this day were thirty-four passengers. Highway 80 was a two-lane road winding through the southern foothills of the Apache Mountains. Because blind curves marked certain stretches of the highway, passing a vehicle in front of you was not advised. It was less advisable given the fog and ice-slick roads that marked the early morning traveling conditions.

Logan's Greyhound bus got behind an Alamo Freight Line semitrailer and trailed the truck for some seven miles. Logan and the semitrailer driver, Hubert Harshaw of San Antonio, turned their lights on to improve visibility. As Harshaw reduced the speed of his freighter to negotiate the curving road and fog, Logan realized he was losing time trailing the truck.

It was 8:30 a.m. when Logan, looking to pass the semi on the two-lane road, shifted his Greyhound into high gear and pushed the speedometer to fifty miles an hour. Because of the ground mist, Ben had slowed his speed to twenty-five miles per hour. From their lane, Ben and Valerie suddenly saw four headlights barreling toward them in the fog. The startled Hogan pulled his steering wheel to his right to avoid a head-on collision, but a concrete abutment blocked his Cadillac from getting off the highway. Yelling "Look out, Valerie!" Ben threw himself across the front seat to protect his wife. Logan tried to yank his bus back into the westbound lane, but it was too late. The 19,250-pound Greyhound going fifty mph slammed into the 3,900-pound Cadillac going twenty-five mph, the left front of the bus collapsing the left front of Hogan's car. Seeing the horrific collision, Harshaw drove into an embankment to avoid hitting the back end of the bus.

Hogan's attempt to save Valerie also resulted in saving himself. The force of the collision caused the steering wheel to be driven into the back seat, its violent movement breaking Ben's collarbone. The car's engine was pushed into the driver's seat, fracturing Hogan's pelvis and rib and damaging his legs. Knocked nearly unconscious, Ben and Valerie lay on the roadside, twisted amid the wreckage before finally being helped from their mangled car. The great golfer was given up for dead; a call was placed to the police telling them two people had been killed in an accident.

Some ninety minutes elapsed before an ambulance arrived to rush them to the hospital. Onlookers covered Hogan's prone form to keep him warm. Valerie endured lacerations on her legs and bruises on her head; Ben, meanwhile, would be hospitalized in El Paso for the following fifty-nine days with a broken collarbone, fractured pelvis and rib, broken left ankle, bruises on his left leg, a cut on his head, and internal injuries. One month into his recovery Hogan got another scare when blood clots formed in his lungs. His condition became so grave newspaper editors began gathering biographical information in the event of his death.

Hogan instead made a heralded comeback, arguably the greatest in the history of sport, and his riveting personal story served to inspire millions of fans and nonfans around the world. "I know that after his accident he was really surprised to find out how much people liked him and cared about him," great niece Lisa Scott says. "All the fan mail he got and the well-wishes, and I think at that point he warmed a little."

Hogan had been Golfer of the Year in 1948 and a man who had won thirty-seven tournaments since returning from service in World War II. Doctors couldn't say with certainty if the thirty-six-year-old champion would reclaim his form, but he defied the odds and became an even greater champion. He was a golfer who majored in guts and grit, and it was not without paying a painful price. "Golf is so hard, and you don't improve without a ton of work," Scott states. "It gave me a newfound respect for how long he practiced and how much work he put into preparing for a tournament. . . . That 1953 season in particular, he only entered into a small number of tournaments. His playing season was such a short period, because after his accident he had to be strategic about when he played."

Hogan lived every day with constant aches, and his circulatory problems were such that he required a three- to four-hour ritual just to be able to compete. He would soak in a tub of warm water and Epsom salts to stimulate circulation in his legs. He applied liniment to his lower limbs and, to reduce the swelling in his legs by facilitating the flow of blood in his veins as he walked, wrapped his lower body in bandages and encased his legs in support hose stockings.

"Hogan," Bruce Devlin says, "was lucky to be alive." Devlin recalls a trip he and his wife took with Ben and Valerie to the 1966 U.S. Open in San Francisco. "I'd known him for four years then," Devlin says, "and I got up enough confidence to ask at dinner one night, 'Ben, do you ever talk much about what happened on the way home from El Paso?' He started out talking about putting his golf clubs in the trunk of the car and by the end of dinner Tuesday night he got to the victory at Merion. Nearly two full dinners before we got the whole story. It was quite remarkable."

The terrible accident having left him with a pronounced limp and slightly blurred vision, Hogan headed to the first tee of the Masters Tournament on Thursday, April 9. The field for this seventeenth Masters was filled with notables—nine Masters champions, nine U.S. Open champions, six PGA Championship winners, two British Open kings, five U.S. Amateur champs, three British Amateur victors, and many of the top twenty-four players from the previous year's Masters.

Augusta National's layout in 1953 spanned 6,950 yards and was a par 72. The course length had been expanded fifty yards prior to the 1952 Masters. It marked the fourth time Augusta was lengthened since its inception in 1934, when it measured 6,700 yards. It remained at that yardage through 1937 before going to 6,800 yards from 1938 to 1947. It expanded to 6,900 yards in '48, and another fifty yards were added in '52. It would remain at 6,950 through 1955 and expand to 6,965 in 1956.

The Masters layout listed ten par fours, four par threes, and four par fives. The front nine opened with a par four measuring four hundred yards, with number two a par five stretching to a course-long 555 yards and hole three a par four listed at 355 yards. The fourth hole was the first par three and the fourth shortest on the course at 220 yards, number five a par four with a distance of 450 yards, and number six a par three whose 190 yards tied it with the sixteenth for the second shortest on the course. Number seven was a 365-yard par four, hole eight a par five with the second longest distance of 520 yards, and number nine a par four measuring 420 yards.

The back nine began with a 470-yard par four, followed by another par four on an eleventh hole measuring 445 yards. Famed number twelve was a par three whose 155 yards marked the shortest hole on the course. Holes thirteen, fourteen, and fifteen combined to mark the longest stretch on the course. Number thirteen was a par five measuring 470 yards, hole fourteen a par four at 420 yards, and number fifteen the final par five listed at 505 yards, the third longest on the course. The closing three holes listed number sixteen at 190 yards and the last par three, the seventeenth a par four at 400 yards, and number eighteen another par four at 420 yards.

Having played Augusta numerous times, Devlin knows well the challenges the course presents. "The greens are a little bit like Oakmont," Devlin states. "In those pine trees that wind can sort of wander around, and you're not quite sure where the hell it's coming from and that can make it quite difficult. Plus, you've got Amen Corner and the lake at 15 and 16."

John Boyette said Amen Corner—the Masters' eleventh, twelfth, and thirteenth holes—was first named in 1958 by Herbert Warren Wind in an article for *Sports Illustrated*. Wind was a jazz fan along with being a golf writer, and Boyette noted that Wind was influenced in his naming of Amen Corner by a jazz song titled "Shoutin' in That Amen Corner."

Over the years, a full one-third of the names of the holes at Augusta National have changed, as the plants and shrubs showcased on certain holes are different from their predecessors. Hole number one, called Tea Olive, was first known as Cherokee Rose. The second hole, Pink Dogwood, was Woodbine. Number four, Flowering Crab Apple, was The Palm, and hole seven, Pampas, was formerly Cedar. Three Pines was the original name for number twelve, now known as Golden Bell. Hole fourteen, currently Chinese Fir, had been Spanish Dagger.

British golf essayist Henry Longhurst visited Augusta in 1960 and wrote that the Masters, a tournament considered by many as the greatest in the world, is a course offering a "tremendous test of nerve and skill" and an atmosphere all its own. Longhurst observed that the course is laid out among a combination of vast pine trees reaching one hundred feet high, shorter firs, and trees and shrubs in full flower, including red, purple, and orange azaleas that bloom magnificently come tournament time. When the spring sun blazes forth, Longhurst wrote, it brings out everything, even spectators, in "gorgeous Technicolor." Augusta's grass is green as can be, said Longhurst, and is "an expensive combination of basic Bermuda, which provides an almost invisible brown and dormant under matting to the vivid green rye."

Reportedly the first player to arrive for the Masters, Hogan was in Georgia two weeks prior to the tournament and brought with him the distinction of being the lone man to have a lifetime scoring average at Augusta under par. His 71.91 was crafted over eleven prior Masters Tournament appearances, an impressive mark that would have been lower but for his rough 74-79 scores in the final two rounds that prevented him from defending his title in '52. As Gene Gregston noted, Hogan acknowledged being "particularly ashamed" of the 79 and was determined to make amends. The stigma of his finish in '52 needed to be erased, and Hogan made it clear prior to the tournament that was his primary intention.

Hogan had fallen prey to the majors in 1952; in '53 he would be the predator. He was the "Hawk," a nickname given by competitors for the intense way he studied and attacked a golf course. His shot-making has impressed generations of golfers, from Bobby Jones, Byron Nelson, and Sam Snead to Arnold Palmer, Jack Nicklaus, and Tiger Woods. Tommy Bolt said that while he saw Nicklaus stop to watch Hogan practice, he never saw Hogan stop to watch Nicklaus practice. Devlin remembers what it was like to play alongside Hogan:

His shots always sounded pretty damn solid. You never saw Hogan hit a 25-yard drive offline. He might miss to the left rough or the right rough, but it was never one of those where he hit it and it was 30 yards offline.

He was working all the time. He never stopped working on the golf course. The one thing he always did to me every time we walked to the first tee was he'd pull my driver out of the bag and shake his head a little bit and say, "Still using the buggy whip, huh?" He used a club that was like a steel rod, it was so stiff. But that was his deal, that's what he liked. I guess the theory is, the stiffer you got it the less you could bring the misses in closer than what they are with a whippy shaft. I think he was unique in that regard. I broke my driver one year and Arnold Palmer gave me one of his spares and that shaft was not as stiff as Hogan's was. You look at the structure of the two men and you'd think Arnold had the stiffer club but that was not the case. For a little guy, Hogan was pretty strong.

Hogan's days at Augusta consisted of an early breakfast, several hours perfecting his precise left-to-right control of the ball at a practice fairway, a short break for lunch, and then several more hours hitting golf balls on the practice fairway. Insular to the point that he was considered by many to be a loner, Hogan pursued perfection with a relentless and religious zeal.

Bolt believed Hogan knew more about hitting a golf ball than anyone. Hogan was the only player Bolt knew who received ovations from fans while on the practice tee. He watched Hogan play practice rounds and realized other pros made up half the gallery. Bolt played rounds in which he recalled Hogan hitting every shot at the flag. The opening day of the '53 Masters belonged not to Hogan, however, but to Chick Harbert, whose four-under 68 led the field. Al Besselink and Ed "Porky" Oliver tied for second at 69, with Hogan and Milan Marusic tied for fourth at 70.

Hogan remained confident. Though he had not competed in a major for nine months following the 1952 U.S. Open, Hogan had been practicing regularly for four months leading up to the Masters. Hogan knew Augusta's fairways were in near-ideal condition. To deal with the difficulty of the greens, he made a physical adjustment, slightly closing his putting stance. Two years earlier, he told *Time* that Augusta's greens "are tricky . . . and there are shots to the green here that paralyze your thinking." Hogan's adjustment paid off, with Gregston noting that Hogan's "confident stroke was once again in evidence when putting the ball." Indeed, Hogan needed just thirty-one putts in Thursday's opening round. Hogan displayed at Augusta what Gregston described as the "attitude of a man with a brisk purpose once more, more of a spring to his somewhat stiff-gaited step, and an air of authority that had been missing the year before."

Fans by the thousands sought out prime real estate to get the best view of the golf legend. The Hogan mystique was real; the Hawk always owned the largest gallery at a tournament. Hogan was cognizant of the crowds, but his focus was such that he would stare straight ahead, fixating his glare on the shot at hand as he took deep drags on his Chesterfield cigarettes. Bolt believed Hogan focused so intently on his own game that he was barely conscious of his playing partner and competitors. Snead said Hogan's conversation on the golf course was usually limited to "good luck" on the first tee and "you're away."

"I think he's a tad misunderstood," Scott says. "Everyone's impression of him is that he's this, he's that. He's sort of everything. Was he serious when he was playing? Of course, that was his job. Maybe he wasn't super friendly; he was concentrating. I can't imagine that if I was interrupted at work, I would be that great about it."

For later generations who would never know what it was like to watch Hogan up close, Jenkins provided a vivid word picture. Hogan, he wrote, "walked from shot to shot quickly as he could, not so much with a limp but as if he were always trudging slightly uphill. He might study a shot for a long moment, drawing on a cigarette, peering coldly into the distance."

Once Hogan chose his club he played quickly, finishing with his trademark swing. Fans at Augusta heard the telltale sounds of Hogan's contact with the ball and read what sportswriter Randy Russell wrote in the *Augusta Chronicle* prior to the tournament that Hogan had spent weeks "tuning up for the Masters."

His preparation paid dividends in the second round on Friday, Hogan shaving a stroke from his score the day before and carding a 69. Halfway through the tournament, he had taken over first place with a two-day total of 139 that was five under par. Chunky, cigar-chomping Bob Hamilton, who also shot 69 on Friday, was one shot back at 140. Harbert followed his 68 with a 73, and he and Ted Kroll were tied for third at 141. Lloyd Mangrum, who shot Friday's low-round score of 68, joined Oliver and Marusic in fifth place at 142.

The second round had begun in a thunderstorm and ended in sunshine, but it was Hogan, not the erratic weather, that stood at center stage. The Associated Press began its coverage of the second round in the following fashion: "Ben Hogan, the grim little golfer who once had a Masters tournament dedicated to him, took charge of another Masters today as he shot into the lead at the 36-hole mark."

Followed by a weekday gallery of eight thousand that the AP called "tremendous," Hogan was taking the measure of a course whose par the AP referred to as "always hard to beat." Yet Hogan was beating what the AP called the "spacious and soul-testing course in the red clay hills of East Georgia."

Hogan's initial birdie of the day came on hole number five, the same hole that began a bedeviling round for reigning champion Sam Snead. Hogan followed with birdies on the sixth, eighth, and ninth, each achieved with what the AP described as "deadly iron shots." Hogan's three-putt on number eleven put him over par for the first time, but he regained lost ground on thirteen when he followed a drive into the woods with his fifth birdie. Hogan went over par again on the short sixteenth, then played cautiously the remainder of the round and recorded pars on seventeen and eighteen.

Gregston called Hogan's golf on Friday "forceful, his shot making brilliant, and his putting consistently fine." Regarding the latter, Hogan required only thirty-two putts in his second round. Snead, meanwhile, was struggling mightily. Slammin' Sam shot a 70 in the first round, and the Virginia country boy might have been tempted to let loose a rebel yell when he had to endure a 71 due to a mix-up on his signed scorecard. Round Two proved more problematic. Unable to control his wood shots, The Slammer shot a 76 that put him at 146, seven shots off the pace.

Hamilton, whose inaction the previous winter had led to his competing just for fun in the first round, grew serious on Friday when he realized he was in contention. He shot 32 on the front nine and was tied with Hogan for first place after eleven holes. Hamilton went over par on twelve, birdied thirteen, but then went back over on fourteen. A par on sixteen would pull him even with Hogan once more, but he three-putted. On eighteen, Hamilton hooked his shot "a country mile," in the words of the AP, and then failed to drain the long putt that would have again put him in a tie for first place.

Mangrum, the pretournament favorite of many, followed his first round 74 with a second round 68. A fashion plate whose colorful clothes could make even Augusta's brightest blooms blush, Mangrum in the 1955 Masters donned an outfit consisting of blue cap, pink shirt, and lavender slacks. *Time* magazine said Mangrum's ensemble "howled like an off-key calliope along the green fairways of Georgia's Augusta National course." Mangrum laughed off the criticisms. "They need a little color around here, since the frost ruined all the azaleas."

Mangrum's flash was not limited to fashion, as his sterling second round at the '53 Masters vividly illustrated. His efficient play could be just as eye-catching, and he climbed into a three-way tie for fifth, with his 142 two under par and three strokes off Hogan's lead. Mangrum said of Hogan that "the little man is the only one in golf I've ever feared."

The little man would show why he was feared in Saturday's third round. The pairing for this penultimate round featured a historic matchup in the matinee and a legendary performance by a proud former champion. Steady rain dampened the expansive greens and blossoming azaleas at the start of the third round. Yet when Hogan strode to the first tee, the storm stopped and was replaced by sunshine and sweet-scented air. Hogan was seeking his second Masters title, Oliver his first, and the two proceeded to give the galleries what Gregston described as "a classic shoot-out to rival any in the history of the game."

The Bantam and Porky may have been an odd couple on the course, but they dazzled onlookers with their precise play. Oliver carded a 34 on the front nine, Hogan a 32. Ben claimed birdies on the second, fourth, eighth, and ninth holes. Porky reclaimed lost ground on the back nine with a 33, bettering the Bantam's 34. To go with his four birdies on the front nine, Hogan produced more of the same on numbers ten, fourteen, and fifteen. The lone smudge on Hogan's card came on sixteen, a bogey resulting from his three-putt from thirty feet.

By the time Hogan had reached the fifteenth, his assault on Augusta had him seven under par. History was beckoning, and the gallery was buzzing. Some seemed unable to comprehend the extremely high level of play they were witnessing. One man watched Hogan drain three consecutive birdies and said he was leaving because he didn't believe what he was seeing. A golfer watched from the clubhouse and announced he was heading outdoors to breathe the same air as Hogan.

For the round, Oliver shot a superb 67 and was still a stroke behind Hogan, whose startling 66 represented his best ever round at Augusta. Hogan's fifty-four-hole total of 205 was eleven under par and a Masters record. It also gave him a four-stroke cushion over Oliver. Hamilton and Harbert trailed Hogan by five and six shots, respectively. Hogan came out for Sunday's final round fully aware of his 79 in the fourth round the year before. "Worst round he'd ever shot," Dan Jenkins told John Boyette. "He didn't play bad; it was just windy and he didn't get any breaks."

Strong wind and drenching rain again lashed Augusta's grounds prior to Hogan teeing off. Once again, the skies cleared an hour before the Bantam approached the first tee attired in his flat, white cap, sharply creased slacks, and golf cleats with the extra spike. His smoldering cigarette jutted forth from his lips, the smoke swirling in front of his dark stare. While the early starters had to deal once more with a deluge, Hogan would again play most of his round in brilliant sunlight.

Even tournament director Cliff Roberts seemed a bit startled by this parting of storm clouds. "Twice we experienced rain," he later wrote, "but on both occasions it ended, and the sun came out just before Ben's starting time."

Heavy morning rains had left the course, in the AP's words, "soggy and slow." Teamed with Nelson, who was always paired with the leader, and accompanied by a gallery of twelve thousand fans eager to witness history, Hogan played in his customary slow and careful style. His birdie four on the second hole came courtesy of a four-wood second shot that hugged the fairway and rolled twenty feet past the cup. A three-iron on number four led to another birdie. Hogan was armed with a lead so comfortable he could shoot over par in the final round and still set a tournament record. He had shot over par in the Masters and U.S. Open in '52, and some might have wondered if he was faltering again when his putting skills deserted him on the sixth and eighth holes and he bogeyed both. With the scent of cigarettes mixing with the fragrant, perfume-like aroma of azaleas, Hogan made the turn with a par 36, one more than the 35 posted by Oliver, whom the AP called "the only player who wouldn't be shaken off."

Oliver fought to make a match of it, carding a birdie four on number two and a birdie three on number three. Fans were hoping for a late afternoon duel amid the pines, but Hogan would have none of it. Making the turn, Hogan continued to sail drives through the dramatic shadows of a Sunday afternoon at Augusta, adding birdie fours on thirteen and fifteen.

"There's no doubt he was not hitting short irons into the par 5s back then," Boyette says "All of the accounts I've read is that when they went for the par 5s on the back nine they were hitting long irons or even fairway woods. Dan Jenkins told me that Hogan would play it out to the right, and then use a 4-wood or something to try to launch it up into the air and hold it onto the green. It was a much different game back then."

For Hogan, the final round of the 1953 Masters was a different game than the one he had played the year before. Claude Harmon was on the eighteenth green in the final round of the '52 Masters when Hogan limped in with a 79. Harmon heard fans stating that Ben's legs were shot, that it was the end for him. Harmon dined with Hogan that night, and while no mention was made of the day's events, Claude could see that Ben had determined that he was not leaving golf with a 79 and was already calculating the amount of work it would take to avenge his loss.

Approaching the final hole in '53, Hogan knew his moment of redemption had arrived. He strode the sun-streaked eighteenth fairway, the scent of spring in the air and the huge gallery at his heels. Snead stated once that striding up the eighteenth fairway with a chance to win the Masters was like "floating on air." Hogan wasn't floating; the tough Texan was limping, courtesy of his car accident.

Just two years earlier Hogan by his own admission had wondered if he would ever win the Masters after failing on his first nine attempts. He finally prevailed in 1951 with a two-stroke victory over Skee Riegel highlighted by a bogey-less 68 in the final round. The latter was particularly satisfying, since Hogan had struggled to conquer the closing eighteen at Augusta. The final round of the Masters, he acknowledged, had become "a complex" with him.

Prior to his accident Hogan had not always been a gallery favorite. Support for him grew following his almost mythic return from crippling injuries. Hogan said his biggest thrill at the '51 Masters came from being able to succeed for the crowd. Every par he recorded resulted in a deafening cheer. "I knew a lot of them were pulling for me," he said later. "I was glad I didn't let them down."

Nor would Hogan let his followers down in '53. They rushed to catch glimpses of him, peering through portable, handheld periscopes as they lined the green on eighteen. The Masters boasts one of the more famous finishing holes of any course in the world. Called "Holly" for the variety of *Ilex opaca*, the hole offers an uphill dogleg right. The morning rain had resulted in a deepening of the lush green expanse and heightening of fragrant aromas from Augusta's flowers.

The watery, pastel-like coloring of this April Sunday produced a spectacular setting, and Hogan rose to the moment. Taking long pulls on his Chesterfields, he coolly closed the show with a birdie three, his fifth birdie against just two bogeys in the final eighteen holes. Hogan had sliced three strokes off his front nine score, shooting a 33 for a 69 and new Masters mark of 274, fourteen under par.

Hogan's reaction to setting the 72-hole record at Augusta was understated. "That's nice," he told reporters, "but I was only trying to win a golf tournament."

Oliver's 279 tied the previous long-standing mark for top score set by Ralph Guldahl in 1939 and equaled nine years later by Harmon, but he was still five strokes behind Hogan. The AP opened its report on Hogan regaining his Masters title by referring to him as "the little man who has made golf a science instead of a game." Hogan's second Masters victory in three years set a new standard, and the AP noted that he "wrapped up the record on the last nine holes."

Hogan predicted prior to the tournament that a new standard would be set if the weather cooperated. It did, at least for Hogan, and he made good on his prediction. New York *Herald-Tribune* golf writer Al Laney believed Hogan would have prevailed even if the weather had not favored him. "There is little doubt that whatever the conditions Hogan would have done what was required of him," wrote Laney. "For this man, besides being one of the greatest golfers of all time, is a competitor without a superior in sports."

Hogan's playing partner, Nelson, had said after beating Ben in their playoff a decade earlier that the Masters was a tournament he wanted to win again before all others. Hogan shared that feeling, and it seemed fitting that Byron was standing alongside Ben when he won again at Augusta. "I hit the ball better—more like I wanted to hit it—than in any 72-hole tournament I've ever played," a smiling Hogan told reporters. "Before the tournament started, I knew I was playing the best golf of my life, and I knew that if I played in the tourney the way I did while practicing I would win. It's the best I've ever played for 72 holes."

Roberts called Hogan's 70-69-66-69 "the best 72-hole stretch of golf ever played by anyone anywhere." He thought it a case of a great golfer taking "full advantage of his opportunity by producing a perfect brand of golf on each of the four days of play."

Gregston wrote that Hogan's four rounds "were nearer perfection than anyone could remember ever being played on a championship-caliber course. So flawless was the execution and so brilliant the results that one had to search to find any shadows darkening the effort. There were no blots, only a smudge here and there." That Hogan needed just 126 putts to successfully navigate Augusta's expansive, undulating greens was "a very skillful exhibition," according to Gregston.

Boyette believes the same. "Augusta National was a far cry back then from what it is now," he says. "Looking at the old photos and seeing some of the wild areas, like around the tributary at Rae's Creek at 13, what he did on those greens, they were not the perfection they are now. There were only two cases of someone breaking 280 at the Masters before Hogan in '53, and he just walloped that by five shots. I think that was kind of like a Secretariat moment, for lack of a better term. This guy was miles ahead of his competition. Hogan said at the time that it was the greatest golf he'd ever played for 72 holes, and it was. He was one shot away from being the first guy to shoot all four rounds in the 60s at Augusta. So it was quite impressive."

Oliver's final-round 70 allowed him to place second, his best finish ever at Augusta. Mangrum's 69 in Round Four put him third at 282. Snead, the defending champ, fell off the pace early and never contended, shooting 75 on Sunday for a 292.

Hogan's historic season was fully underway. Two weeks after the Masters he headed to Mexico City and claimed the Pan American Open. He tied for third in the unofficial Greenbrier Pro-Am, finishing four strokes behind Snead, then returned home and defended his championship at Colonial, winning by five shots.

The next major challenge for Hogan would come in June in what he called "the biggest tournament in the world"—the U.S. Open. The steel-nerved Hogan would trek to a Steel City suburb, Oakmont in western Pennsylvania, seeking to secure his record-tying fourth U.S. Open title. It was a feat accomplished to that point only by Willie Anderson and Bobby Jones.

Few knew it at the time, but Ben told Valerie after the Masters that he was thinking of doing something he had never yet done—enter the British Open. It was a tournament Hogan had never played in, but he told his wife he would do so. He did, however, add a condition. "If," he stated, "I win the U.S. Open."

Hogan acknowledged later that his words "If I win the U.S. Open" constituted a big "If." Lying in wait was a course considered by competitors to be bleak, brutal, and bullish on even the greatest golfers.

4

Oakmont

Oakmont in 1953 was a brute and had been since its opening in 1904. Course historian Marino Parascenzo considers Oakmont not only a great course but a beast.

Bruce Devlin agrees. "Oakmont is an extremely difficult golf course," he states. "It's a course where you better think. There are places where if you miss a shot into a green with a particular pin placement in the wrong place, you've got no chance of getting it up there, unless you make it from 20 or 30 feet."

The speed of Oakmont's greens is legendary. Devlin remembers that the first time he played Oakmont, his caddie told him in a practice round, "Bruce, you better not hit it past the flag. If you do, there's a chance you'll putt it off the green."

"I thought he was nuts," Devlin recalls. "I happened to hit my second shot seven or eight feet behind the hole, and I lipped it out and then chipped it for my next shot. You got more chance of making a chip short off the green then you do having to putt from behind the hole. And the bunkers, you drive it into those Church Pews and it's like putting it into the water."

Designed by Henry Clay Fownes and his son William Clark Fownes Jr., Oakmont was built over the course of one year by the sweat and muscle of 100 to 150 men and two-dozen horse-and-mule teams. Unlike most course architects who construct their layouts based on the existing topography, Henry Fownes first drew up his plans for the ideal course and then went in search of the property that would best accommodate him. What emerged remains the pride of Pittsburgh.

Henry Fownes was born September 12, 1856, in Pittsburgh, born into the steel business that became his life. Henry's father, Charles, owned a foundry, and following his father's untimely passing, Henry left school and learned the family business from his uncle, who owned the Solar Iron Works. Henry learned quickly and became a leader in the city's steel business. He and his brothers developed several successful businesses, prominent among them the Carrie Furnace Company, a blast furnace located along the Monongahela River.

Carrie Furnace was sold in 1898 to Andrew Carnegie, the titan of industry and philanthropy who had begun building an empire in the steel business in 1875. The sale and incorporation of Carrie Furnace into the Carnegie Steel Company founded six years earlier left Henry financially secure.

Henry began playing golf in 1898, reportedly being introduced to the game by Carnegie. The latter was a native of Scotland, having been born in Dunfermline in 1835 and emigrating at age twelve to America with his parents. Fownes loved golf, and an excerpt on the founding of Oakmont Country Club from its twenty-eighth anniversary on September 22, 1928, states that Fownes played his first round of golf on the six-hole course situated on the cricket grounds of the Pittsburgh Field Club.

Fownes became an accomplished golfer, playing in the National Amateur in 1901 in Atlantic City and earning a victory over the Philadelphia city champion. He eventually competed in five U.S. Amateur championships. His sons, William and Charles, likewise became enamored of golf, and the Fownes family came to be ranked among the top players in western Pennsylvania.

With the six-hole course of the Pittsburgh Field Club proving too small, Henry and William joined George Ormiston, E. Z. Smith, and others to create the Highland Country Club. Its nine-hole course adjoined Highland Park and opened in 1900. Once again, the club course proved too short and too easy. Henry and William longed for the layouts Carnegie spoke of that existed across the Atlantic in Scotland and England, eighteen-hole courses that were testing and long. Their search for a large tract of land outside Pittsburgh to accommodate their course began in 1902, and with the aid of Oakmont resident George S. Macrum, Henry and William found such a property in 1903. It was a tract of farmland comprising 191 acres and overlooking Oakmont, a borough located fifteen miles northeast of downtown Pittsburgh. The land sat at the top of Hulton Hill, also known as White Oak Levels.

Oakmont was so named in 1816 when Michael Bright, a farmer, purchased the land and the deed read in part, "Beginning at a black oak on the bank of the Allegheny River. . . ." In 1899, Oakmont was incorporated from the second ward of the borough of Verona.

Henry and business associates Joseph F. Guffey, Joseph B. Shea, Edwin Z. Smith, and F. T. F. Lovejoy applied for a charter for the Oakmont Land Company. On May 15, 1903, the charter was granted, and the Oakmont Land Company bought the land for $78,500, an amount that in 2024 would equal more than $2.75 million. According to a 1928 excerpt from the *Anniversary Journal,* "stockholders subscribed sufficient funds to pay for the land, build the course and erect the present club house." Concurrently, an application was submitted for a charter for the Oakmont Country Club, which was granted on October 24, 1903. Membership in the club swelled, as members from the Highland Country Club, Westmoreland Country Club, and Pittsburgh Field Club switched to Oakmont.

With Oakmont CC an official establishment, work began on September 15, 1903, on building a course that harkened back to Old World layouts. The farmland Fownes invested in offered a rolling landscape situated on a plateau above the Allegheny River. White Oak was populated with oak trees. As Fownes had a passion for Scottish and English courses that were virtually free of trees, he ordered the land to be cleared. Modeling Oakmont on the dune-strewn links of Europe meant Fownes's new course would be a Sahara of sand. Construction began in the fall, workers hand digging the first twelve holes of the only course Henry ever designed. Six weeks saw the course cleared up to the twelfth fairway. Work was halted in winter, and the last six holes were dug the following spring. Seed was planted, and on October 1, 1904, Oakmont was opened to play.

When the Fownes family and fellow golfers from Highland Country Club, Pittsburgh Field Club, and Westmoreland Country Club first stepped foot on the grounds, they found themselves surveying a course unique to their sporting experience. "Bleak and windswept, it was also endless—eight par fives, one par *six*, a total of par 80!—and endlessly menacing," wrote Oakmont historian James W. Finegan.

Mirroring the links courses of Great Britain, Oakmont's design is that of an "inland links" course, its layout far removed from any large body of water. Large, undulating greens provided part of the problem golfers faced, but the real menace were the bunkers, more than two hundred in all. Because of their high number, it was not possible to avoid every one of them. Once trapped, wrote Finegan, it was "embarrassingly difficult" to get free.

Henry Fownes not only favored bunkers; he favored bunkers with a nasty attitude. The hazards were furrowed with grooves that Finegan noted were "deeper than the diameter of a golf ball and perpendicular to the line of play."

Workers maintained the furrowed sand with rakes specially fitted with teeth seven inches long and across their heads a thick, flat piece of steel. Jimmy Demaret said that if one combed North Africa with the rakes in World War II, Germany's "Desert Fox," Field Marshal Rommel, wouldn't have advanced past Casablanca.

Located just outside Oakmont's limits in the borough of Plum, Oakmont CC added a clubhouse in 1904. Following the Scottish influence of the links course, Edward Stotz, a renowned Pittsburgh architect, modeled the clubhouse after the farmhouses of Scotland.

Turning Oakmont into something of an anomaly among its blue-blooded brethren on the country club circuit was a railroad that sliced across its grounds. In time, the Pennsylvania Turnpike eventually covered the same straightaway as the railroad tracks, with holes two through eight on the eastern side of the highway.

Oakmont hosted its first prominent tournament in 1919, club member Davidson Herron defeating seventeen-year-old wunderkind Bobby Jones 5 and 4 in the final to capture the U.S. Amateur championship. Three years later, the *New York Times* reported in its August 14 edition that the "eyes of the golf world will be focused on the Oakmont links beginning tomorrow, when the cream of the professional golfers of America will start out in their annual tourney to determine the PGA championship."

Gene Sarazen seized the title, defeating Emmet French 4 and 3 in the final. Sarazen's victory came in the fifth PGA Championship played to that point, its match play field of sixty-four participants qualifying via sectional championships. It was the first time the field listed sixty-four players, double the size of each of the four previous P G A Championships. The tournament opened on August 14, its match play format listing ten rounds over five days. Each of the first two rounds was an eighteen-hole match played in the morning and afternoon of the opening day. With the field reduced to sixteen following Monday's first two rounds, the following four days were used to hold thirty-six-hole matches in the third round, quarterfinals, semifinals, and finals.

The twenty-year-old Sarazen was fresh off the first of his eventual seven major victories, this coming in the U.S. Open one month earlier at Skokie Country Club in the Chicago suburb of Glencoe, Illinois. Before a gallery of two thousand fans, The Squire shot a final-round 68 to finish one stroke ahead of Jones and John Black. When the final ended on the thirty-third hole, Sarazen, the Highland Club pro, was carried to the Oakmont clubhouse on the shoulders of Pittsburgh fans.

The Squire successfully negotiated Oakmont's troublesome greens and bunkers, matching French in drives and outdoing him on approaches and on the blazing fast greens. He took just one putt on thirteen of the greens and more than two on only one. French, whom observers felt seemed to have a "hoodoo" curse hounding him as he consistently fell short of fame despite being one of the game's best, was off target on several short putts.

Sarazen shot 74 in the morning round to own a two-shot lead over French. Both struggled in the afternoon and made the turn with French leading by a stroke, 42-41. Sarazen picked up three strokes on the back nine, and both were over the green on number fifteen. Sarazen chipped back to within a foot of the cup to win the match.

Defending P G A winner Walter Hagen did not play at Oakmont in the '22 Championship due to scheduling conflicts with his exhibition schedule. One year later, The Squire and The Haig would meet in a much-anticipated matchup of titlists in the 1923 P G A Championship at Pelham Country Club in New York. Sarazen emerged triumphant over Hagen in thirty-eight holes for his second straight P G A title and third major championship overall.

The two champions were tied at 77 strokes following the morning round of the final. The stocky Sarazen went up two with three holes remaining. Consecutive bogeys left them even again, and a pair of par fours halved the thirty-sixth hole. The first extra hole resulted in clutch birdies by Sarazen and Hagen. On the thirty-eighth hole Hagen's tee shot landed twenty feet from the hole but in the sand. Sarazen's ball was fifty feet from the cup and in the rough. While Hagen failed to free himself from the bunker, Sarazen pitched out of the rough and to within four feet of victory. The Squire sealed the deal with a pressure putt for birdie. Disappointed in defeat in what had been a tremendous matchup, Hagen would bounce back and claim the next four PGA Championships en route to his career total of eleven major titles.

The *New York Times* described an outcome that was unprecedented:

Gene Sarazen, the young Highland Club professional, added to his unique and unparalleled collection of golf titles here today when he vanquished Emmet French, stalwart home-bred pro at the Youngstown (Ohio) Country Club, by 4 & 3. . . .

The victory of the young star, who only a few years ago was an unknown caddie toting clubs around Westchester links, easily stamps him as one of the stars of all time, for it marked his third conquest of the present year, a feat never before equaled in the history of golf.

By the time the U.S. Amateur returned in 1925, *Time* magazine was referring to Oakmont as one of the most difficult courses in the world. *Time* wrote that the "greens-gang" kept the landscape at its "pinnacle of horticultural impeccability" and wondered how competitors "liked the way they had drawn some of the already-retiring tees still further back."

Jones had established himself as one of the game's premier players, the twenty-one-year-old earning his first major championship by defeating Bobby Cruickshank by two strokes, 76-78, in an eighteen-hole playoff at the 1923 U.S. Open at Inwood Country Club in New York. One year later Jones claimed the first of his five U.S. Amateur titles, returning to Merion Cricket Club, where eight years earlier he had made his Amateur debut. Having taken to heart a letter from USGA President George H. Walker that Jones would have to tame his temper before competing in future USGA national championships, Bobby took control of his emotions, and it showed in his pressure-ridden playoff against Cruickshank.

At the 1925 U.S. Amateur championship at Oakmont, it was another Atlanta phenom who set a match-play record by winning fifteen straight holes in his thirty-six-hole opening match. Watts Gunn, a twenty-year-old member of the same East Lake Golf Club as Jones, took Bobby's advice to accompany him to Pittsburgh to compete in the Amateur at Oakmont. Due to criticism that the Amateur was too long, for the first time since the 1897 championship at Chicago Golf Club the match-play bracket was reduced from thirty-six players to eighteen. All matches were thirty-six holes, thus reducing the chance that a "fluke" win would occur. Former champs Herron, Francis Ouimet, and Charles Evans failed to make the cut, but qualifying were Jones and 1921 and '22 champs Jesse Guilford and Jess Sweetser, respectively, as well as 1924 finalist George von Elm.

Nicknamed the "Southern Hurricane," Gunn advanced to meet Jones in the final. It remains the only time in U.S. Amateur history that two members of the same club reached the championship. Despite playing one fifty-hole stretch in even par, a remarkable feat at Oakmont, Gunn was a prohibitive underdog to Jones, who in practice had bombed drives of three hundred yards and carded a 67 and then tore through his first three matches. Yet it was the Southern Hurricane who held the early advantage and had Jones wondering why he had begged Watts's father to send him to Oakmont.

Rare film of the tournament shows the two clubmates attired in nearly identical clothes—white shirts, black belts, white plus-fours, and light-colored socks. The major difference in their dress was that Jones wore a long, dark tie that flapped in the breeze, while Gunn donned a dark bowtie.

The match turned on the twelfth hole, called the Ghost Hole. Six years earlier in the Amateur final at Oakmont, Jones trailed Herron by three and was at the top of his backswing on his second shot when a gallery marshal bellowed, "Fore!" into his megaphone. Startled, Jones bunkered his shot, lost the hole, and eventually the title to Herron.

Trailing Gunn in the opening round, Jones found himself in a greenside bunker on the twelfth while Gunn was on the green. Jones knew that if Watts took the twelfth he would not catch him. Watts, he thought, was playing the most ferocious brand of golf Bobby had ever seen. Watts was two under and on the verge of taking another hole. Still, Jones remained unflappable. His slicked-down hair parted neatly down the middle, Bobby steadied himself for a final charge. Blasting out of the bunker on number twelve, Jones got to ten feet and drained the putt to halve the hole. Jones's remaining rounds read 3-3-4-3-3-4, and he finished two under and four up on Watts. Bobby settled the matter by starting the afternoon round 4-3 and would always believe that the match turned on the ten-foot putt on the Ghost Hole.

Jones's comeback victory at Oakmont started him thinking about his legacy. If he could hold an Amateur or Open championship for six straight years, he could retire. Bobby would do just that.

Two years later, Tommy Armour of Scotland took the title in a playoff in the second U.S. Open held on Fownes's now famous course. For the 1927 U.S. Open, the course length of 6,965 yards and par of 72 was dramatically more difficult than the 6,707 yards and par 74 of the 1922 PGA Championship.

Originally called the "Sterling Scot" but known in '27 as the "Silver Scot" for his graying hair, Armour engineered an eighteen-hole playoff win over "Lighthorse" Harry Cooper to decide the championship. Eight past champions—including Jones, Sarazen, and Hagen—were in the field; seven made the cut. Yet it was Scotland native Harry Hampton and American amateur Jimmy Johnston who led the field with 73s following the first round on June 14. Johnston, the 1929 U.S. Amateur champion, followed with a 74 to remain atop the leaderboard; Hampton slumped and shot a 78 to slide to fifth place. Shooting a 74 for the second straight round, Sarazen moved into second place, and Armour, who carded a 78 in the opening round, climbed into contention with a one-under 71.

Johnston's downfall began in Thursday morning's third round, his two double bogeys on the front nine and three straight sixes leading to a disastrous 87. Taking over the top spot was the twenty-two-year-old Cooper, the native of Leatherhead, England. Lighthorse Harry, so named because of his quick play, produced a 74 to match his first-round score and put his fifty-four-hole total at eight-over 224. The thirty-two-year-old Armour's 76 left him one stroke off the lead, followed by Hagen, who was two shots back. That Armour could contend despite being partially blind in his left eye and having shrapnel in his shoulder due to his time served in the British Tank Corps in World War I spoke to his determination.

A crowded field of contenders headed into the final round. Cooper carded a 77, and Armour 76 to tie for first. The playoff wasn't a certainty until the eighteenth hole, the straw-hatted Armour sinking a ten-foot birdie putt. The AP dissected the tense final round and previewed the playoff:

> It was a battle to the finish among the professional stars of Britain and America as the amateur phalanx was broken. . . .
>
> Armour knew he had to finish the last six holes in one better than par to tie Cooper and his shots were as straight as a string as he reeled off this tripod and troublesome stretch, the Waterloo of most other hopes, in the astonishing figures of 3-4-4-3-4-3. . . .
>
> There was less thrill but just as much workmanship to the performance of "Lighthorse" Harry Cooper, whose meteoric flights of scoring have been confined to the west heretofore.

Jones, providing commentary on the tournament for Bell Syndicate, wrote that the feature of the day was Armour's gallant finish.

Cooper took a two-shot lead early in Friday's extra round, but a birdie by Armour on thirteen and Cooper's bogey on fifteen evened the match. Light Horse Harry followed with a double bogey on sixteen, allowing Armour to seize a late two-stroke lead. He secured the title with a 76, Cooper coming in at 79. Cooper suffered a fate like what Jones had endured at Oakmont in 1919. Looking to get out of a bunker on sixteen, Cooper was into his swing when a voice screamed, "Down in front!" Cooper followed with a double-bogey 5 to Armour's 3. Both birdied the seventeenth, but Armour's 4 on eighteen secured the three-stroke win.

The title was the first of two major victories for Armour, who would go on to win the 1930 PGA Championship over Sarazen at Fresh Meadow Country Club in Flushing, New York. Cooper's thirty-one PGA Tour wins are the most by a player who did not win a major, and Light Horse Harry is often called the best golfer to never win a major.

The testament to the toughness of Oakmont could be found in Armour's 301 being the highest winning total since Hagen recorded the same score in a one-shot win over Mike Brady in an eighteen-hole playoff at Brae Burn Country Club in West Newton, Massachusetts, in 1919. It was the first U.S. Open since 1916, with 1917 and '18 being canceled due to World War I. Oakmont's difficulty could also be found in Bobby Jones sharing low amateur honors with Eddie Jones and, for the only time in his career, Bobby finishing outside the top ten in a U.S. Open. Two-time champ Bobby became entrapped in a bunker on the fourth hole in the opening round, took three shots to get out, and endured a double bogey that led to a 76.

Observers at the time considered the '27 Open the greatest in history. Oakmont yielded but one round under 70, with Al Espinosa shooting 69 in the final round. Armour's 301 also marks the last time the U.S. Open's winning score surpassed 300. The Silver Scot would be the last foreign-born player to win the U.S. Open for thirty-eight years, South Africa's Gary Player breaking the skein in 1965 at Bellerive Country Club in Missouri.

For the 1935 U.S. Open, Oakmont was lengthened to 6,981 yards while maintaining a par of 72. Hole twelve stretched to a massive 621 yards. Compounding the scoring problems was inclement weather, which increased during the final round on the afternoon of Saturday, June 8. Pennsylvania native Sam Parks Jr.—a relative unknown in a field filled with past champs Armour, Hagen, Sarazen, and defending champ Olin Dutra—shot 299 to finish two ahead of Jimmy Thomson and three ahead of Hagen.

The twenty-five-year-old Parks hailed from Bellevue near Pittsburgh, was an alumnus of the University of Pittsburgh who helped found the school's golf team a decade earlier, and was club pro at the South Hills Country Club in Pittsburgh. Parks was familiar with Oakmont, and for a month prior to the tournament he played a practice round on the course every day.

After shooting 77 in Thursday's opening round, Parks followed with a 73 to place fourth at 150, four shots behind Thomson. Butch Krueger's one-under 71 gave him the first-round lead, and his 77 on Friday dropped him to second, two strokes behind Thomson, who began the tournament with back-to-back 73s.

Parks continued his ascent in Saturday's morning round, his sixty-foot eagle giving him a 73 and a tie with Thomson. Hagen grabbed the lead in the afternoon but was betrayed by four consecutive bogeys. Hagen wasn't the only one struggling, with wet weather conditions worsening to the point that 73 was the lowest score of the final round. Parks's knowledge of the course prepared him well. He three-putted only twice over the four rounds. The rainy weather contributed to the highest winning U.S. Open score since the 1927 tournament, also hosted by Oakmont.

Associated Press sports editor Alan Gould wrote that Parks was a home-town golfer who made good. "The youthful Pittsburgh professional came from behind to conquer the country's foremost shot makers and capture the United States open golf championship in a stumbling, rain-soaked finish," he said. Gould noted that Parks was the lone player among the all-stars to break 300 on Oakmont's "terrifying, storm-tossed layout."

Parks became golf's ultimate dark horse, a reputation he would come to relish. "It gave me a tag to my name that lives on," he would say. The 1935 U.S. Open was historically significant for several reasons, including inspiring Stimpmeter, a device created by Edward Stimpson Jr. that quantifies the speed of a putting green. A graduate of Harvard University, Stimpson captained the golf team in 1925 and '26. He graduated from Harvard in 1929 and mixed his time between business and amateur golf. Stimpson heard horror stories emanating from the '35 Open and believed the greens at Oakmont to be too fast. Since no device had previously existed to accurately measure the slickness of a putting surface, Stimpson's device provided for officials the speed of the green. Resisting the urging of friends to patent his device in 1936, Stimpson would write a letter to the USGA in 1963 and refer to his revolutionary instrument as "a labor of love and not for profit." Finally adopted by the USGA in 1977, the Stimpmeter established standards for tournament play in the U.S.

Also of note, Kanekichi Nakamura became the first Japanese player to make the cut at the U.S. Open. He shot 325 and finished fifty-eighth.

Three years later, Oakmont hosted the U.S. Amateur for the third time, with Willie Turnesa taking the title, one of seven famous golfing brothers. Willie's brother Joe was runner-up by one stroke to Jones in the 1926 U.S. Open at Scioto Country Club in Columbus, Ohio. Another brother, Jim, won the 1952 PGA Championship. The Turnesa brothers were featured in a 1938 newsreel filmed by RKO Pictures. In 2000, the *New York Times* referred to the Turnesa brothers as a "golf dynasty."

Willie Turnesa's win in the 1938 U.S. Amateur was noteworthy in that he implemented a new instrument to battle the beastly Oakmont. Years earlier, Sarazen had developed the sand wedge, but the instrument was still something of a novelty. Danny Galgano, a friend of Turnesa, told him that the wedge would help him deal with Oakmont's infamous bunkers.

Turnesa's plan for the sand was to use his nine-iron, but Galgano told him that Oakmont's furrowed bunkers would neutralize the nine-iron. Galgano had a wedge given to him by a sportswriter, who reportedly received it from Sarazen. Turnesa took the wedge to Oakmont, and it paid dividends, as he found himself in a bunker thirteen times. He also emerged victorious from a twenty-hole duel in the third round with 1936 Amateur champ Johnny Fischer. For his skilled shot-making with the new club that he had to be talked into taking to Oakmont by Galgano, Turnesa was named by the press "Willie the Wedge."

In 1951, the PGA Championship returned for the first time to a course it had been previously played on. The format listed 216 holes played over twelve rounds in seven days. It began on Wednesday and Thursday, June 27–28, with thirty-six-hole stroke play qualifiers, eighteen holes each day. The first two rounds of eighteen holes each were held Friday, followed by thirty-six holes in Saturday's third round, thirty-six more in Sunday's quarterfinals, thirty-six in Monday's semifinals, and the final thirty-six in Tuesday's finals.

Nine past PGA winners populated the field, including Snead, who was seeking his third PGA title after winning in 1942 at Seaview Country Club in New Jersey and again in '49 at Belmont Golf Course in his native Virginia.

Reigning champ Chandler Harper fell in the first round in dramatic fashion to Jim Turnesa, their match going twenty-three holes. Snead advanced with a win over Jack Burke Jr. in the quarterfinals and defeated Charlie Bassler in the semifinals. The Slammer's opponent in the finals was Walter Burkemo, a chunky club pro who was playing in his first PGA event. Riding an unorthodox swing, the Michigan-born Burkemo beat Reggie Myles in the quarters and in the semis got past Ellsworth Vines in thirty-seven holes. Wearing his trademark fedora, Snead cruised in the final, winning 7 and 6 before a crowd estimated at 6,500–7,000, most of whom were rooting for the underdog Burkemo, whom the crowd called "the kid" in comparison to the "old pro" Snead.

The PGA title was the third for Slammin' Sam, who at thirty-nine became at the time the tournament's oldest winner. Two years earlier, he had set the previous record by winning at age thirty-seven. It also marked the fifth of Snead's eventual seven major victories.

Snead's record as oldest PGA champ lasted less than one year. The following June 25 Jim Turnesa, who finished second to Sam in '42, won at Big Spring Country Club in Louisville, Kentucky, and became at age thirty-nine and six months the new oldest champion.

Snead said the rains that slowed Oakmont's treacherous greens made putting easier for him. The Slammer started fast in the final, earning an eagle on a chip-in on the first hole. Burkemo, described by Phil Gundelfinger in the *Pittsburgh Post-Gazette* as "a blonde dark horse," used his own solid putting to stage several rallies. Comebacks were nothing new to Burkemo, an infantry sergeant in World War II who was wounded twice, including once at the Battle of the Bulge, and earned two Purple Hearts.

Gundelfinger reported that Snead played at twenty-two under for 166 holes of match play and carded but three bogeys in the fifty-eight holes of the semifinal and final matches. Three up at the break, Snead sank birdie putts of six and twenty-five feet to go up five. He maintained a comfortable lead throughout.

Henry Fownes wasn't alive to see Snead's triumph. Not long after Parks claimed his dramatic victory at the '35 U.S. Open, Fownes took ill with pneumonia. He died five days later, having just turned seventy-nine. Henry's impact on U.S. golf remains long-lasting. Because of him, championship golf has become a fixture in western Pennsylvania. His son William would follow in his father's footsteps. Born on October 22, 1877, to Henry and Mary Fownes, William was named after Henry's brother. William earned a degree in chemical engineering from the Massachusetts Institute of Technology, but his career in the steel and iron industry ended early, heart problems causing him to retire at age thirty.

William, however, found balm for this by excelling in golf. He won his first Western Pennsylvania Amateur Championship in 1904 and repeated as champ the following year. He followed with titles in 1907, '09, '10, '11, and '13 and advanced to the semis in 1914 and 1919. In 1916, William won his record eighth Western Pennsylvania Amateur Championship and gained his first title in the Western Pennsylvania Open Championship. His 1910 campaign saw him claim the West Penn Amateur, the Allegheny Men's Invitational, the Pennsylvania Amateur, and the U.S. Amateur, a "grand slam" season.

Beginning in 1911, William oversaw the Oakmont course as head of the grounds committee. Following Henry's death in 1935, William took over as club president of Oakmont. While he wanted to remain true to his father's desire that Oakmont be not a social club but a golf club, William knew that for the club to prosper, they would have to transform into the former.

William became a fixture in golf, not only in western Pennsylvania but nationally as well. He played a role in the creation of the Walker Cup Matches, and in 1921 he headed a team of the best amateurs in the U.S. against their counterparts from Great Britain. He served as the first captain of the U.S. team, which won the Walker Cup over Great Britain and Ireland. William served as vice president of the USGA Executive Committee in 1924 and two years later was USGA president. He also served on the USGA's Implements and Balls Committee from 1924 to 1948, focusing on the tools of the sport. As such, he was acutely aware of the advancements being made in equipment that could lessen the severity of what his father saw as the most difficult course in the world.

Jones would later write of his experience at Oakmont in 1919 that it was the setting for the highest group of qualifying scores of any national amateur championship he ever played in. After winning the U.S. Open in 1927, Armour called Oakmont "a cruel and treacherous playground." Armour's 301 was 5 to 13 strokes higher than the winning scores at other U.S. Opens played in the 1920s and 7 to 15 higher than in U.S. Opens into the mid-1930s. When the tournament returned to Oakmont in 1935, Parks's 299 dwarfed the winning marks of the prior seven Opens.

William was determined to fulfill his father's dream of keeping Oakmont a course to be feared. Finegan thought it possible that William's instinct was to be even more punishing than Henry. "Par was to be dearly bought," Finegan wrote. "One suspects that he would have preferred it to be beyond price."

William spent time walking the course with greenskeepers seeking ways to toughen the layout. He and greenskeepers John McGlynn and Emil "Dutch" Loeffler added bunker upon bunker until the course became so pockmarked it listed close to twenty hazards per hole and 350 in all. "A shot poorly played," reasoned William, "should be a shot irrevocably lost."

Finegan noted that William's revisions included far more than additional hazards. Holes were lengthened and ditches dug in the rough. Greens were cut very short, to a reported three thirty-seconds of an inch. William's attention to the greens included having eight men push a 1,500-pound roller over them to keep them firm and fast and, as Finegan stated, "all but unmanageable" to even the most skilled golfers.

Finegan believed Oakmont became the nonpareil of penal golf course design. "And if it prompted little in the way of affection (at least from those who confronted it only when their careers depended on it), it did earn universal respect," wrote Finegan. "It was impregnable. It was implacable."

Oakmont remained a brute as golfers began arriving in the Pittsburgh suburb for the 1953 U.S. Open. *Sports Illustrated* in the summer of '62 called the creation of Henry and William Townes "awesome . . . a desert of sand and some huge, fast greens that rise and fall like dunes." *SI* declared Oakmont a "Championship Trial on a U.S. Sahara." Herbert Warren Wind was blunt in his description of the course. Oakmont, he wrote, "is the toughest golf course in the world."

What made this Steel City layout so treacherous, so menacing, were the numerous challenges embedded in its expansive layout. It is a course, wrote Alfred Wright in *SI*, "with pitfalls galore—acres and acres of sand border its sloping fairways and embrace its immense greens." Oakmont had rough that *SI* labeled "vicious," and Wright said there were greens where one "can drop a ball vertically from the height of your forehead and watch it roll slowly but inevitably right off the green and possibly into a bunker."

While Wright wrote this in advance of Oakmont hosting the 1962 U.S. Open, it was just as true when Hogan, Snead, and others prepared to deal with what *SI* called in its cover story "The Horrors of Oakmont." As spring arrived early in '53, the greens promised to be perilously fast. The number of bunkers had been reduced from 350 to 250 by 1953, but the trademark deep furrows remained. As Wright explained, once the furrows snared a shot, the harried golfer's only hope was to sacrifice a stroke by blasting it free of the sand to a safe lie. The furrowed bunkers were both penal and practical. Drainage issues demanded Oakmont's hazards not be deep, and greenskeepers realized they needed to deal with rain settling in the bunkers and hardening the sand. Their response was to rake deep furrows into the sand.

"Church pew" bunkers are another signature of Oakmont. *SI* described them as "tiers of deep and beckoning bunkers" that may cause their inhabitants to "fall from grace." Write referred to them as "a series of long, narrow hazards running perpendicular to the fairway and separated from one another by only a strip of sod." The church pews crowded the left side of the third fairway and boasted parallel bunkers stretching some fifty yards and strategically placed to catch drives.

At 6,916 yards, Oakmont would play longer for the 1953 U.S. Open than it had for the 1951 PGA Championship (6,882) and '22 Open (6,707) but shorter than it had for the Opens in '35 (6,981) and '27 (6,965). The Open was returning to Oakmont, but William, unfortunately, would not be there to witness the game's greats take on the beast he and his father had developed. William passed away from heart disease at age seventy-two on Independence Day, 1950. He shared his father's satisfaction that their course was one of the truest tests of championship golf in the world.

When Snead won the PGA Championship in 1951, he was glad he won at Oakmont because he had grown tired of hearing how he, Hogan, and Nelson had been setting records on what critics called "pitch and putt" courses.

By the summer of '53, fans across the country were waiting with great anticipation to see how Hogan and the proud pros would deal with a course on Hulton Hills that was so hellish it was called the "Hades of Hulton."

5

Abandon All Hope

Ben Hogan arrived for the U.S. Open and promptly began probing the punishing course in his practice rounds. "Oakmont," Hogan told reporters, "requires as much thinking as any course I've ever seen."

Accompanying the former U.S. Open champion was writer Arthur Daley of the *New York Times*. Daley told readers that from the first practice round, he had a ringside seat for Bantam Ben's battle with the Oakmont beast. Daley stood on the first tee and watched Hogan slice one drive to the right, hook another to the left, and lash the next down the middle. The former champion followed with second shots from each initial drive and then chipped to the green. Daley watched as Hogan putted each of the three balls and studied each ball's movement on the swift, undulating greens.

Daley wrote that Hogan played an entire round in that fashion, "filing away in his mind every phase of the terrain." Hogan even estimated pin placements and how he would attack from various spots. The engrossing experience afforded Daley what he described as "a rare glimpse inside Ben Hogan. It was almost as if Blazin' Ben raised up his motor hood for the very first time and exposed to view the intricate, delicate mechanism of sports' finest golfing machine."

That the taciturn Texan would provide so rare a glimpse into his preparation for a major championship made the experience even more memorable for Daley. The writer looked forward to the coming collision between the man he considered golf's "analyst supreme" and "ferocious Oakmont, the impregnable, par-resistant course."

Decades following Daley's descriptive term, Marino Parascenzo of the *Pittsburgh Post-Gazette* previewed the 1978 PGA Championship by writing that Oakmont's reputation was so terrifying the gates to its club should contain a sign, "preferably in smoldering sulphur, moaning the awful directive of that tormented Italian poet: 'All Hope Abandon, Ye Who Enter Here.' For these are the Gates of Hell."

Hogan had dueled dark forces before. Two years earlier, he engaged in brutal combat with the Monster of Oakland Hills. Hogan endured an early beatdown but battled back with a sizzling 67 in the fourth round to bring the Monster to its knees. Dan Jenkins called Hogan's final round in the 1951 U.S. Open "the greatest eighteen ever played." He thought it Hogan's "Rembrandt." Hogan also considered it the greatest round of his life considering the pressurized atmosphere of the U.S. Open and severity of course architect Robert Trent Jones's seemingly unconquerable layout. The Monster, Hogan said, was the toughest course he ever encountered.

Hogan's customary plan for the U.S. Open was to arrive a week ahead of the scheduled first tee. An early arrival was even more imperative in 1953, since the USGA had announced the previous June 12 that everyone would have to submit to a thirty-six-hole qualifier. That included Hogan, who had won three of the past four U.S. Open tournaments he competed in since 1948. Reigning champion Julius Boros would be the lone exemption.

The *Pittsburgh Post-Gazette* trumpeted the news with a bold headline on an Associated Press story that reported, "Playing procedure of the National Open Golf Championship was sharply revised today, effective in 1953, to restore 36-hole qualifying at the site of the tournament." The *Post-Gazette* added the following:

> These are the changes in qualifying which will be effective in next year's event at Oakmont in Pittsburgh:
>
> 1. After the usual 36-hold sectional qualifying rounds, 300 players will be qualified instead of the present 162. Present exemptions will be continued.
> 2. All the 300 except the defending champion will compete in a 36-hole qualifying competition on Tuesday and Wednesday, June 9–10.
> 3. As a result, 150 players, including the defending champion, will qualify to compete in the 72-hole championship June 11-12-13.

4. Next year, the Pittsburgh Field Club will be used along with Oakmont for the 36-hole qualifying.

Located in Fox Chapel, Pittsburgh Field Club hosted the 1937 PGA Championship, won by defending champ Denny Shute, who beat Harold "Jug" McSpaden in thirty-seven holes to claim his third and final major title. Shute would be the last player to win consecutive PGA Championships until Tiger Woods matched his feat in 1999 and 2000.

Hogan didn't complain about qualifying because he knew he would have to play exceedingly poor to fail to be one of the 150 qualifiers. He secured a berth with rounds of 77 and 73. Ben then opined that this U.S. Open would be won not by one of the tournament's seven former champions in the field but by an "unknown." He also stated that beastly Oakmont would not surrender a winning score lower than 292. Hogan was, in fact, favored by experts to unseat Boros and win his fourth U.S. Open title to tie Willie Anderson and Bobby Jones. Hogan's chances, however, were thought to be reduced after he wrenched his back in the first round of qualifying.

National wire stories dated June 9 reported that "Chick Harbert, the recognized Babe Ruth of modern golf, seized the first round qualifying lead in the National Open Golf Tournament today while the ranking favorite, Ben Hogan, suffered a back injury which could rob him of his fourth championship." Harbert blasted booming drives through the Field Club's gun-barrel fairways and carded a course record 66. Harbert's score was two strokes better than the previous mark of 68 recorded in 1937 by Byron Nelson and Paul Runyan.

Hogan played his first qualifying round at Oakmont and injured his back in the right shoulder area on hole number seven. According to reports, Hogan said that for the rest of the day he was struck by a sharp pain every time he made a back swing. A wire story called Hogan "one man against the field" and stated that while his 38-39-77 was five over par and disappointing, it likely wouldn't threaten his chances of qualifying. Still, the Bantam's style of play wasn't, in the words of one observer, "the old errorless Hogan golf. . . . The grim, silent Hawk—as his fellow pros call him—made miscues that weren't characteristic of Hogan and putted poorly."

Hogan said after his round that while he wasn't concerned with qualifying, he was worried about how his injured back would fare. "I'm afraid it will stiffen up," he told reporters. "That would bother me."

Players changed courses the following day. Those at the Field Club on Tuesday went to Oakmont on Wednesday, and those at Oakmont headed to the Field Club. The low 149 scores and those tied for 149th would qualify for Thursday's opening round. Hogan headed to the Field Club and shaved four strokes from his previous day's total at Oakmont. He had his injured back treated and according to reports didn't notice the pain again until later in his round. It was at that point that Hogan tired and shot five over par. Though his rounds were ordinary, and his back was injured, Hogan was still seen by sportswriters as "the man to beat."

Hogan wasn't the only contender dealing with injuries and pain. Sam Snead had been suffering from hand injuries all spring and summer, and Lloyd Mangrum injured his right hand while making a shot in Wednesday's qualifier. No bone fractures were found in the x-rays, and the debonair Mangrum told reporters he did not anticipate the injury affecting his performance.

The revised format fell flat with the pros and was abandoned the following year. The qualifying rounds did claim two former champs: Pittsburgh's Sam Parks Jr., the 1935 winner, and Billy Burke, who finished first in '31. Burke shot 158 and Parks 162. Hogan, Boros, Mangrum, Gene Sarazen, Lawson Little, Lew Worsham, and Cary Middlecoff were past winners who qualified for the championship proper. Jimmy Clark led all qualifiers with a 138, achieved via a 72 at what sportswriters called "cozy and hilly" Pittsburgh Field Club and a record 66 at "broad and rolling" Oakmont.

Writing for the Associated Press, Hugh Fullerton Jr. stated that the two experimental qualifying rounds showed that the "manufactured monster, Oakmont, can be mastered like any mechanical toy." Clark, a thirty-two-year-old blond-haired, broad-shouldered Marine, paced a field that Fullerton said proved "Oakmont can be licked." Clark's record round resulted in six birdies and twelve pars. He missed just four greens, and his longest putt came on number seven and traveled twenty feet.

Oakmont Country Club is 2.5 miles east of the Pittsburgh Field Club, and Snead, still seeking an elusive first U.S. Open title, told listeners that a "tougher" course than Oakmont was not far away—the Pittsburgh Field Club. Described by reporters as "narrow and deep roughed," the course measured 6,712 yards and was a par 71. Sportswriters seemed to agree with Snead, noting that while Oakmont remained long and rolling, Pittsburgh Field Club "proved a tougher scoring proposition." Three of the four qualifying scores in the 60s were carded at Oakmont and par was broken more often there than at the Field Club.

Still, Oakmont's demanding layout did take a toll on some. Harbert shot a record 66 at the Field Club but blew up at Oakmont, carding a ten-over 82. The muscular Michigan champion suffered a seven on the par-four tenth, prompting him to admit he completely lost interest.

Snead qualified with rounds of 73-72-145 and joined Hogan, Demaret, Mangrum, et al. in what was expected to be a heated battle between men and beast. Snead was well-acquainted with the horrors of Oakmont, and The Slammer prepared a strategy built on booming drives off the tee and guerilla attacks on the greens. It was a strategy that worked two years earlier when he won the PGA Championship at Oakmont. *Time* magazine called Snead's tee-to-green game the best in golf at that time. Heading into the final match of the PGA, Slammin' Sam was bloodying brutish Oakmont to the tune of seventeen under par. Snead himself was impressed, telling reporters he didn't know if he'd ever scored better.

Al Abrams, sports editor of the *Pittsburgh Post-Gazette*, wrote that "golf's greatest attraction played a powerful game as he ripped and tore Oakmont's par of 72 to tatters."

Oakmont, Abrams stated, "was made to order for Snead, especially the front nine, as most experts thought it would be." The heavy rains at the championship softened the greens and slowed the slick carpets. Snead, wrote Abrams, played Oakmont's first nine as if he owned it. "He just overpowered his opponents on the long, arduous 3,473-yard terrain on the front nine, then would try to match them stroke for stroke on the back nine," observed Abrams.

Including the qualifying rounds, Snead played the front nine in 24 under par for the tournament. The back nine he played to a total of three over. Having defeated what *Time* noted were five "topflight" opponents, The Slammer outdid himself in the final against Walter Burkemo. Snead's sky-scraping drive and strategic approach shot placed him on the fringe of the green, forty feet from the cup on the par-five, 483-yard first hole. Burkemo birdied the hole, and Snead sank the putt for an eagle three.

Time quoted Snead and his down-South drawl as stating that unless Burkemo went "hawg wile, ah'd be OK. Ah thought if a man can't win six up, he oughta quit and go home."

Snead eventually won 7 and 6, the largest winning margin since The Slammer lost to Paul Runyan and his popgun attack 8 and 7 in the 1938 PGA Championship, also in Pennsylvania but in the northeast, at Shawnee Country Club in Smithfield Township in the foothills of the Pocono Mountains.

Returning to the sight of one of his most impressive victories, Snead was wary. He had experienced Oakmont's caffeine-quick greens—"I put a dime down to mark my ball," he said, "and the dime slid away"—and endured the pain of close losses in the U.S. Open. The tournament had become his personal bug-a-boo, bedeviling Snead as it would Phil Mickelson decades later.

Making his U.S. Open debut at Oakland Hills in 1937, Slammin' Sam started the final round tied for second place with Ralph Guldahl. Front-runner Ed Dudley fell off the pace with a 76. A long-ball hitter on a long-ball course, The Slammer was in perfect position to capture the Open in his first attempt. The course played to more than seven thousand yards and Slammin' Sam was one of golf's great siege guns. He won five times that year and bombed a 360-yard drive in the West Virginia Open. Despite having the ideal course to match his strength, Snead shot a 71 to finish two strokes behind Guldahl.

Two years later Snead was at the Philadelphia Country Club when he suffered one of the notable late collapses in U.S. Open history. Following a bogey on seventeen, The Slammer headed to the par-five seventy-second hole determined to atone with a birdie. It went bad from the beginning. Snead hooked his drive, then topped his two-wood and sent his shot spinning into a fairway bunker. His game going sideways, Snead became urgent. His first attempt to free himself from the sand failed; his next shot sailed into a greenside bunker. Snead finally made it to the green, then three-putted for a triple bogey. His freefall landed him in fifth place.

In the 1947 U.S. Open at St. Louis Country Club, Snead led Worsham by two strokes on the sixteenth hole of their eighteen-hole playoff. Worsham birdied sixteen, and Snead followed with a bogey on seventeen, tying the tournament for the final time. On eighteen, The Slammer was preparing to tap in a three-foot putt for par when Worsham suddenly called for a ruling. Seemingly rattled, Snead missed his short putt. Worsham drained his putt, and another Open had slipped through Sam's grasp.

Snead made a gallant late charge at Medinah in 1949, rallying from six strokes down in the final round to finish one shot behind Middlecoff. It was one more missed opportunity, one more close call that frustrated one of golf's more misunderstood players. Those who thought Slammin' Sam had a natural swing, that he didn't work hard at it, were unaware that when he was young, he played all day and deep into the night, practicing by the glare of car headlights.

Snead also had a reputation for being tight with money, and with this he didn't disagree. But most didn't know that when Sam was a kid his biggest Christmas came one year when he found fifteen cents and a pair of socks beneath his breakfast plate. "Poverty," Snead said once, "will make you respect money."

When he won at Oakmont in 1951 and pocketed $3,500, Snead's smile was so wide that he made the Cheshire Cat look like Mona Lisa. He signed autographs "$am $nead." Despite what some thought, Snead was generous with his winnings. While his manager, Fred Corcoran, said Sam's arms grew shorter when it came time to pick up a tab, Snead spent plenty on people who needed help. Guy Yocom of *Golf Digest* noted that Sam purchased homes for poor families, tipped lavishly, and did so much for the people of Bath County that a sizable stretch of Virginia's Route 220 was named after him.

One more interesting fact about The Slammer. Despite endorsing tobacco—Chesterfields, Granger Pipe tobacco, Lucky Strikes, Viceroys— Snead was not a smoker. Years later he would detest those endorsements so much he made The Greenbrier remove his tobacco ads from their walls.

Writers called the lanky Snead "the golfin' hillbilly from West Virginia." His receding hairline led to another nickname—"Old Nude Knob"— bestowed upon him by fellow pros. It was the reason Snead was rarely seen without his straw fedora. The headwear was but one ornament of Slammin'

Sam. His silky-smooth swing was another. Golf writer Nick Seitz once observed that "cashmere should be so smooth." Yocom wrote that even if Snead was "wrapped in crinkly cellophane, you had the impression he'd swing without making a noise." Writer Bill Fields compared Snead's swing to a Faulkner sentence: "It was long, laced with the perfect pause, and blessed with a powerful ending."

Chi Chi Rodriguez called Snead's swing the greatest ever, and Tom Watson modeled his swing on The Slammer. Jack Nicklaus said that when he was a young player, he would close his eyes and envision the perfect golf swing, and it was Snead's. Snead's swing was self-taught, but he was far from being a natural. Snead told Seitz he hit as many as two million practice shots in his life and that his swing looked natural because he worked hard to keep it simple. The simpler the swing, Snead reasoned, the easier it is to repeat.

Born May 27, 1912, Samuel Jackson Snead entered this world within six months of the births of Hogan and Byron Nelson. They would become golf's "Big Three," the great triumvirate of their era and one of the best in their sport's history, as they claimed a combined 197 PGA Tour victories. Byron said Sam proved that a golf ball can be hit both hard *and* straight. Nelson thought Snead had great rhythm and the best turn of anyone. "Turn and burn!" was what Snead would instruct young golfers to do. "Turn and burn!"

Snead's power off the tee allowed him to drive the ball twenty yards longer than many competitors on the tour. He stands with the great power golfers of all time—Ted Ray, Arnold Palmer, Jack Nicklaus, Tom Weiskopf, Greg Norman, John Daly, Tiger Woods, and Bubba Watson.

Sam was part of a farming family that struggled financially, and he saw sports as his way out of Ashwood, Virginia. Snead wanted to be a football star, but a back injury ended that dream. To help bring in money he caddied at a local resort, the Cascades, which was two miles from his home. He left the Cascades in 1934 when he was in his early twenties for White Sulphur Spring, West Virginia. Snead became club pro at the Greenbrier, and in 1936 he won the West Virginia Closed Pro and finished fifth in a PGA event in Hershey, Pennsylvania.

One year later, the native of rural Virginia heeded Horace Greeley's call to "Go West, young man," and with three hundred dollars in his pocket, he earned his first Tour victory: the Oakland Open. A San Francisco newspaper headlined his win with "Unknown Sam Snead beats par; wins Oakland Open." Over the course of his career, Snead's celebrated swing and sky-scraping drives helped popularize the PGA Tour. He captured his first major at the 1942 PGA Championship, won the British Open in 1946 when contractual ties demanded he play St. Andrews, and claimed his first Masters title in 1949. From 1937 to 1946 Slammin' Sam won at least two tournaments every year. "In my prime," he said once, "I could do anything with a golf ball I wanted. No man scared me on the golf course."

That included Hogan, despite the oft-repeated Snead quote that the three things he feared most in golf were "lighting, Ben Hogan and a downhill putt." In 1991, Snead told Fred Robledo of the *Los Angeles Times* that he never feared Hogan. The Slammer stated that a lot of things written during his era weren't true. He said Corcoran quoted him and others and would sometimes get the right quote but the wrong source. When his game was on, Snead told Robledo, he feared no man.

Snead's game was outsized, and so too were stories of his southern family. Snead would say his mother was forty-seven when she gave birth to him and that a great uncle named Big John Snead, a Confederate soldier in the Civil War, stood 7-foot-9, weighed 350 pounds, and boasted a size twenty-seven shoe.

One thing about Snead that wasn't exaggerated was his athleticism. Snead in his youth was a multitalented athlete who was reportedly timed at ten seconds in the hundred-yard dash, played halfback in football, and was a pitcher in baseball. Snead also did some boxing, defeating a professional, "Hurricane" Hite, in a decision in 1936. It was said by friends that Snead liked fishing more than golf, but he couldn't make any money fishing.

Slammin' Sam stood 5-foot-11 and weighed 185 pounds, and it's part of his legend that even at eighty years old, he was still so athletic he could kick the top of a seven-foot doorframe. Reportedly double-jointed, Snead would pluck his ball out of the hole without bending at the knees. He could sit in a clubhouse chair and, bending forward, touch both of his elbows on the floor. Snead was supple enough to press the thumb of his left hand against his forearm. Sam was also strong enough that he could reportedly flex the steel shaft of an iron with his hands.

Snead set a record for PGA Tour victories with eighty-two that Tiger Woods tied, yet Sam remained in the shadow of Hogan. The Bantam would retire with nine career major victories, two more than The Slammer, and when Snead in 1950 won a career-high eleven events, it marked the third most in a year behind Nelson's eighteen in 1945 and Hogan's thirteen in '46. Snead also set a mark with a scoring average of 69.23 that stood until Greg Norman averaged 69.10 in 1990. Yet it was Hogan who was named "Golfer of the Year" following his inspirational comeback from life-threatening injuries and dramatic victory in the U.S. Open at Merion Golf Club in Ardmore, Pennsylvania. Snead said that instead of naming Hogan Golfer of the Year, they could have given him a six-foot high trophy that read, "Great Comeback."

Snead wasn't the only champion golfer overshadowed by Hogan. Burkemo, a member of the U.S. Open field in '53, would likewise be bumped from the spotlight by Ben later that summer. A native of Detroit, Burkemo was the youngest of thirteen children born in 1918 to Norwegian immigrants who settled in Michigan. At age eight he began caddying at Lochmoor Country Club and three years later was competing. In 1938 Burkemo medaled in the stroke play qualifying rounds in the Amateur Public Links Championship and was called by United Press International "a 20-year-old unemployed Detroit youth who crams his golf in between odd jobs." He earned his first pro win with a victory in the 1938 Southern Florida Open.

Like many of his era, Burkemo lost some of his prime years to military service. Returning to the tour following the war, he struggled the remainder of the decade, due in part to his war wounds. His career turned in 1951 when he won the first of four Michigan Open titles. That same year, he was runner-up to Snead in the PGA Championship, and he became one of the most consistently successful golfers on the tour, finishing in the top ten on numerous occasions, including eight times in majors.

Burkemo would win the 1953 PGA Championship and 1955 Michigan PGA Professional Championship and play on the 1953 U.S. Ryder Cup team. Excelling in match play, Burkemo built a 27–6 record and is tied with Nelson for the highest winning percentage among golfers who played at least fifteen PGA Championship matches. *Time* called Burkemo "one of the game's canniest match players."

In its coverage of the 1953 PGA Championship, the Associated Press wrote that Burkemo "tamed the Toy Tiger"—Felice Torza—with pressure putting. Nicknamed the "Toy Tiger" for his size—5 feet 8.5 inches and 135 pounds—and grit, Torza battled thirty-five mile-per-hour gusts for control of his tee shots. He also dueled an erratic putter, and Burkemo seized control of the final and closed the match with a par four on the thirty-fifth hole.

His success in the 1953 PGA Championship prompted Spalding to create a Burkemo-branded golf set and signature golf balls. Burkemo's success is more remarkable considering he only played on the tour part-time. He was the head pro at various Michigan country clubs, all of them in his native Detroit area. He also owned a prosperous driving range that allowed him to be selective in his tournament play. The AP remarked that when Burkemo did compete, he more than made expenses. He usually played fewer than ten tournaments each year but impressed fellow golfers with his steady—and heady—play.

Golfer Bob Toski admired Burkemo's course management, how he kept the ball in play and was a good putter. He thought Burkemo was a consistent, solid player and a great guy. Popular with players and the press, Burkemo was called by the AP the "people's choice" and the "blonde belter." Spending winters in Palm Springs, Burkemo golfed with A-List personalities, including President Eisenhower and Hollywood celebrities Bob Hope and Bing Crosby. Nicknamed Wally or Sarge, the latter for his service as an infantry sergeant, Burkemo was considered by contemporaries one of the game's straightest drivers. When he was at the top of his game, Burkemo rarely missed fairways and the USGA Journal called him an "amazingly straight shot maker."

Burkemo was said by the AP to own "a quick, jerky swing" but was regarded highly by other pros for his bold play. "He hits strong and goes for the big blow," the AP said. "He is not an exceptional putter ordinarily but has a knack for ringing in the long ones when they count." Clutch play was part of Burkemo being, in the AP's words, a tenacious young battler, a pug-nosed, round-faced, local pinup boy who "doesn't know when he's beaten."

Like Burkemo, George Fazio was part of a large family whose parents were European immigrants. Also, like Burkemo, Fazio made his living as a club pro and played alongside Hollywood's rich and famous. Born in Norristown, Pennsylvania, a suburb of Philadelphia, Fazio began his pro career in the mid-1930s. He nearly gained a notable win in the 1950 U.S. Open at nearby Merion. He finished third in an eighteen-hole playoff behind Hogan and Lloyd Mangrum. Fazio did earn PGA Tour victories in the 1946 Canadian Open and 1947 Bing Crosby Pro-Am.

The head pro at half a dozen different clubs in the Philadelphia area, Fazio supplemented his income with ownership in driving ranges and a Ford automobile dealership, due to the generosity of William Clay Ford, and had business interests in scrap iron. He was one of eight children born to Italian immigrants and began caddying and golfing at nine years of age. Fazio secured an assistant pro job a decade later and began earning wins in area tournaments. In 1940 he became the head pro at Glendale Golf Club in Havertown, then went to Cedarbrook Country Club as the playing pro.

Fazio became one of the faces of Philadelphia golf. He operated and leased semiprivate golf courses in the Philadelphia suburbs and became a playing professional from prestigious Pine Valley before undertaking another challenge in 1955 and renovating Cobbs Creek Golf Club in Philadelphia for a PGA Tour stop. Several years later he created and designed Waynesborough, a private course that he would own and operate.

Working with his nephew, Tom Fazio, George designed sixty-four courses, some of them ranking among the top layouts in the country. Pinehurst number six, Jupiter Hills in south Florida, Hershey East, Edgewood on Lake Tahoe, and Palmetto Dunes on Hilton Head Island, South Carolina, are Fazio designs. He had an idea of how a golf hole should look, play, and blend into the landscape, and his emphasis as an architect was on tough, technical courses, their layouts looking to expose a player's weakness. Butterfly and cloverleaf bunkers were signatures of his designs.

Fazio's multiple careers flowed from his belief that a person should do multiple things in their lifetime. "What are you going to do, hit golf balls for the rest of your life?" he once asked. "I'm not saying it's wrong, but for me, it's boring. I don't think anybody should take more than five years to do anything." From 1950 to 1953 Fazio was a leading contender at the U.S. Open, claiming three top-five finishes. Not surprising, perhaps, since he ranks as one of the best golfers ever from Philadelphia. After learning the game as a caddie at Plymouth Country Club in his native Norristown, he won the Philadelphia Open five times.

Just as Fazio had things in common with Burkemo, Frank Souchak shared similarities with Fazio. Both were Pennsylvania natives, Souchak hailing from the famous high school football town of Berwick. Owning amateur status in 1953, Souchak was known more for his prowess playing football for the University of Pittsburgh than for playing golf.

A member of Pitt's golf team, the solidly built, 6-foot-0, 205-pound Souchak gained notoriety for football. Named All-America in 1937, he was a two-way starter for head coach Jock Sutherland and paced the Panthers in catches and interceptions. He was a member of Pitt's legendary 1936 squad that whitewashed Washington 21–0 in the Rose Bowl, its sixth shutout in ten games, and was named national champion. Pitt went 8-1-1 that season, its tie coming on Halloween against Fordham in New York's famed Polo Grounds. Fordham featured its formidable "Seven Blocks of Granite" line, which listed a future coaching legend in Vince Lombardi.

Souchak would play in the 1938 East–West Shrine Game and was selected in the sixth round of the 1938 NFL draft, forty-eighth overall, by the New York Giants. He spent one season in the NFL, playing for the Pittsburgh Pirates, who were renamed the Steelers in 1940.

He won the 1946 Western Pennsylvania Amateur, and a year later claimed the first of four West Penn Four Ball titles. In 1967 he would team with his younger brother Mike to win the Bing Crosby National Pro-Am. Along with Frank, Mike helped put the Souchak name on the golf map. Will Grimsley of the AP called Mike "the hottest commodity on the U.S. pro tour." He was featured on the January 16, 1956, cover of *Sports Illustrated* and its story on the Bing Crosby Tournament at Pebble Beach. Grimsley said Mike, a 5-foot-11, 215-pound long ball hitter, was Arnold Palmer before Arnold Palmer. Mike teamed with Gene Littler to form what Grimsley called "a version of the 'Gold Dust Twins' in leading a tough new contingent known as the 'Trailer Kids.'"

Sports Illustrated stated in 2002 that Mike was built more like Chicago Bears linebacker Dick Butkus than Hogan. If Souchak played on the modern PGA Tour, *SI* surmised, he would be "heckled about steroids."

Frank's and Mike's strength and physical build were natural. They may have inherited them from their father, who made a living in Berwick's blue-collar industrial surroundings by driving rivets in subway cars. Mike never did any weight training, only calisthenics. He was a gunner in the U.S. Navy in World War II before enrolling at Duke University on a football scholarship. He helped lead the Blue Devils' golf team to the Southern Conference championship in 1948 and '51 and served as captain of the golf team in 1951 and '52. Souchak starred for Duke at the time that Palmer played for Wake Forest. In football, Souchak was a kicker and starter at both offensive and defensive ends on the football team under coach Wade Wallace. Casey Stengel–like in his inability to remember names, Wallace called Souchak "Shoe Lace." Mike's talent on the gridiron was such that in 1950 he gained All-Southern honors from both the UPI and AP.

When Mike joined the pro golf tour in 1954, he was part of the "Trailer Kids," golfers who traveled the tour in trailers with their families. Souchak, Littler, Don January, Billy Maxwell, and Dow Finsterwald were all members of the "Trailer Kids" contingent.

Winning tournaments and setting scoring records that stood for decades, Mike's success on the tour led to fifteen victories and eleven top-ten places in majors. He would earn fame for his sterling performance in the 1955 Texas Open. Played in February amid near-freezing weather, gusty winds, and a muddy course at the Brackenridge Park Country Club in San Antonio, Mike tied a tournament record with a one-under-par 60 in the first round highlighted by a 29 that wasn't matched until Andy North in 1975 and Billy Mayfair in 2001.

He blistered the 6,400-yard course with follow up rounds of 68, 64, and 65 to card a 257, twenty-seven under par, and eclipse the low score for a seventy-two-hole tournament by two strokes. Nelson set the prior mark of 259 at the 1945 Seattle Open, and Chandler Harper tied it in 1954 at Brackenridge Park. Mike's 60 remained a record until Al Geiberger shot 59 at the Danny Thomas Memphis Golf Classic in 1977. His seventy-two-hole record low lasted even longer, with Mark Calcavecchia finally surpassing it by a stroke with a 256 at the 2001 Phoenix Open.

Frank and Mike Souchak were prototypes of the modern golfer. Their athletic skills made them long off the tee and helped elevate their sport's profile at the outset of the age of television. Frank would bring his athletic skills in play in an attempt to beat the beast of Oakmont. He joined Hogan, Snead, Burkemo, Fazio, and others in seeking to conquer the Hades of Hulton.

6

Hades of Hulton

The early morning hours of Thursday, June 11, 1953, saw the world's greatest golfers approach a green expanse situated on a hill northeast of Pittsburgh. That this famous, and feared, tract of land looked down on a serene Allegheny County was ironic given the heated battle soon to take place between men and beast.

Golfers nosed their cars along a driveway that breaks off Hulton Road and flows between stone pillars stately in appearance. Metal plates on the pillars state "Oakmont Country Club" in their welcome to competitors. Golfers, however, knew better. This was hardly a welcome sign, more like a warning, for this entrance was a highway to golfing hell.

Oakmont is as much a battle front as it is a golf course. Players go there preparing for combat at the country club. Oakmont historian and author Marino Parascenzo wrote that golfers "crawl off Oakmont, spent and reeling. They curse the bunkers. They cry of treacherous subtlety. They whimper of quicksilver where the greens should be, of putts that overrun their shadows. Oakmont is a midnight walk in a graveyard, something furry in a dark room." Bob Ford, former head professional at Oakmont, called the course "certainly one of the most penal courses in the world. It's a fair test of golf, but errant shots are treated as errant shots."

Oakmont bills itself as the "ultimate examination of championship golf." It remains one of the most difficult courses in the United States, with a bevy of bunkers, the challenging Church Pews, tough greens that tilt away from players, and narrow fairways that demand precision and accuracy.

It's called the Hades of Hulton for good reason. Players know it, and Parascenzo wrote that "Oakmont's reputation whips you, not Oakmont herself."

Reputation no doubt destroyed some golfers, but the quick, quirky course claimed its share of victims as well. As former *Pittsburgh Press* sports editor Pat Livingston noted, Oakmont had more victims than winners. It began in the 1919 National Amateur, when Oakmont—"this sand-scarred Hades of Hulton," Livingston called it—claimed its first prominent victim, a budding legend from Georgia named Bobby Jones.

It was just the start. "Oakmont," wrote Livingston, "has been beating those who would conquer its massive, intimidating sand traps and slick, deceptive greens ever since." Hall of Famers Jones, Harry Cooper, and Arnold Palmer are among the greats who have been burned by the Hades of Hulton.

Ben Hogan had successfully dealt with hellish courses before, the Monster of Oakland Hills in 1951 being the most intense and terrifying experience any field of golfers ever endured. Oakmont was daunting and could be demoralizing, but when the opening day of the tournament dawned, there stood Hogan on the first tee, defiant and determined.

The field at Oakmont was driven to win. Hogan, however, was driven by something more, something that went beyond winning. He was driven to settle a score. "It was part of his makeup," John Boyette recalls Dan Jenkins telling him.

Hogan strode to the first tee wearing a heavy gray cardigan sweater despite sweltering conditions. Because of the wrenched back he suffered in the qualifying rounds, Hogan wore the sweater to keep his muscles warm. Reporters noted that he smelled of ointment, Hogan having coated his back to keep him limber and loose. Sizing up the green expanse of Oakmont, the Masters champion tugged on his white cap and took deep drags on his Chesterfields.

Surrounded by swirling smoke, the Hawk trained his dark glare on a layout that ranks among the most impressive in the world. Oakmont boasts famous features in its lightning-fast greens and Church Pew bunkers but is far from being a tricked-up course.

Oakmont's first hole is considered one of the best of any course in the world. The putting skills of Hogan and the field would be tested immediately as they sought to negotiate the hard, slick greens. Because the green slopes front to back and right to left, second shots to the hole would be challenging. Oakmont owns arguably the toughest first hole in golf.

Most golfers seemed resigned to the idea that they would produce a five or more on the opening hole. The immense length of the hole—at 493 yards, it was outdone in 1953 only by numbers four (544) and twelve (598)—can be intimidating for starters, and drives off the tee are confronted by a fairway flanked by the Fowneses' famous bunkers. An errant shot into rough that reaches skyward to the accustomed height sought for the U.S. Open leaves golfers searching for ways to get on the green, whose slope is downhill and away from the player and is so steep that a ball won't easily come to rest.

Oakmont's number one had seen moments of glory. Two years prior to the '53 Open, Sam Snead's eagle in the final match of the PGA Championship gave The Slammer a lead he never lost. Sound strategy for surviving number one called for a midiron into the green and three putts for par. Number two (par four, 355 yards) is short but still dangerous. Approach putts would be manageable, but putts from behind the hole required a surgeon's skill. Anything less would lead to a three-putt or worse.

The storied "Church Pews" have long been the flashy feature on number three (par four, 428), but golfers couldn't ignore the severe fairway bunkers on the right. The elevated green sloped slightly from front to back. The Church Pews came into play again on number four (par five, 544), as did the bunkers on the right. This could be a birdie hole for Snead and some of the other big guns, and for Hogan, who could play power golf as well.

The Church Pews are one of the ornaments of Oakmont. George Peper of GOLF magazine wrote in 1994 that "Christian charity was the farthest thing from the mind of H. C. Fownes when he conceived the pitiless pit of sand known as The Church Pews. Of the nearly 200 bunkers at Oakmont, surely this is the most fiendish of all."

Oakmont's Church Pews are not only one of the more famous bunkers to be found anywhere in the world; they're also one of the more menacing. That they can affect play on not only one hole but *two* makes this hazard even more hideous. The Church Pews sit left of the fairway on number three and number four. The two holes run side-by-side, and the bunker perches between them. Either way, it lies in wait for errant drives that miss their mark.

The Church Pews got their name from their design—a sandy oasis featuring eight rows of grassy berms stretched straight across like pews in a church. The Church Pews did not exist in Fownes's original planning; six smaller separate bunkers did. From 1930 to 1934, the grass on the fringe was removed so that by the time golfers headed to Oakmont for the 1935 U.S. Open, the smaller bunkers had been melded into the much larger and more intimidating Church Pews.

A golfer seating his ball in the Pews might as well instruct his caddie, "Say a prayer for me." There is little that is heavenly about these Church Pews, and it's ironic that their devilish design is an integral part of one of the cathedrals of golf. Make a bad decision in the Pews and a poor soul would feel relegated to golf purgatory and seeking divine intervention. Peper wrote of the dreaded Pews sprawling "in the two acres of rough twixt holes three and four, its greedy green fingers ready to trip and grip a missed shot from either tee."

Jill R. Dorson noted in a 2016 article on Oakmont that the vaunted and vexing Church Pews were originally known as the "Snake Mounds." The "Snake Mounds" served as snake pits for golfers, and Oakmont historian Gerry Hickel told Dorson the phrase "Snake Mounds" first appeared in a 1934 caption accompanying a photo of the bunkers. Dorson writes that the term "Church Pews" appeared in a 1962 newspaper article and has remained ever since.

Number five (par four, 384) was challenging and called for long irons off the tee and short irons to the green. Playing short of the fairway bunkers was key, as was negotiating greens dangerous enough to deal three putts. The initial par three came on number six (183 yards). An errant attempt to the right would lead to a trap shot requiring a deft touch or resulting in a bogey.

A solid drive on number seven (par four, 387) could escape harsh fairway bunkers left and right. A midiron for the second shot put players on a green that sloped left to right, but a faulty shot to the left would be dire.

Described as "a monster" par three, number eight (253) was one of Oakmont's more difficult pars in prior majors. Not only is it very long for a par three, but one of the biggest bunkers found on any course in the world—a hundred-yard-long sandy expanse called "Sahara"—guarded the large green on the left and also served to intimidate some golfers. A blind uphill tee shot awaited the field on number nine (par five, 480). The fairway sloped left to right, with a ditch on the left and bunker on the right. The green was expansive and could be reached readily, but the serious undulations demanded proficient putting. As it could produce any score from a three to a seven, it was a hole that was expected to produce much excitement.

Oakmont's front nine played to 3,507 yards and a par 37. The back nine would play to 3,409 yards and a par 35. It began on number ten (par four, 470). A wasp-waisted driving area was flanked by fairway bunkers. Competitors were confronted by a troublesome green similar to number one in that it sloped front to back and right to left. Because it would be immensely difficult to handle the high-speed green, par would be a welcome result.

Number eleven (par four, 372) offered the opportunity to reach a flat plateau on the left side of the fairway and an approach to a green that slopes back to front and is well guarded. Number twelve (par five, 598) is the last par five and the longest hole on the course by fifty-four yards. Trouble is a constant companion. An undulating fairway slopes right, and there's a fall-away green that tilts away from the player and is bunkered on both sides. Approach shots and putts need to be precise on a hole that boasts severe difficulties.

Oakmont's longest hole is followed by its shortest. The narrow, hourglass green on thirteen (par three, 161) makes for a scenic and exciting hole. Golfers could play short and go for a birdie putt, but they would have to deal with an undulating, tilted green with bunkers in front, right, and left. Birdie opportunities are available on number fourteen (par four, 362). Surrounded by sand, the large green is deep and rolling and slopes from right to left. Seeking an uphill putt for birdie, players would look to stay left of the stick.

Number fifteen (par four, 458) is considered not only a great hole but perhaps Oakmont's best. A smaller Church Pews bunker—known as the Mini Church Pews or Little Church Pews—lines the left side of a fairway that slopes left to right. The Mini Pews combine with grass pews on the right to demand a straight drive. Enormous bunkers surround both sides of a large green. A long two-putt will be needed if the correct iron is not selected for the second shot to the green. Number sixteen (par three, 234) features an elevated tee to an expansive green that slopes left to right. Missing left and sending a shot to the right of the green could lead to major problems.

Number seventeen (par four, 292) is another exciting hole, an uphill dogleg left to an elevated green with a bunker on the right. Number eighteen (par four, 462) is Oakmont's most picturesque and historic hole. It's also considered by some the best finishing par four of any course anywhere. Golfers would look to drive the fairway to avoid bunkers left and right. An uphill approach to an undulated green finished a hole that has played a prominent role in golf history.

This rugged Steel City course required a steely competitor to conquer it. Hogan would seek to oblige. When the USGA declared there would be no furrows in Oakmont's bunkers, club officials nearly became apoplectic. Oakmont wouldn't be Oakmont, they countered, without furrowed bunkers. The impasse wasn't settled until just forty-eight hours prior to Thursday's opening round. The heavy river sand in greenside bunkers would be allowed; fairway bunkers would be smoothed by rakes with extralong tines.

While some golfers seemed ready to stage a wildcat walkout, Hogan dismissed the furrowed bunker controversy as so much Shakespearean drama—much ado about nothing. "I don't care whether they rake the bunkers in furrows or not," he declared. "I don't plan to be in them."

Time wrote that as the tournament teed off, the guessing at Oakmont "ran hot and heavy on two questions":

1. Could anyone crack Oakmont's tough par of 288 for 72 holes— something never done in two previous Opens at Oakmont?
2. Could anyone stop Ben Hogan, who had won three of the last five Open Championships?

Time noted that "Bantam Ben himself, complaining that he was a creaking 40 and his back ached, undertook to answer both questions."

With his aching back warmed by a cardigan and his putter red-hot, Hogan scorched the sun-spangled surroundings with a 67 that was five strokes below par and would be the low round of the tournament. Hogan did not go over par once in his opening round and might have set a competitive course record had three of his putts not stopped on the lip of the cup. As it was,

Hogan carded four birdies and five pars on the front nine and made the turn with a four-under 33. On the back nine he recorded eight pars and a birdie for a 34.

United Press sports editor Leo H. Petersen led his story that day by stating that the field "started chasing Ben Hogan, who held a three-stroke lead, in the U.S. Open golf championship today and the betting was that no one in the star-studded field would catch him over the rolling fairways of the Oakmont Country Club course. Blazing Ben, who burned up the rugged layout in a first round 33-34-67, five under par, was in a good position to prove to any remaining skeptics that he is the greatest golfer in history." Petersen added that the way Hogan played on opening day showed that the mechanical man of golf meant business. "Insisting that he felt great despite a pulled back muscle, Hogan was the master of one of the toughest golf courses of them all," wrote Petersen.

Hogan's blitz began early. He attacked Oakmont's downhill first hole with a solid drive. His second shot found the rough, and he followed with a pitch forty feet past the hole, then drained the putt for a birdie four. Holes two and three led to what author Robert Sommers described as "routine, though well-played par 4s." Two solid shots on number four brought another birdie, and he salvaged a par on number five when his second shot freed him from a bunker and his chip shot hit the flagstick. A well-crafted iron on six led to a four-foot putt and a birdie two. Hogan carded another birdie on seven with an eighteen-foot putt, and pars on eight and nine had him four under par at the turn. His blistering first round allowed him to end the day with a three-shot lead.

Hogan's booming drives carried the day, and Randy Jacobs says people who caddied for Mr. Hogan believed the sound of his shots was distinctively different from other golfers. "I suspect it might have had something to do with his equipment as well as the quality of his striking," says Jacobs:

> His clubs were extremely stiff, and of course he had the chord grips. The way he turned his body into the ball he generated a lot of speed, so it may have been a function of that.
>
> You can analyze his swing, but if you don't look at his equipment, you're only getting half the story because his equipment perfectly

complemented his golf swing. He set his equipment up to exactly complement what he was doing with his swing.

He was obviously very knowledgeable about equipment. If you have a soft, spongy rubber grip, it tends to absorb the shock that's coming up the shaft from the strike. If you have a really hard chord grip like he did, you're getting all the vibrations coming up the shaft into your hands, and it tells you exactly that you hit that right on the money or you hit low in the face. I'm sure that's one reason he always stayed with those hard chord grips because it gave him 100 percent feedback when he hit the ball. There were all kinds of grips then and most of them weren't as hard as the ones he used.

His equipment was different than the norm. Everything he did had a well thought out, distinct purpose to achieve an objective. He didn't mail anything in. You could just tell that's how he did everything in his life.

As was his wont, Hogan at Oakmont was insular, mostly maintaining a sphinxlike silence that vividly illustrated the intrigue surrounding the mystery man. Bob Hackett was an Oakmont resident since the age of five and would become a club member in 1964. He was a boy when his aunt and uncle took him to the famous 1927 U.S. Open, and while he was too young to fully appreciate walking the fairways with Jones, Sarazen, Hagen, and Armour, Hackett was fully aware of what he was watching in 1953 as he followed Hogan around the course. Hackett thought Hogan's concentration was so intense it prevented him from even recognizing the gallery.

Snead said Hogan didn't like to talk much when he was playing. Ben wasn't one to walk on the course and say, "How's the family?" Hogan, Snead said, was out there to beat you.

Chuck Pollock caddied for Hogan when Ben played on the West Coast and said Hogan rarely talked to his caddies either. Pollock thought Hogan was very prepared and didn't need much from caddies except to check for pin placements. Hogan might turn to him and ask if he had ideas about a particular shot, but it was rare, Pollock said, that Hogan asked for help. He thought Hogan was like a computer on the course, his every shot having been planned before the round.

Hogan said once his pretournament preparation was essential to maintaining his standard. In an article previewing the 1994 U.S. Open at Oakmont, Hogan stated that he tried to play to his standards even in social games. Golf is great, he said, because of its challenges and the different shots required. He found pleasure executing shots and perfecting shots. He would play a course first to find out which shots it required.

"They're the shots that give the edge—like the 10th at Oakmont," he said in '94. "I've practiced three days at a time just hitting high 4-woods or punch shots that skip to that green. You're not out there just trying to hit a ball to a caddie." Hogan's planning paid off in an eighteen for the ages. Jenkins wrote that Ben "butchered" the course that day, "romping through Oakmont's furrowed bunkers and lightning greens like they didn't exist."

Among the field of 157, the closest to Hogan were George Fazio, Walter Burkemo, and amateur Frank Souchak. The trio was three shots back at a two-under 70 and tied for second. Jimmy Demaret and dark horse pro Bill Ogden tied for fifth at 71.

Only six members of the field broke par the first day; four more tied it. Snead was among the latter group, with The Slammer coming in at 72 and finishing in a four-way tie for seventh with Jay Hebert, Jerry Barber, and Lou Barbaro. Petersen wrote that as far as Snead was concerned, it appeared the only major Slammin' Sam had never won was going to escape him once again. "Fine shotmaker that Snead is," said Petersen, "no golfer figures to spot Hogan five strokes and then catch him."

Hogan knew better, knew he was going to be in for a prolonged fight, most likely with Snead. Hogan returned to the course for Round Two on Friday, outfitted again in his cardigan to subdue back spasms. Picking up where he had left off in the first round, Hogan started in sizzling fashion, reaching the green on number two in two shots and birdieing the first two holes, the latter coming courtesy of an eight-foot putt. His two-wood second shot on number four was just shy of the green and his eight-iron left him three feet from the cup. His birdie put him at three under, but he lost a stroke on number five when he sent his tee shot into a trap. A three-putt on number eight resulted in another lost stroke.

Hogan rebounded on the back nine, sinking a ten-foot putt to birdie four-teen, and moved to two under heading to the sixteenth. Missing the green, he spun his ball twenty feet past the cup and two-putted for a bogey four. Hogan approached the eighteenth, where a gallery of six thousand fans flanked the fairway. His three-iron approach was short, and his chip was likewise short, by some twenty feet. Reports described him as appearing fatigued as he trudged up the hill to the green. Putting for par, Hogan's shot slid two feet beyond the hole. Ending his day with a bogey, Hogan carded an even par 72 and a two-day total of 139. He had prodded the Oakmont brute, and his lead had been trimmed to two strokes.

Thoughts of the previous year's U.S. Open, when Hogan struggled on Saturday, shimmered in the minds of some. He shot 74-74 in the morning and afternoon rounds, Jenkins telling Boyette that Hogan "lost it on the sixth hole of the morning round."

A pair of future champions failed to make the cut in their U.S. Open debut—amateurs Arnold Palmer and Ken Venturi. Palmer, granted a military furlough by the Coast Guard to play in this Open, was from nearby Latrobe and would have a long and bittersweet relationship with Oakmont CC. He shot 84-78-162 to miss by nine strokes. Venturi was much closer, his 78-76-154 missing by just one shot.

Snead's 69 on Friday, capped by a clutch chip shot on eighteen, was three under and would be the only other sub-70 round of the tournament. The sterling round allowed The Slammer to move into a second-place tie with Fazio with a thirty-six-hole score of 141. The easy win for Hogan was now no longer expected. Open Saturday, with its thirty-six holes of championship golf, was going to be Showdown Saturday.

"I feel better than a year ago, and I'm not tired," Hogan told reporters. Asked about his chances of holding off Snead, Fazio, and a surging field of contenders that now included Lloyd Mangrum (143), Hebert (144), and several others, Hogan remained cautious. "Anyone within 10 strokes of me now may be able to win."

That included Snead, who was determined to snap his skein in the U.S. Open. The morning round saw Hogan donning a short-sleeved polo shirt to accommodate the scorching summer sun. Yet it was Snead who was warming to the task, heating up amid the June weather. He tied Hogan on hole three and took a two-shot lead on number five. Snead held a one-shot lead over Hogan at the turn. They had played 45 rounds, and there was little to separate them. By round's end, Hogan had rallied and regained his advantage, but The Slammer succeeded in slicing another stroke off the Bantam's lead, with Sam shooting 72 while Ben posted a 73.

The 1953 U.S. Open would come down to a duel in the sun between two golfing greats. Hogan's fifty-four-hole total of 212 fronted the field, but Snead was only one back at 213. Tied for third were Demaret, Fazio, and Hebert, who at 218 were far enough back that they weren't expected by fans to be a factor.

This was Hogan versus Snead, mano a mano, with a major on the line. The past three years had seen them trade titles at Augusta—Hogan in '51, Snead in '52, Hogan in '53. Now they were colliding amid the sunshine and heat in the U.S. Open at a time when their rivalry was, as Snead said, "hot and heavy."

Snead thought this the most dramatic and the most personal U.S. Open he ever played, the reason being his duel with Hogan. Both were seeking to make U.S. Open history—Hogan for a record-tying fourth title that would put him in rarefied air; Snead for his first Open championship and a coveted career slam that would make he and Sarazen the only players at that time to achieve the modern Grand Slam. Snead knew, too, that a victory would tie him with Hogan for career majors with seven.

Time reported that Slammin' Sam sounded jubilant during the luncheon break between the third and fourth rounds. Snead "had plumbed Oakmont's secret. In his best hillbilly drawl, Sam explained: 'You gotta sneak up on these holes. Effen you clamber and clank up on 'em, they're liable to turn around and bite you.'"

Hogan seemed less jubilant. Encircled by sportswriters, he opined that this tournament could be decided by the final three holes. "And that's where the real danger is," Hogan warned, "particularly if you need to go for a birdie."

The afternoon round commenced, the final eighteen holes to decide the championship. Hogan teed off an hour ahead of Snead. Teeing off first could present problems as one could only speculate on the meaning of the roars from the gallery behind him. Since Snead would know what Hogan was scoring on every round ahead of him, the advantage was with Sam.

Snead held at least two other seeming advantages as well. He was in great shape for the thirty-six-hole marathon that made up Open Saturday, while Hogan was limping on legs permanently weakened by his accident. Playing thirty-six holes in one day was a physical grind for Hogan, particularly on ground baked so hard by the summer sun it could have served as a suitable training ground for General Patton's desert army. Snead also drew confidence that he had twice played Hogan head-to-head and won. The first victory came in a match-play tournament in San Francisco, the second in the LA Open.

Because Hogan and Snead rarely spoke at length to one another, newspapers promoted a rivalry and sought to make readers believe the two didn't like each other. Snead said he and Hogan were like brothers because each made the other better. The two men were vastly different, but they had tremendous respect for one another.

Their differences were highlighted by those handicapping the climactic eighteen. Snead was seen as a superior athlete with a tremendous swing. Hogan was favored for his mechanical precision and course management.

Snead thought Hogan more scientific, though he believed Ben thought *too* much. Snead knew his swing was more natural but lacked Hogan's control. The Bantam had power off the tee, but not as much as The Slammer. Snead believed Hogan thought of him as "a prima donna, the favorite of the photographers. . . . Man, he hated picking up the morning newspapers and seeing 'Snead' everywhere he looked."

Snead felt Hogan didn't like that when Ben drove the ball, the gallery looked to the fairway to see *where* he hit the ball. When Sam was teeing off, fans watched to see *how* he hit the ball.

Fellow pros knew they could get a rise out of Hogan and Snead by making comparisons. Ed "Porky" Oliver thought no golfer matched Snead when it came to hitting the ball. But when it came to concentration, Oliver opted for Hogan. He thought the way Hogan set himself up for a tournament made him tough to read. Yet he favored Snead's swing over Hogan's. Oliver opined that if Ben quit golf for six months, he'd be nothing. He also believed that Snead, by contrast, could quit for a year and still be great.

Denny Shute emphasized to *si* that Hogan and Snead were different types. He called Snead a natural golfer who always swings the same. Hogan's swing was manufactured, and he didn't make many mistakes because he practiced hours upon hours.

Bob Toski believed one had to consider physical, mechanical, and mental ability. He chose Hogan, he told *si*, because Snead lacked the one quality that would make him the greatest player of all time—concentration. Toski thought Hogan had greater nerve control than Snead, was a better judge of distance, and performed better in championship conditions.

How well Hogan would perform in the afternoon round was dependent in part on his physical health amid the summer conditions. "There was a lot of trying to get his body ready," says John Boyette. "I don't know how much time he had between rounds on the 36-hole day, probably no more than an hour or so."

Pat Ward-Thomas, who covered golf for the *Manchester Guardian* from 1950 to 1977, wrote in 1953 that the playing of two rounds on the last day can considerably aid a great golfer, since he has two chances at the same pin position. Small errors of judgment in the morning round can be changed to accommodate the afternoon round, especially, Ward-Thomas stated, "when a man has the certainty of shot-production of a Hogan."

This had been proven true on several occasions, Ward-Thomas said, "notably his classic victory at Oakland Hills in 1951. This was a ferocious test, perhaps the severest that has ever been for an American Open, and Hogan's scores in order were 76, 73, 71, 67. The wonder of this performance can be appreciated from the fact that, of 220 rounds played by the competitors who completed the championship, there were only four scores of 70, and one 69, by Clayton Heafner."

A gallery reported at ten to twelve thousand fans surrounded the first hole when Hogan opened with a birdie. Snead started some sixty minutes later, and the huge crowd raced between the two men as they dueled for the title. A three-putt bogey on number seven and a trapped-drive bogey on number eight left Hogan at one-over 38 heading into the back nine. Oscar Fraley of the United Press wrote that "there were times on Ben's final round when it appeared that he might waver just a bit too much."

Snead made the turn at one over as well, and Hogan held grimly to his one-stroke lead. Nine holes remained, nine holes of the championship pressure that Toski said Hogan handled better than anyone. Fraley called it "a two-man race down the tremendous stretch at old Oakmont."

A year earlier, Hogan had come unglued in the U.S. Open. Playing for keeps at Oakmont, Hogan recalled in a 1994 article that the tenth hole would be one to worry about in the final round.

"A par there would put me in shape where I'd be hard to catch," Hogan remembered for Robert Sommers, and he made his par four. Hogan ratcheted his game up another notch on number thirteen. His five-iron from twenty-five feet successfully negotiated the rolling green and found the cup for a birdie. Ben bogeyed fifteen when his two-iron second shot was trapped, putting him one over par. He knew he was still leading Snead, but he didn't know by how much.

Observers wondered how many strokes constituted a safe lead when The Slammer was within striking distance. Hogan said later that all anyone can do in such a situation on the finishing holes is to "try to play as well as you can, one hole at a time."

In Jenkins's words, Hogan "floated a brassie shot" on sixteen that settled "safely onto the center of the green." Gene Gregston thought it "a fine wood shot" that placed the ball on the green 234 yards out. It was, in Hogan's estimation, his "best shot of the day." It was a clutch shot on a hole that concerned Hogan. The ball sliced through the summer breeze and came to rest twenty-five feet from the pin, and Hogan followed with a two-putt for par that he considered crucial. "The wind was blowing from right to left," Hogan told Arthur Daley of the *New York Times*, "and so I had to cut the ball a little bit in order to hold it into the wind." Daley thought no detail too insignificant for Hogan: "He not only outgolfed everyone else. He also out-thought them."

Hogan seemed pressure-proof, but he was not immune to the tension of championship golf. He flicked his cigarettes with such force they bounced off the baked ground. The more efficiently he played, Hogan recalled once, the more nervous he became. "I think the problem in those 36-hole U.S.

Opens," Boyette says half-jokingly, "was that he was worried about driving it into his divot from the morning rounds."

Hogan was one over par when he headed to seventeen, where he hadn't driven the green in any of the three previous rounds. He had been playing it short to avoid the bunkers, staying out of the dreaded sand as he had stated he would. He preferred being in the high grass, where he could wedge out and play for par.

Daley considered the seventeenth one of the more challenging holes on the course: "a tricky par 4," he called it. "It's too long for anyone to drive the green," he wrote, "especially since it's an uphill hole with the fairway sloping down from left to right." The hole played tricks on the mind; the pin was there but hard to find. "Yawning traps surround the green everywhere but a narrow alley in the left corner, and the pin was placed in the right corner behind the biggest and deepest trap," Daley observed.

Analyzing the difficult hole, Hogan told Daley there was no way to get to the pin unless one used a bow and arrow. It couldn't be done with a golf club, Hogan stated. "So I decided I'd deliberately drive into the rough, short of the green and to the left," Hogan explained to Daley. "Then I'd have a chance to attack in the only way possible. The rough didn't scare me. It still was a more advantageous shot than from the fairway."

Dramatically changing tactics for this afternoon round, Hogan attacked the beast of Oakmont—"that ugly old brute," Herbert Warren Wind called it—and drove the green. "I hit it with everything I had," he told Daley. The Hades of Hulton remained daunting, but Hogan, who drew pleasure from conquering courses, wasn't content to merely survive the horrors of Oakmont. He wanted to destroy them.

The Hawk's drive through shimmering sunshine carried 292 yards and landed hole-high, "40 feet from the pin," Fraley noted. Another estimate put it at thirty-five feet. Jenkins thought Hogan's drive was "arrow straight, it rammed through the slender entrance to the green and left him pin-high with a 30-foot putt for an eagle deuce."

The drive reminded Gregston of Hogan's two-iron second shot onto the green at eighteen at Merion three years earlier. "He cranked out his best pop of the tournament and flew the ball between the sentinel traps and onto the green," wrote Gregston.

Said Hogan later, "I had never reached the green from the tee, but that day I drove the green." His putt from eight feet stopped a reported six inches shy, Daley put it at eight inches, and Hogan tapped in for birdie, having barely missed an eagle. The Hawk was flying high, rallying in what Fraley called "that old Hogan manner."

On to eighteen and the final hole in Hogan's grueling battle with brutish Oakmont. Sun and heat bore down on golfers and spectators alike, the Hades of Hulton fully in evidence. Thousands of spectators lined the eighteenth from tee to green; the scent of cigars, cigarettes, and Coppertone sunscreen filled the summer air. Facing one of the great finishing holes in golf, Hogan hit what Jenkins called "a monstrous drive" that split the fairway and traveled the middle of the fairway three hundred yards out. He followed with a five-iron; "rifled his approach six feet from the flag," Fraley wrote. Some estimated it at eight feet, others at nine. It was reported that thousands of "gasping fans" formed "a tight, tense circle" around the chain-smoking Hogan.

With a championship riding on his putt, Hogan carefully studied his shot for more than a minute, dropped his Chesterfield to the sun-soaked ground, then calmly sent his shot spinning toward the cup, the ball rolling gently in for what Fraley called a "great big birdie." Hogan shot two under par on the final three holes and earned five thousand dollars for his victory.

Vintage film captured the highlights of Hogan's furious finish, which some fans strained to see through their handheld periscopes. Daley considered Hogan's dissection of diabolical Oakmont educational. "This one sloped away from the left so he'd deliberately hook into it," wrote Daley. "That one sloped away from the right so he'd fade a slice into it. On another he'd take the risk of landing in a trap because it still was the best way of getting at the hole. On still another he'd take no chances because safe play was a sounder stratagem."

Paired with Dick Metz for the final two rounds, Hogan would walk across the fairway any time Metz was shooting first and position himself alongside Metz's caddie to learn what club was being used. When Daley asked later if that meant anything, Hogan grinned.

"Of course, it did," he said. "If Dick was short with a 2 iron, I'd use a 1. Or if he was long with it, I'd switch to a 3. He helped me make up my mind. We agreed most of the time although he did use the wrong club on the 18th."

Daley noted that Metz overclubbed into a trap and Hogan found the green for a birdie. He saw Hogan as outthinking Snead as well and pointed to their respective strategies for number seventeen. Snead had boldly attacked the hole in the morning round, watched his ball roll past the hole on an attempted eagle two and card a four. Hogan, wrote Daley, would take an eagle but would first make certain of a birdie.

If Hogan was to err, Daley said, it would be on the side of shortness. Where Snead's putt had skirted eight feet beyond the hole, Hogan's rolled to a stop eight inches shy. Thus Ben got his birdie.

Calling Hogan the "Little Killer of the Fairways," Fraley wrote that Ben closed with two "smashing" birdies. Combating the horrors of Oakmont, the heat of the day, and the heightened tension, Hogan shot 3-3-3 on sixteen, seventeen, and eighteen. Jenkins wrote that the shots Hogan hit on those final three holes, "under the Open gun, were among the best of his career and beyond the ability of any other mere mortal."

Looking back, Sommers wrote that even Oakmont, with its narrow fairways, deep and dense rough, and fast, frightening greens, "yielded to the steady, forceful and often inspired play of Hogan. . . . This was the most dangerous fourth-round player in the game, and he staggered Oakmont with a blistering finish."

Hogan said later he believed he prepared for the 1953 U.S. Open more than most of his competitors. He had played more practice rounds because he knew Oakmont's reputation and didn't know what to expect.

Oakmont enhanced its reputation when it snared Snead on number twelve. The Slammer, putting forth what Fraley called a "now or never effort," played an aggressive second shot on the nearly six-hundred-yard hole. He was errant with his fairway wood and required three to reach the green. Once on the green, Snead three-putted for a catastrophic bogey six. Putting was a weakness that cost Snead two U.S. Open titles. In 1948 he had tried eighteen different putters to find the solution to problems that plagued him once again in the final round of the '53 Open. He carded a 76 to place second at 289, six shots off Hogan's pace. It was the fourth time Snead had finished as runner-up in the U.S. Open.

"I guess it's just not meant to be," Snead sadly told reporters. Fraley called it "an old familiar tale to The Slammer." Fraley noted that with nine holes still to play Hogan was holding a slender lead. "But then the little man from Texas put Snead to the test and found him wanting."

It wasn't just Snead who was found wanting. Mangrum finished with a 75 to place third at 292. Demaret and Fazio tied with Pete Cooper for fourth at 294. Defending champion Julius Boros carded a 299 and finished out of the top ten.

Henry Longhurst wrote once that if "Hogan means to win, you lose." Hogan meant to win at Oakmont, and he exhibited the look Longhurst knew so well—"the tightening of the lips, the discarded cigarette, and one more shot dispatched on its way."

Hogan's 33 on the back nine gave him a one-under 71 and a winning 283 total that was five under par and a stunning eleven shots better than Oakmont's course record. The Hawk was the first golfer to beat Oakmont's 288 par in competition. Hogan's score was also sixteen shots better than the 299 Sam Parks Jr. produced in winning the 1935 Open at Oakmont. Hogan had succeeded in joining Anderson and Jones as the only four-time U.S. Open titlists. Unofficially, it was Hogan's fifth U.S. Open, if the 1942 National Open held during the war at Chicago's Ridgemoor Country Club counted, as Hogan and others believed it should.

Following his victory, Hogan strode into the clubhouse and jauntily remarked, "Where's everybody been all week?" "If you would look up once in a while," one competitor answered, "you might see somebody."

Oakmont's Steel City course was conquered, but it had taken the steely edged Hogan to do it. Fraley called Hogan's late surge "chilled steel." "Battling Ben Hogan," he wrote, "staged another of his chilled steel finishes Saturday to win the U.S. Open Championship for the fourth time in six years and once again send Slammin' Sammy Snead down golf's heartbreak highway."

Time wrote that under pressure Hogan and Snead "stroked one-over-par 38 on the outgoing nine. Coming in, and knowing Snead was still hot on his heels, Hogan characteristically closed the Open with a brilliant finish."

Bob Harlow, then editor of *Golf World* magazine, had been in golf since the 1920s as a writer, player agent, and PGA tournament director and was particularly impressed with Hogan's win. "If additional evidence was needed to prove that Hogan is the golfer of the decade and the golfer of the century he provided the details at Oakmont," wrote Harlow. "Four out of five Opens may not be as spectacular as a Grand Slam, but for accurate play against the toughest fields it looks like the top achievement in competitive golf. The fact is, Ben just beats the hell out of the other players and naturally this does not improve his opponents' morale."

Hogan was the U.S. Open's first wire-to-wire winner in thirty-two years since England's "Big" Jim Barnes, playing what sportswriter Walter McCallum called "a remarkable brand of golf," shot 69-75-73-72 for a total of 289 at Columbia Country Club in Maryland in 1921. Hogan's six-stroke margin marked the largest in fifteen years, matching Ralph Guldahl's total at Cherry Hills Country Club in Colorado in 1938. Hogan also became the first American pro to win the U.S. Open four times, Bobby Jones having been an amateur when he won in 1923 and '26.

Snead said Hogan had done himself proud in winning his fourth U.S. Open title and his third since the accident. "An amazing feat," said Snead.

Still, tough Oakmont had taken its toll on Hogan. Asked by reporters if he would seek to repeat his triumph at Baltusrol in 1954, the weary champion was noncommittal. "I may not," he said. "I don't want to say I'm retiring. I love golf. I want to play as long as I can. But I'm getting awfully tired. Someday there has to be a stopping point."

Hogan was feeling his years, but he hadn't yet reached his stopping point. "When I get so I can't prepare for a tournament, then I'll retire," he told reporters. "I think preparation is very important for a championship tournament."

Preparation would never be more important than for Hogan's next championship tournament—his first-ever appearance in the British Open. It would take all of Hogan's famed preparation to conquer Carnoustie, a course so difficult it would come to be called Car*nasty.*

7

Carnoustie

Writing for *Time* magazine in a July 2007 article titled "Golf Is Hell" that previewed the British Open's return to Carnoustie, Eben Harrell stated that if one mentions Scotland's sea-swept course to pro golfers, their response is to compare the brutality of it to war. Survivors of the 1999 "Open"—as the British championship is often called—at Carnoustie "muttered and clutched their heads like traumatized veterans," Harrell wrote.

The analogies to war are understandable, Harrell noted, since Carnoustie sits some fifteen miles from an air force base and just five hundred yards from an army firing range. The soundtrack of the course often includes the soaring sound of fighter jets and the rapid fire of machine guns. Historic battles serve as the names for holes on one of Carnoustie's three courses.

Harrell noted that Gordon Lang, a Scottish author, wrote in his book on twenty-first century warfare that his creation of the term "Carnoustie Effect" best fits what he calls the "psychic shock experienced on collision with reality by those whose expectations are founded on false assumptions."

Making his way to Carnoustie for the first time was a golfer whose mental toughness was unquestioned. Writer Michael S. Clark stated that Ben Hogan's appearance in the world's oldest major tournament and on the toughest course in the British Open rota "had Sunday golfers salivating and seasoned pros trembling at the knees." Yet there were some who felt Hogan was setting himself up to experience the dreaded Carnoustie Effect.

The champion of American golf had been urged to accept the challenge European golf presented, to travel to the birthplace of the sport and test his game against a course and in conditions he was unfamiliar with. Fellow American champions Gene Sarazen and Jimmy Demaret were among those who told Hogan that while he was regarded as the best golfer in the world, he would not be considered a legend until he played The Open Championship. Sarazen, a seven-time major champion, had taken the challenge and conquered it, The Squire winning the 1932 Open at Prince's Golf Club in Sandwich, England. Two weeks later in his native New York, Sarazen joined Bobby Jones as the only men at that time to win the U.S. Open and British Open in the same year.

Golf history beckoned to Hogan. So too did the Scots, their journalists pleading for the enigmatic American to travel to their shores and take on their seaside course. One month following his record-setting appearance in the Masters, an article titled "Hogan, the Master—Come Over" appeared in the May issue of *Golf Monthly*, which was published in Edinburgh, Scotland. The piece pleaded with the American golf king to come to Carnoustie to prove his greatness:

> The man who was shattered to the verge of death in a motor smash, who fought back from an encased body lying rigid for months in a hospital, to win the American Open championship thrice in the last five years, and has again won the Masters Tournament, is becoming a legendary figure to the golfers of Britain.
>
> Carnoustie, did he come and triumph, would impress the seal on Hogan's fame. In phantasy we see Hogan, the enigma, silent, austere, resolute, battling out on the windswept links of the Angus seaboard, one of the massive tests of the game in the whole world of golf. Do not leave it too late, Ben, to take your place amongst the immortals of golf and the supreme honour in the game. Scottish golfers, and especially Carnoustie, whose sons did so much for golf in your homeland, will take you to their hearts.

The year 1953 was a memorable one in the UK. It witnessed the Coronation of Queen Elizabeth II, and the conquering of Mount Everest by Sir Edmund Hillary and a sherpa named Tensing. Now another iceman cometh, the champion of the Masters and U.S. Open. A British writer stated that the drama of Hogan playing in the British Open was stirring the "imagination of golfers in all lands." Players and fans of two hemispheres, *Golf Monthly* stated, would be heading to Carnoustie "in a big way!"

The magazine said South African Bobby Locke, battling for his fourth British Open Championship, and Egyptian champion Hassan Hassanein would be "focal figures of all Africans," and bold challenges by Argentinians Antonio Cerda and Roberto de Vicenzo would arouse the "liveliest interest in the vast regions of South America." A gallant bid by the youthful Peter Thomson would rivet New Zealanders and Australians alike. The British Broadcasting Company would broadcast from the Open ten times each day of the tournament, and Columbia Broadcast of America would make a direct service on their own circuits. For the first time, television would take into the homes of viewers images from The Open Championship. Never before had an international sporting event been more widely described with banner headlines, articles, feature stories, photos, and illustrations as this tournament would be.

Trevor Williamson, a Carnoustie caddie, clubmaker, and ambassador of the historic course, was ten years old at the time of the 1953 British Open and recalls the excitement surrounding the buildup of Hogan's trip to the UK: "We get the Open and there's this expectation about everything, the expectation of Ben Hogan coming over," Williamson remembers. "This was an era where we had nothing like the media of today. We had Pathe News, which you could see every night at the cinema. We had newspapers, but as far as television went, there weren't that many. And we had very few visitors from the United States at that time. To see an American golfing at Carnoustie in those days was like, 'Oh, there's an American out golfing!' Hogan being from Texas, we would think of all the western movies we had seen, and we had all these visions of Americans we had seen in films. We had read about Hogan's abilities in the golfing magazines and how he had won all those tournaments that year."

The Scots' interest was further piqued by the contrast between American and British golf and the coming confrontation. While some implored Hogan to play in The Open Championship, others goaded him to take on the rough-hewn links golf that dated back centuries and was exposed to a variety of elements—stormy sea winds, cold climes, rain, sleet, and even hailstorms. Hogan acknowledged that critics didn't think he could win under such conditions.

Bernard Darwin, a grandson of the British naturalist Charles Darwin and an amateur golfer, thought Hogan's presence was such that even if he did not win The Open Championship, the "small colossus" still bestrode and dominated it. It was Hogan, Darwin said, who was selling tickets in the thousands, leading to crowds of twelve to twenty thousand, the largest to witness the Open to that point. And it was Hogan, said Darwin, who would be filling the parking lots with rows of shining cars. He hadn't played in his only previous trip to the UK, and few British fans had ever seen him in person. Thus, wrote Darwin, it was Hogan the Scottish fans would be coming to Carnoustie to see.

Thus the stage was set when *Time* magazine went public in the wake of his win at Oakmont that Hogan would indeed play in the British Open. "Hogan's winning 283 whipped Runner-Up Snead by six strokes, Oakmont's par by five," *Time* stated. "Ben's fourth title tied the record first set by Willie Anderson just after the turn of the century, later tied by Bobby Jones when he completed his 'grand slam' in 1930. Would Ben try for a record-breaking fifth next year? Maybe. But this week, concentrating on one title at a time, Ben was on his way to Carnoustie, Scotland for his first crack at one of golf's most venerable titles, the British Open."

Hogan had, in fact, mailed his entry for the British Open prior to playing in the U.S. Open. He knew when he mailed it he would head to Scotland whether or not he won the U.S. Open. Hogan would play in the British Open for various reasons, but bringing the Claret Jug back to the United States was not chief among them. The main reason, Hogan said, was to satisfy the wishes of so many fans who were hoping he would play in the UK. He believed that if people had faith in him and wanted him to represent America in the British Open, he should do so.

The second reason Hogan went to Scotland was the challenge of playing Carnoustie. He knew it was one of the most difficult courses in the world, and that the weather was unique enough to pose problems that golfers in the United States didn't have to deal with. Its most famous hole, the sixteenth, is the Barry Burn and marks the first of a trio of dangerous finishing holes.

Deep bunkers protect a green so narrow that a Canadian amateur described his group having to walk single file to get on it. The tee is elevated slightly, providing a view across land that Scottish writer Malcolm Campbell called "rough and uncompromising." To the left is the Barry Burn, which stands ready to swallow up shots pulled from the tee. The undulations of the green are such that balls can be thrown back at virtually any landing spot, and a series of sandy pits are spread around the green. Campbell said the grouping of sand traps strikes fear in the hearts of those who test it, as the ability to thread a shot between the barriers of sand is a gift given to very few.

The changing nature of the course is what makes Carnoustie so challenging. Campbell said the course does not contain even one simple hole, and its most demanding holes rank among the most ferocious anywhere. The difficulty of the course on a given day is governed by the weather, and when the Angus links are buffeted by strong winds, Carnoustie becomes unrelenting, unforgiving, and unplayable. It is not a place, Campbell wrote, for the faint of heart. Walter Hagen called Carnoustie the greatest course in the British Isles, and others have ranked it second only to the Old Course at St. Andrews.

Carnoustie is what the Scots call a bloody difficult beast, a course with teeth and without let up, an unrelenting series of menacing holes with unpredictable rain and wind but predictably massive, penal bunkers, tall rough, and finishing holes that put intense pressure on those who dare to challenge.

Hogan dared. "I wanted to try my hand at it," said the man accustomed to conquering courses. He was also eager to see if he could succeed playing the British ball. More than once he heard it said that his clubs were not suited to the ball that Hogan's friend and American broadcaster John Derr once recalled as a "90 compression, English-size Titleist No. 2."

Claims that even the great Hogan could not win under the conditions he would face at Carnoustie were heard by Ben time and again. Darwin listened to fans in the UK murmuring that Hogan might master the inland courses in America, "but let him wait till he comes over to play the great Carnoustie course in a Carnoustie wind."

It was enough to motivate Hogan. One of the driving forces of his life was proving his detractors wrong. Writer Bob Brumby, a friend of Hogan's, thought Ben's claim to international fame was lacking one element. "He had to win the British Open," Brumby wrote.

A third reason for his trip to the United Kingdom, Hogan said, was that the USGA and the Royal and Ancient Golf Club of St. Andrews had for the good of golf made their rules identical, the size of the ball notwithstanding. That meant Hogan's putter would no longer be banned from British play.

Finally, there was the fact that the timing of the British Open in 1953 did not coincide with any commitments Hogan had in the U.S. His damaged legs would not allow him to play in the PGA Championship held at Birmingham Country Club in Michigan, the match play format calling for twelve rounds—216 holes—spanning seven days. The PGA Championship would end July 7, while the British Open would tee off the following morning, and it involved two days of qualifying rounds.

Still, Hogan had delayed sending in his entry even as the June 6 deadline approached. Part of the reason may have been that Valerie was prone to travel sickness and didn't relish the thought of an overseas trip. Hogan's mother, Clara, told her son she didn't think he should go, recalling his illness during his 1949 trip to Great Britain for the Ryder Cup.

Normally arriving a week early for a tournament, Hogan and Valerie would set foot in Scotland two weeks ahead of time to acclimate themselves to their surroundings. As their departure date approached, Hogan began feeling a kind of pressure he had never before experienced prior to a tournament. He didn't have a fear of losing; what he did have was an anxiety that his critics would be proven right, that he couldn't win the British Open, and that fans in the UK would believe that American players weren't as good as advertised, especially when playing Britain's brand of rugged golf.

Hogan knew many fans believed he would win whenever he wanted. That wasn't the case, he said. Hogan felt that if a golfer can win 1 percent of the tournaments they play they're lucky. Luck would not be enough to win at Carnoustie, and Hogan was aware of that. Precise preparation would play a pivotal role. Sam Snead believed no golfer ever prepared for a tournament better than Hogan.

Brumby believed the same but doubted Hogan would win at Carnoustie. Ben had been driving himself since the Masters, Brumby thought, and was very tired. Carnoustie would not take pity, nor would it take prisoners. Hogan by his own acknowledgment was not known as a great wind player, and the wind at Carnoustie was so fierce it forced upon golfers who first tried to conquer it a swing aimed at keeping shots low to the ground. Harrell had seen "breeze-hardened seagulls swept across fairways like errantly sliced golf balls." Constantly playing shots low to the ground on a course that stretched to 7,200 yards and featured eleven holes at 406 yards or more proved problematic, so golfers sought a swing that could whip the ball through the wind.

To compensate, players developed the Carnoustie Swing, seen now as the start of the modern swing thanks to the emigration of Carnoustie golfers. Between 1898 and 1930 some three hundred pro golfers emigrated to America from Carnoustie and taught the Carnoustie Swing at clubs across the country. Harrell called it "quite a feat for a town that then had a population of only 5,000." The émigrés provided several of the sport's earliest ambassadors, and these golfing missionaries spread their game's gospel to many distant lands. Sons of Carnoustie won championships in Britain, America, Australia, Canada, and South Africa and claimed every state title in the United States. It was for this reason that Herbert Warren Wind stated that while St. Andrews is the home of golf, Carnoustie is the home of Australian and American pro golf.

Among the Scottish émigrés was Stewart Maiden, who sailed from Carnoustie in 1907 and settled in Atlanta. His brother James had left in 1901 to become an assistant pro at Nassau Country Club in New York, and another brother, Allan, left home for Australia and became the pro at Melbourne's Victoria Golf Club. Stewart became head pro at Atlanta's East Lake Golf Club in 1908.

Called "Kiltie" because of his penchant for wearing kilts as a young boy playing barefoot on the cobbles of Carnoustie, Stewart was born in February 1886 to James Sr., a payroll clerk at a local metal foundry, and Elspeth Maiden. While at East Lake, Stewart met a young Bobby Jones and made for him his first set of matched clubs.

Photos and film of Stewart show him wearing a cap, dark sweater, and gray slacks and with a cigarette protruding from his lips even as he was in full swing. The impressionable Jones followed Stewart around the East Lake course and became so impressed by the Carnoustie Swing that he later called it "the finest and soundest style I have ever seen." Bobby would grow up swinging like Stewart Maiden, who became the only coach to one of golf's great legends.

Jones used elements of the Carnoustie Swing to become the only man to win four major titles in the same year. He would reportedly contact Maiden at times to help him with issues concerning his swing. Maiden accompanied Jones to St. Andrews in 1927 when Jones defended his British Open title with a wire-to-wire six-stroke victory and in Jones's 1930 Grand Slam season when Bobby won the U.S. Open, U.S. Amateur, British Open, and British Amateur.

Years later Jones credited his mentor further, saying the greatest stroke of luck he ever had in golf was Maiden coming from Carnoustie to coach at East Lake Golf Club. The success Maiden had in teaching American pros influenced generations of golfers. Sportswriter O. B. Keeler said once that the Stewart Maiden style "stood out like the Washington Monument" over the field of competitors.

The principles Maiden taught have been followed by golfers ever since. American golfer Harvey Penick, who coached numerous Hall of Fame players, called Maiden the best golf teacher of all. Maiden likewise had a mentor, and it can be said that he learned elements of the Carnoustie Swing from Archibald Simpson. Born in 1866 in the village of Earlsferry (next to Elie in Fife, Scotland), Archie entered a world that Bernard Darwin said might have been a small one where golf was concerned but a busy one nonetheless, at least in Earlsferry.

Darwin noted that there were golfers who carried abroad the fame of Earlsferry, notably the Simpson family's brothers, headed by Jack and Archie. Robert Simpson, Archie's older brother and the fifth eldest of the six Simpson boys, moved to Carnoustie in 1883. Robert started the Simpsons Golf Shop, believed to be the world's second oldest golf shop, and seventeen-year-old Archie relocated to Angus to join his brother at the shop. Favoring a checkered woolen cap and bristling mustache, Archie rapidly rose to local fame as an outstanding player, club maker, teacher, and course architect. Though Archie would never win the Open as Jack did at Prestwick in 1884, he did make sixteen straight appearances in the tournament from 1885 to 1900, was twice runner-up, and was a top-fifteen finisher every year.

Darwin declared that Archie owned one of the most graceful swings of his day, and it was Archie whom Richard Goodale credited in *Golf Course Architecture* for being the model for the famous Carnoustie Swing. Goodale wrote that young golfers would follow Archie around Carnoustie, seeking to mimic his swing. It was a swing exported around the world, most notably by Maiden, who passed it on to Jones.

Just as a young Jones followed Maiden around the Atlanta course and studied his style, so did Maiden in his boyhood days tag along behind Simpson and learn his swing. And just as Jones joined forces with famed course architects in America, Simpson worked with Old Tom Morris designing layouts in Scotland.

Maiden and Simpson were among the more influential Carnoustie exports, as were the Smith brothers—Alex, Macdonald, and Willie. Alex and Willie claimed a combined three Claret Jugs, and in 1899 Willie became the first of the Smith brothers to take America's national championship when his 315 at Baltimore Country Club produced an eleven-stroke victory. It remained the largest margin of victory for more than one hundred years, until a fifteen-stroke victory in 2000 by Tiger Woods at Pebble Beach.

The Smith brothers recorded another historic first in 1906 when Alex won the U.S. Open with a score of less than 300, shooting 295 at the Onwentsia Club in Illinois to win by seven strokes over Willie. Four years later Alex won his second U.S. Open, outdueling Macdonald and Johnny McDermott in an eighteen-hole playoff at the Philadelphia Cricket Club.

Macdonald shared a British Open fate like that of Sam Snead in the U.S. Open, enduring a string of close calls. He came within three shots of winning the British Open or U.S. Open eleven times between 1910 and 1936, including placing second in the U.S. Open in 1930 and British Open in '30 and '32. Macdonald's near misses in the British Open occurred in three-year clusters, 1923–25 and '30–'32. They were more spread out in the U.S. Open, where he came close in 1910, '13, '30, '34, and '36. He is arguably the greatest golfer to have never won the British or U.S. Open. Macdonald's most devastating defeat came in the 1925 British Open at Prestwick, where a 78 on the final eighteen would have clinched his first Open title but he instead shot 82 and finished fourth behind champion Jim Barnes.

Archie Simpson, Stewart Maiden, the Smith Brothers, and others are integral parts of golf's rich history in Carnoustie. The game has been played in the Angus town for more than four centuries, dating to at least 1560, when parish records referenced the game of "gawf" on the Barry Links adjacent to the current course and a local man named Sir Robert Maule, who may have been Carnoustie's first golfer. Born in 1497, Maule was a landowner and gentleman given to, as the records state, "hawking, hunting, and the gawf."

No mention was made of exactly where Maule and his fellow sportsmen practiced "gawf," but it is on record that the Carnoustie Golf Club was formed by 1839, dating it to the early years of Queen Victoria's reign and making it the world's oldest artisan golf club. Allan Robertson, considered the first golf pro and the best golfer of his time, laid out the initial Carnoustie course, a ten-hole design that was lengthened to eighteen by Old Tom Morris in 1867. That same year, Old Tom was proud that his son, sixteen-year-old Young Tom, took on all comers on Carnoustie's new course and won.

"Auld Tom," as he was called in Scotland, is widely regarded as the "Grand Old Man of Golf." Born in 1821 in St. Andrews, he moved to Prestwick in 1851 and was known as Keeper of the Green. He returned to St. Andrews in 1864 and for the next forty years took care of the venerated Old Course. Distinct in appearance with his flat cap and full white beard, Old Tom won Open Championships in 1861, '62, '64, and '67 and is rated by some historians as the greatest golfer ever. A devout Christian who set high standards on and off the course, he read his Bible daily, refused to play "gawf" on the sabbath, and was said to immerse himself every day in St. Andrews Bay, regardless of the weather. While he is most closely linked with St. Andrews, Old Tom ranks among the more famous contributors to Carnoustie's history.

Carnoustie got its name from nouns of Scandinavian origin—*car*, which means "rock," and *noust*, which translates to "bay." Some citizens of the town, however, prefer the legend that Carnoustie takes its name from the Battle of Barry, a bloody encounter waged in 1010. It was then that Malcolm II, the Scottish king, drove back Danish forces fronted by their leader, Camus. The great Dane general's death remains marked by a cross at the spot where he is buried in the soil of Panmure Estate.

Local lore states that the Norse gods were offended by the Dane's death and cursed the area by sending forth to Barry Sands crows numbering in the thousands. Like a scene out of Alfred Hitchcock's 1960s horror film *The Birds*, the crows took over the Buddon Ness woodland to the point that the village was called "Craw's Nestie," which later became Carnoustie. In 1899, the village was given burghal status, and area officials, in an homage to the legends, adopted a crest in which three crows are depicted flying over a tree. The latter is the Dibble Tree, which is more than two hundred years old and located in the middle of the town. Carnoustie is said to have been built around the leafy tree, and the crest adopted long ago still serves as the Carnoustie Golf Links logo.

More than half a century passed between Carnoustie's conversion to an eighteen-hole course and its readiness to host The Open Championship, which it did for the first time in 1931. Credit for Carnoustie's renovation goes to James Braid, like Maiden a native of Earlsferry. Born in 1870, Braid grew up golfing near venerated St. Andrews on the links of Elie. His impact on the sport has been said to be almost without equal. Braid's introduction to the game came as a caddie, and his talent was evident at an early age when he won a caddie tournament at age eight. A year later he came to the attention of three-time Open winner Jamie Anderson, who told the young Braid that he had the talent to become a top golfer.

By age sixteen Braid was a scratch golfer and member of Earlsferry Thistle Golf Club. The club featured several talented young golfers, including Archie and Jack Simpson and two-time Open Championship runner-up Douglas Rolland. Five years later Braid was finishing first in area tournaments and breaking course records. He transitioned to the pro ranks in 1893 and played his first Open Championship a year later. He finished tenth behind champion J. H Taylor, who combined with Harry Vardon to win six Open titles in seven years through 1900.

In 1901 Braid beat Vardon and Taylor to claim the first of his five Open Championships and turn the great tandem into the famed "Great Triumvirate." Long before the great American trio of Hogan, Snead, and Nelson, Braid joined with Vardon and Taylor to form "The Great Triumvirate" that ruled British golf. Darwin believed the conduct of Braid, Vardon, and Taylor raised the standing and reputation of professional golfers from what he called the "lowly levels of the 1800s."

Braid's strength was the distance of his drives. Like Snead he could reach holes others couldn't, and he became known for sudden strikes. Like Hogan, he was a strategic player whose determination, hard work, and practice made him a champion. From 1901 to 1910 Braid won five British Opens and finished second three times. Braid, Vardon, and Taylor combined to win the Open sixteen times in twenty-one years, but that was not the boundary of Braid's legacy. He was a man of character, and it was said of him that while he had many opponents, he was without enemies.

Future British Open champion Henry Cotton said that everyone who knew Braid recognized in him modesty, dignity, reticence, wisdom, and kindliness. Braid's reputation was such that he became the first president of the Professional Golfers' Association following its founding after World War I.

Braid was prolific as a course designer. He is connected to more than two hundred UK courses, and his layouts have become more famous than he. While nearly forgotten by all but the most devoted golf fans and historians, the course designs of the great Open champion include beloved Brora Golf Club; Gleneagles King's, arguably Scotland's best inland course; Lundin Golf Club, a unique combination of parkland and seaside links; Southport and Ainsdale, which in 1937 served as the host site for the first Ryder Cup won on foreign land; and Carnoustie.

Considered the first course to be designed at least in part by an Open champion in Old Tom Morris, Carnoustie was redesigned in sweeping fashion by another Open king, Braid. With his woolen cap low on his brow, thick walrus-like mustache, and gray jacket pulled over a white collared shirt and dark tie, Braid began revamping Carnoustie in 1926. His work was comprehensive, as virtually every one of the eighteen holes was redone by Braid, described by the James Braid Golfing Society as a "thinking" course designer.

Like all great course architects, Braid was able to see in his mind's eye how to create each hole from the natural topography. His use of hazards was said to challenge shots from even the top golfers that were slightly errant. The Braid Society states that he thought deeply about variety, wind direction, turf condition, green size, and tee positions in his twin desire to provide both pleasure and challenge to golfers.

Carnoustie ranks as Braid's crowning glory, the course being called "golf's greatest test" and the toughest on the Open rotation. As would be the case at Carnoustie in future Open Championships, the 1931 inaugural contained a fair amount of drama. Two decades prior to Hogan's arrival at Carnoustie, Tommy Armour was a celebrated champion who stepped forth to battle Braid's design. Born in Edinburgh in 1896, Armour was a native Scot who sharpened his skills on Edinburgh's Braid Hills before emigrating to the United States in the 1920s. Like Bantam Ben, the Silver Scot was battling both a difficult course and a physical challenge, having lost an eye in a mustard gas attack as a member of the British Army in World War I.

Armour won the 1927 U.S. Open and 1930 PGA Championship. Shooting rounds of 73, 75, and 77 in the 1931 British Open, the popular Scottish-American was tied with four others five shots back of Argentinian Jose Jurado heading into the final eighteen. Despite a cold wind that buffeted the field and caused large crowds to bundle against the elements in warm coats and hats, Armour, attired in cap, dark sweater, and tan knickerbockers, rode solid shot-making and clutch-recovery play to a course-record 71.

Grainy black and white film of the tournament shows the Prince of Wales, an avid golfer, among the largest gallery to go to Carnoustie to that point. The first of the great Latin American golfers, Jurado, wearing a white sweater and dark knickers, approached the final hole believing he needed a four to win and a five to beat Armour, who had missed a short putt on seventeen. Following a solid drive off the tee, Jurado decided to play it safe and not attempt to carry the burn but lay up short of the water. Jurado's mental mistake left him a shot back of Armour, who made up for his lost stroke on seventeen with a clutch putt on eighteen.

Armour's dramatic putt gave him a 71 for the final round, one shot ahead of Jurado. Hard-luck Macdonald Smith finished tied for fifth. The Silver Scot's 296 total marked the highest winning score since 1925, when Jim Barnes won at Prestwick with a 300.

The Open Championship returned to Carnoustie in 1937, and Braid's design was updated and extended from 6,701 yards to 7,200 by Thomas Wright, links committee chairman. Just as Robert Trent Jones would do at Oakland Hills in 1951, Wright adapted to the modern game and eliminated bunkers and hazards that had been rendered obsolete by modern equipment. Though he added some five hundred yards to the course, Wright, an accountant, stressed that quality rather than length was the objective.

The drama in '37 focused on a man considered a colossus of British golf. Henry Cotton captured the British Open three times at a time when no Brit was able to hoist the Claret Jug more than once. Cotton's first Open Championship victory came in 1934 when even a disappointing closing round of 79 at Royal St. George's could not stop him from winning by five shots.

Three years later Cotton was back to battle a Carnoustie course that had brutalized him in '31, leaving him fourteen over par and tied for tenth. This time, however, Cotton and his competitors would be tested not only by Britain's toughest course but also by steady showers that saturated the grounds on the final day. The rain wreaked havoc with many scores. Byron Nelson shot 74, Snead 76, both making their British Open debuts. Fellow Americans Henry Picard and Denny Shute trudged in with 80s. With the fairways becoming mud baths, tournament officials seriously considered canceling the remainder of the day's round. Vintage film shows workers pushing brooms to try to clear the greens of excess water.

Down three strokes at the beginning of the final eighteen, Cotton made the turn with a 35 and one-stroke lead. Dressed in a light-colored cap and windbreaker, he pushed his advantage to three shots before losing a stroke on eighteen. Cotton's 71 amid the drenching downpour that nearly made the course unplayable put him at 290, two strokes ahead of Reg Whitcombe, who bore the brunt of the storm. That Cotton also held off the cream of America's Ryder Cup team—Nelson, Snead, Sarazen, Horton Smith, Ralph Guldahl, et al.—who had thrashed Britain, added luster to his second of three British Open titles. Considering the watery conditions, Cotton's round is one of the best in Open annals and ranks with the course record 66 he carded in the second round at Muirfield in 1948 when he won his third Open Championship.

The Open wouldn't return to Carnoustie until the summer of 1953. The tests facing Hogan and the field would be like the puzzle put to Armour and his challengers in 1931 and Cotton and his competitors in '37. The world's toughest links course is a nasty brute known to reduce champions to literal tears. Hogan would be striding the same barren, unforgiving land trod decades earlier by Stewart Maiden, Archie Simpson, and the Smith brothers. The legendary American would be linked with past champions as he sought to solve a course first laid out by Old Tom Morris a century before.

Carnoustie would present a fickle foe. *Time* wrote once that it is "a beautiful spot to play . . . when the wind keeps low." Should the elements take a turn for the worse and gusty winds whip through, as they did in the '31 Open, or soaking rain similar to '37, then high scores would follow.

Williamson remembers Carnoustie the course and the town as it was when Hogan arrived:

> The Barry Burn was home to golf balls, brown trout, sticklebacks, minnows, flounders and on the banks the water voles had their burrows. When disturbed, you would hear them plopping into the water. In early spring you might catch the larger sea trout as it came up from the North Sea, but not often. August brought the eels, the burn fishers ultimate pest!
>
> And such was the excitement of the crowd during this event, that several men on one occasion in the early stages of the Open practise days, fell in and for a short time joined the fishes!
>
> Since the late 19th century, Carnoustie, like many other seaside towns, was used to large crowds coming from all parts of the UK for their summer holidays, but there was a special reason for the nongolfers to find their way to the golf course, they had a chance to see some show business stars up close, and perhaps get an autograph or two. After all, Frank Sinatra and Bing Crosby were coming, the papers said. [American singer-songwriter] Frankie Laine, another big star from the States, and Britain's own [singer/actor] Frankie Vaughan had both been spotted.
>
> Carnoustie in the 1950's was a thriving town. From the west end to the east end there were around 125 thriving businesses, and one of the highest amounts of licenced premises per population in the area. There were shows for all the family all throughout the summer. These were at the

Beach Hall, on the links, and the beach, where there were loads of fun things for the kids and mums, and two cinemas showing the latest films.

Such is Carnoustie. Clark wrote that the small coastal town serves as golf's holiday home just as St. Andrews serves as the sport's spiritual home. Yet Carnoustie is also a place where golf can be such a grim experience that the course itself has come to be considered "Carnasty" by even the worldliest pros.

Writer Gwilym S. Brown noted during the 1968 Open Championship that the course sits on a flat stretch of sandy soil between the town and its small cottages and the spacious beaches bordering the North Sea. Flat plains do not make for smooth fairways, Brown wrote, and he compared the Carnoustie fairways to rolling waves of green surf that were as hard and dry as marble.

This was the challenge that awaited Hogan. In his attempt to become the first man to win the modern slam in the same year, the American champion might have drawn inspiration from Arthur Machen, a Welsh author of the early twentieth century. "It was better," Machen wrote, "to fail in attempting exquisite things." There could be no more exquisite thing in golf than what Hogan was attempting—an unprecedented Triple Slam featuring the Masters, U.S. Open, and British Open titles.

Fig. 1. This photo composite clearly illustrates Ben Hogan's classic golf swing circa 1953 as he teed off on the Concord Hotel golf course in Lake Kiamesha NY. (Library of Congress, Prints and Photographs Division, NYWT&S Collection)

Fig. 2. (*opposite top*) Following his disappointing 1952 campaign, Ben Hogan launched his Triple Slam season in style in April 1953 with a record-breaking win in the Masters Tournament at scenic Augusta National. Spectators peered through handheld periscopes to follow the flight of Hogan's shot in the sunshine. (Source unknown)

Fig. 3. (*opposite bottom*) At his historic victory in the 1953 Masters, champion Ben Hogan is photographed at Augusta National with (from left) friendly rival Byron Nelson, U.S. president Dwight D. Eisenhower, and Clifford Roberts, co-founder of the Masters and Augusta National Golf Club. (Library of Congress, Prints and Photographs Division, Photo by Morgan Fitz, LC-USZ62-122977)

Fig. 4. (*above*) One month after his victory at Augusta, Ben Hogan shot a final-round 67 to defend his title in the Colonial National Invitation in his hometown of Fort Worth, Texas. It marked one of five times in his career that Hogan captured the Colonial crown. (Source unknown)

53rd OPEN
CHAMPIONSHIP
OF THE
UNITED STATES
GOLF ASSOCIATION
AT
OAKMONT
COUNTRY CLUB
OAKMONT, PA.
JUNE 9 thru 13
1953

OFFICIAL
PROGRAM
50 CENTS

Fig. 5. The sterling silver U.S. Open men's golf trophy adorns the cover of the program for the 1953 championship at renowned Oakmont Country Club in June. (Oakmont Country Club Archives)

Fig. 6. Displaying the grim visage noted by reporters covering the 1953 U.S. Open, Ben Hogan battles an Oakmont course called the "Hades of Hulton." The large gallery that framed Hogan was several thousand strong, prompting many to use handheld periscopes as evidenced in this photo to get a glimpse of the legendary champion. (Oakmont Country Club Archives)

Fig. 7. Ben Hogan hands in the winning scorecard after conquering the tough Oakmont layout at the 1953 U.S. Open. (Oakmont Country Club Archives)

Fig. 8. Ben Hogan is all smiles as he holds up four fingers signifying four U.S. Open titles following his history-tying victory in the 1953 championship at Oakmont Country Club. (Oakmont Country Club Archives)

Fig. 9. Bundled against Carnoustie's cold climate and with his ever-present Chesterfield cigarette dangling from his lips, Ben Hogan blasts out of a trap and sends a spray of sand skyward in his first and only British Open appearance in July 1953. (Source unknown)

Fig. 10. (*above*) Surrounded by Scots several thousand strong, Ben Hogan coolly dissects a Carnoustie course so demanding and difficult it has been called Car*nasty*. The course is considered the most challenging of the British Open Championship venues. (Source unknown)

Fig. 11. (*opposite top*) Ben Hogan was awarded the coveted Claret Jug following his historic victory in the 1953 British Open. Always a model of decorum, Hogan insisted on putting on a jacket for the trophy presentation and photo. (Source unknown)

Fig. 12. (*opposite bottom*) Ben Hogan returned to the United States a conquering hero following his victory in the British Open. Hogan's Triple Crown season was an accomplishment so rare he was treated to a homecoming parade on Broadway in New York City's celebrated Canyon of Heroes. Photograph by Dick DeMarsico. (Library of Congress, Prints and Photographs Division, LC-USZ62-115559)

Fig. 13. Hogan's unprecedented Triple Slam year yielded impressive trophies and awards for Ben Hogan and is arguably the greatest season in PGA history. (Source unknown)

Fig. 14. The year 1953 was both busy and happy for Ben Hogan. Along with recording a stunning Triple Slam with victories in the Masters, the U.S. Open, and the British Open, Hogan started his own golf company and was photographed displaying his new company-made clubs. (Source unknown)

8

"A Beastly Test"

Ben Hogan was a transcendent talent, and the summer of '53 was showcasing his skills. On their way to Oakmont for the U.S. Open, Ben and Valerie had stopped in New York City to visit with Paul Shields, a friend of the Hogans and renowned yachtsman.

Speaking with *New York Times* sports columnist Dave Anderson years later, Valerie recalled Paul asking Ben: Had he "given any thought to playing in the British Open this year?" Hogan replied that he hadn't given it much thought. He told Shields he really didn't want to make the trip to Scotland and joked that his friend just wanted to go over there to see him get beat. If he won the U.S. Open at Oakmont, Hogan said, maybe he would think about the British Open. Valerie told Anderson that while she had never tried to influence her husband when it came to golf, she turned to him and said, "I would think you would have a curiosity to want to go."

Hogan was nothing if not practical. Asked following his U.S. Open win at Oakmont why he was considering traveling to Carnoustie for the British Open, he said it was because "so many people want me to." Among those was Jimmy Demaret. Writer Bob Brumby believed Hogan might not have played in the British Open had Demaret not spoken to him about it during an exhibition played at Jimmy's home course at the Concord Resort at Kiamesha Lake, New York. Brumby wrote that Demaret "took Hogan to task" for refusing to go to Scotland, the ancestral home of golf.

Hogan's response was as forceful as his drives off the tee. "What would I want to go over there for? What would it prove? I don't like boats. They say the food is bad and a hotel room is next to impossible to get. Besides, what have I to gain?"

Demaret told Hogan he owed it to his sport, that the Bantam wouldn't be considered one of golf's greatest champions until he claimed the Claret Jug, an ornately decorated silver trophy whose history dates to its birth in Scotland in 1872. "You're a legend over there," Demaret told Hogan. "People want to see you. Carnoustie is where golf came from and it's a great course."

Said Hogan, "I don't see you going over."

"A fellow like me still has to earn a living," Demaret replied. "You could pass Fort Knox without having to tip your hat."

Despite Scotland being the birthplace of golf, many U.S. pros were not enamored of the thought of leaving the New World for the Old. Byron Nelson played at Carnoustie in 1937 and considered the trip a losing and lengthy proposition. Finishing fifth behind winner Henry Cotton and earning only $187 had something to do with Nelson's negative viewpoint, and so did the drenching downpour on the final day of the tournament. Nelson also had to take a month's leave of absence from his position as head pro at Reading Country Club, sail for six days across the Atlantic, use four days to recover from the journey, practice, qualify, play the tournament, and then sail home. Add it all up and it was close to a month's time.

Like Nelson, Snead played the Open in 1937 and traveled to St. Andrews in '46. Slammin' Sam won at St. Andrews, but at first sight he thought so little of the famed layout that he wondered if it was a course that had been abandoned. Snead's payoff for the victory was five hundred dollars, which covered just one-quarter of his expenses. Asked by the Scots if he was coming back, The Slammer didn't mince words. "Are you kidding?" Snead replied.

Cary Middlecoff thought the primary reason for playing The Open Championship in those years was for the glory that goes with winning golf's oldest major. But he knew that one had to finish first to even begin to make ends meet financially, and there was no glory in finishing second, since few remember the runner-up.

Like most American golfers, Hogan considered the British Open less important than its U.S. counterpart and the Masters. The prize money had been increased, but it would still be just $1,400. He would also have to drag his sore legs through a demanding thirty-six-hole qualifier. Still, Hogan had sent in his entry prior to playing at Oakmont, so the fact that he could become the first man to win three majors in one year was more a happy coincidence than a premeditated strategy.

One plan Hogan did have was to dress warmly for the unpredictable Scottish weather, which could blow both warm and chilly depending on the day and sometimes the hour. Prior to flying from New York, Hogan mentioned to the media that he needed long underwear—"long handles" in his Texas language, and preferably cashmere—to combat the cold climes overseas. A week later, Abercrombie & Fitch wired a response to Hogan. The New York clothier specialized in sports apparel and told Hogan that it carried the long underwear he was seeking, and that the price was ninety-five dollars per pair. Adjusting for inflation, ninety-five dollars in 1953 equals $1,091 in 2024.

Hogan was accustomed to paying top dollar for fine clothes and the comfort they provided. Contacting Shields, he asked his friend to purchase two pairs of cashmere long underwear and have them sent to the hotel in New York that he and Valerie would be staying at prior to departing for Scotland.

It wasn't just Abercrombie & Fitch contacting Hogan regarding his clothing for his historic trip. Other companies and fans sent him long underwear as well. Hogan received two pairs of cotton and wool long handles colored red; from BVD he received three pairs. He received so many packages of clothing from well-wishers that paying duty on them, Hogan joked, almost broke him financially.

One other gift came courtesy of Bernard "Toots" Shor, the famed proprietor of Toots Shor's Restaurant in Manhattan. The establishment was more of a saloon and nightclub than restaurant and since its opening in 1940 served as a favored hangout for America's rich and famous. Celebrity entertainers Frank Sinatra, Jackie Gleason, and Charlie Chaplin mingled with star athletes Mickey Mantle, Whitey Ford, and Frank Gifford. Joe DiMaggio shared a table with Marilyn Monroe at Toots's, and Yankee great Yogi Berra met writer Ernest Hemingway, prompting Yogi to ask the famed novelist, "What paper you work with, Ernie?"

Baseball, football, boxing, billiards, and horse racing were frequent topics of conversation at Toots's. Brumby wrote that golf was mentioned "only in whispers at Shor's." That was until Hogan came along. The garrulous Shor, a Philly native, had an affinity for the silent Texan; Toots called Hogan "the little guy." For Hogan's trip to Scotland, Shor handed a friend a St. Christopher medal given to him by baseball great Rogers Hornsby. "Give it to the little guy," Shor said. "Tell him I'm praying for him." Toots would spend the days of the tournament listening to radio reports issued on site by broadcaster John Derr.

Hogan inspired that kind of respect. Movie producer Sidney Lanfield, who worked with Ben on the Hogan biopic *Follow the Sun*, had such an interest in the 1953 British Open that he told Brumby he was heading to Scotland to watch Hogan play. Brumby wrote that Lanfield had been impressed with Hogan when the two worked together on the film. Hogan served as technical advisor, and Lanfield thought him the hardest worker on the set. Even though he hadn't fully recovered from his auto accident, Hogan drove himself hard because he wanted the movie to be accurate. Lanfield told Brumby he had never seen a more conscientious person than Hogan, and because of Ben's input, thought it difficult to find a technical flaw in the film.

The last time Hogan headed to the UK he was the nonplaying captain of the 1949 U.S. Ryder Cup team. Travel accommodations had been made for the squad, and due to rationing restrictions and lack of meat in England in the post–World War II years, food for team members and their wives had been sent from the United States to England. This included steaks, which were in short supply in the UK, and caused controversial remarks to fly back and forth between Hogan and the British media. Hogan considered having three weeks' worth of meat and vegetables frozen and shipped to Carnoustie to coincide with his trip but decided against it. He didn't want the British media making a big deal of it as they had in 1949.

For The Open Championship, Ben and Valerie made their own travel arrangements. They would fly to Prestwick, a town in South Ayrshire on the west coast of Ayrshire in Scotland, some thirty miles southwest of Glasgow. They would then drive to Carnoustie, where they would spend three weeks. Following the tournament they would take a week's vacation in Paris and sail back to New York on the ss *United States*. Upon their arrival in Prestwick, Hogan agreed to meet with UK reporters. One man was chosen as spokesperson, and Ben had trouble deciphering the accent. The reporter would ask a question and Hogan wouldn't know how to answer. He would have to think for several minutes to figure out what was meant by the question, Hogan said later, because the Europeans didn't word their queries in the same way as Americans.

The reporter asked if there was special significance to the tie he was wearing. Hogan said no, but the reporter noted that the American champion's tie was red, white, and blue. Hogan's attire may not have been by happenstance. Randy Jacobs says everything Hogan did had a reason behind it. "He paid attention to the little things," Jacobs remembers. "His clothes were meticulous."

The Hogans' arrival remains vivid to Trevor Williamson. "Ben, Valerie, golf clubs, and a great pile of luggage arrived at Carnoustie at 1:30 p.m. on Tuesday, the 23rd of June 1953," he says. "Both were exhausted after a 24-hour journey to Prestwick airport. The Hogans were booked into the Bruce Hotel, Carnoustie's top hotel at the time, situated on Links Parade, and only a good golf shot from the first tee of the Championship Golf Course. This seemed to be the ideal establishment for them to stay. However, this was not to be."

The hotel opened in 1892 and was named after its proprietor, Mary Bruce. Originally called the Bruce's Hotel, it housed several bedrooms, three parlors, a dining room, billiard room, and smoking room. The baths in the Bruce Hotel drew salt water from the nearby sea. Following Miss Bruce's death in 1905 the hotel was run by Janet Hendry until her retirement in 1929. James Walker then took over and made a minor change in calling it the Bruce Hotel.

Upon looking over the hotel, Valerie had a question for the manager. "Where is the bathroom?"

"It's right this way. Down the hall."

"Down the hall?" she asked, recalling the moment for Anderson.

"No, no," said Ben, who had to soak his legs daily in a private bath. "If the bathroom is down the hall, we can't stay here. I'm sorry."

Valerie asked about a room with a bath and was told by the manager the room next door had such an arrangement. The room proved too small, however, and Valerie recalled Ben being ready to return home and forego the British Open. "Let's go back to the airport," he said.

"Wait a minute, Ben," Valerie replied. She asked her husband if he had the card given to him by a friend containing the phone number of another place to stay that was nearby. Ben did, and called the number of Miss Pettie, who had a spacious place in Dundee, approximately eleven miles from Carnoustie and said to be Scotland's "sunniest city." Valerie told Anderson that Ben talked on the phone for several minutes with Miss Pettie, then hung up, turned, and smiled. "She's been expecting us," he said.

A friend of Ben's had made a reservation without the Hogans knowing about it. When they arrived that day, Valerie and Ben were impressed by what Valerie told Anderson was "like Shangri-La, a big, beautiful house with big, beautiful grounds and a big beautiful upstairs room with a big, beautiful bathroom." It was the Taypark House, and Valerie would recall for Anderson that it "wasn't really a hotel, it was the National Cash Register's guest house for its Scottish executives and clients." Executives and business personnel went to Dundee because the National Cash Register (NCR) Company had a factory there. Hogan, who had been ready to leave Scotland just half an hour earlier, was pleasantly surprised by his accommodation. "I can't believe this," he told Valerie.

Derr later revealed that after having to convince his CBS bosses to let him cover the tournament, it was he who got the Bruce Hotel room that the Hogans vacated. Valerie recalled to Anderson that she and Ben were given a chauffeur, John Campbell, to drive them in their rented British Humber automobile on their daily trips from the NCR house. "NCR was a big factory in the city of Dundee," Trevor Williamson says. "They got to hear about what happened and got in touch with Hogan and said you can have use of our mansion if you stay in Dundee. They got hundreds of workers at the factory who were interested in golf to come out and Hogan did a marvelous exhibition for them. And they got to see Hogan acting funny."

Willie Park Sr. won the British Open's inaugural tournament in 1860, one of just five golfers to that point to emerge victorious in their initial attempt. Hogan, seeking to become the sixth to do so including Park, planned for two weeks of practice to acquaint himself primarily with the Carnoustie course, called by many golf's greatest test, and also with the Burnside course, which would serve as a host site for a qualifying round.

Because of his victories in the Masters and U.S. Open, Hogan was a 6-4 favorite, the shortest priced favorite on record, according to the Scottish newspaper the *Courier Evening Telegraph*. Still, Hogan would have to acclimate to the changing seaside weather and the smaller British golf ball, which at 1.62 ounces weighed the same as the American ball but whose 1.62 inches in diameter were .06 smaller. Gregston wrote that while the difference in figures is minute, the difference in distance, especially in a heavy wind, would be "enormous." Hogan was playing the Titleist ball, and the company produced dozens that were the same size as the British ball for him to use in Scotland.

It wasn't just a different ball Hogan had to familiarize himself with. This was a championship played on foreign soil, with rules different from those back home. As such, Hogan could not leave anything to chance in his preparation. He would have to learn the British game of links golf inside and out and diligently study the unfamiliar fairways and greens. "A whole lot of things came into play—the weather's different, the course is different, the British ball is different—so he's got to get attuned to all of that," says Williamson. Peter Alliss, who would compete against Hogan at Carnoustie, said there would be a need for the Masters and U.S. Open champ to "learn the pitch and run; to play off highly uneven stances; to hit from hard ground; and perhaps to accept that perfectly struck shots are frequently punished by unlucky bounces into rough and on through a green into trouble."

Hogan's first look at the Carnoustie course left him with feelings like Snead's at St. Andrews seven years earlier. Its color was a mix of brown and green, and there was a decided lack of trees. Even Alliss thought the terrain bleak and gaunt. This was land, Hogan thought, that looked as if it hadn't been developed since its original formation.

Cecil Timms, a tall, strapping, sandy-haired professional caddie and pro soccer player who had worked for American amateurs Dick Chapman and Harvie Ward in previous British golf events, approached Hogan on his first day at Carnoustie. In what was described by Herbert Warren Wind as an "earnest, English Midlands voice," Timms asked Hogan for a trial run as his caddie.

Timms had been recommended to Hogan by Chapman and Ward, and Cecil's initial interview with Ben was reportedly brief and to the point. "I want you only to carry my bag, son, and keep very quiet."

"Aye, Mr. Hogan. So you dinnae want me to club ye, Sir?"

"No, son. Keep the clubs clean and your mouth shut. Is that completely understood?"

"Aye. Shall I read the greens for ye, then?"

"No."

Timms caddied for Hogan for five of his practice days and was told that Mr. Hogan was not particularly satisfied but would give him one more opportunity. Timms became so anxiety-ridden that Hogan relented and told Timms he could be his caddie for the championship.

The talkative Timms would prove satisfactory to the silent Hogan, although Ben felt him to be a bit nervous. Still, Hogan thought Timms—whom he called "Timmy"—to be a good caddie. Cecil took Ben's black golf shoes home every night and polished them and kept his clubs clean and shining like "crown jewels," Hogan said later. Timms grew nervous whenever Hogan struggled to make his shots, and the more excited Cecil became, the more he talked. Hogan would have to pause play to settle down his caddie.

Born in the village of Lapworth in Warwickshire, England, Timms was seven years old when he began caddying. He made his pro debut as a caddie in the 1935 British Open at Muirfield in Gullane, East Lothian, Scotland, and became a regular in The Open Championship and British Amateur, missing only the 1950 Open at Troon Golf Club in Troon, South Ayrshire, Scotland. Timms became known internationally in 1951 when he carried the bag for Chapman in his winning effort in the British Amateur at Royal Porthcawl Golf Club in Porthcawl, Wales, and in the following year's French Open Amateur. *Time* magazine would call Chapman "the Ben Hogan of amateur golf."

Timms told Wind there were half a dozen essential things a caddie should do. The first is to refrain from speaking to the golfer unless spoken to. The second is to wipe the golfer's clubs following every shot to keep them clean. Number three is to hustle after the ball following the shot to prevent fans from disturbing it. The fourth essential thing, said Timms, is to study the elements of the shot—the lie, turf, wind, and target—to have an informed opinion ready prior to the player's arrival. Fifth, a caddie must study his player's game closely enough so that after four or five holes, he can offer the correct club. The sixth and final essential is to know the course and how it's playing. Timms thought most new courses took three or four days at the minimum to learn. St. Andrews, he said, took longer.

So would Carnoustie. Hogan was eager to test himself on the famed links course that sits across the Firth of Tray from St. Andrews on Scotland's east coast. He found the noise from the nearby army firing range to be extremely loud, so he headed to the Barry course between Carnoustie and Dundee, since it afforded more privacy.

Carnoustie was a culture shock to Hogan, wrote Malcolm Campbell, a resident of Scotland. It was as much a contrast to Hogan's native Texas as it could be. He disliked Scottish food, though he sometimes joined John Derr for lamb stew.

Hogan established a daily routine of eggs and bacon for breakfast, followed by a drive to Barry for sixty to ninety minutes of morning practice, then lunch, and an afternoon round of golf at Carnoustie. Dinner capped their days, though Ben and Valerie did find time to take in two movies during their stay. Practice rounds saw him playing three balls on every hole. Hogan found he could hit the British ball some twenty-five yards farther than the American ball. His greatest difficulties, he thought, were getting used to the distance he could hit the smaller ball and judging distances on the course. Hogan would practice more with his woods for the British Open than for tournaments in the United States.

Williamson remembers in detail the first time Hogan played the Carnoustie course:

> It was a nice, sunny day. It was a working day for most, however, a crowd of around 200 had gathered. So for the first time they cast their eyes on the hero from across the water. He had a Chesterfield cigarette in his hand, he was a big smoker.
>
> Hogan and Frank Stranahan, using the back tees and a little guess work, played the course at an incredible 7,200 yards. This would be the length of the championship course for the week, making it the longest in Britain at that point.
>
> In a round of two and a half hours, [Hogan] had six birdies and one eagle, if you give him the five-foot putt on 16 that he didn't bother

to play, he shot a 69, and this included a great display of putting to wow the crowd. Ben Hogan came to Scotland to win the Open, and he gave the impression this might be true.

Hogan kept finding himself taking two clubs less than he would with the American ball. The result was that he hit the ball harder than needed. He memorized what club he should use from different spots on the fairway, accounting for weather and wind, rather than trusting his judgment. Hogan realized that the wind coming in off the North Sea was heavier and contained more moisture than what he was accustomed to in the United States. He also found that par changed from hour to hour with the wind. Play a hole with the wind at his back in the morning and it was a par four. Play the same hole in the afternoon with the wind in his face and it was a par five.

As Carnoustie offered a barren landscape, it lacked the trees, borders, hedges, and fences that marked courses in America and made for what Hogan called "target golf." Where U.S. fairways were well defined, Hogan found it difficult to discern where the fairway ended and the rough began because the topography was all of the same color. He walked the course backward nearly every day, starting at the eighteenth green and finishing at the first tee, to familiarize himself with its unique features and layout. "He walked the course backward to see what he had to avoid," John Boyette says. "I think that was very telling. There's nobody that dissected the course more than Hogan and plotted his way around."

Hogan felt that when the Brits build a course, they seed a tee, seed a green, mow a fairway between them, and leave the rough the same. Fairways were hard and rolling, and because they were loaded with mounds, there were few level lies. Hogan called it "bounce golf." He'd hit a shot and not know which way it might bounce when it landed. Stray off the fairways and send a shot into the rough and Hogan would have to deal with an abundance of heather and gorse. The former tolerates sea spray and poor soil, thriving in coastal areas like Carnoustie. Growing in thick clumps, it can reach as high as eight to twelve inches. Gorse is a spiny, thorny, yellow-flowered shrub that at Carnoustie grew tall and wide, "waist- to head-high," Hogan said. Hit that rough, he thought, and one would go for a 77 every round.

The fairways were scarcely better. There were sand traps everywhere, and six of the holes had them in the middle of the fairways to catch drives at the expected distance. Hogan realized in practice he needed to find a way around those fairway traps. Play them short, he knew, and his second shot would not reach the green.

Additional hazards included two creeks—Barry Burn and Jockie's Burn—that Hogan thought added to Carnoustie's difficulty. He considered the course "burn-happy." Eben Harrell would write in *Time* that a watery ditch "zigzags through the course like a World War I trench, and cavernous traps dot the landscape like bomb craters." There were other ditches and trenches as well, and Hogan tried to locate them all. He knew if he spun a shot into one of them it was a one-stroke penalty. But there was also the matter of self-preservation. Hogan was wary of being in the rough, where he might fall into a ditch and break his legs. More than once he wondered, "What am I doing here?" Jacobs says of Hogan at Carnoustie,

> He was out of his routine. He had all of these logistical problems to overcome. He was Masters and U.S. Open champion and he had to qualify for the British Open. Isn't that crazy? That's always fascinated me. Even if you win, you probably lose money, and you're not even guaranteed a spot in the field.
>
> At Augusta he would have to hit the ball higher. Raymond Gafford told me that when he was preparing to play his first Masters, Mr. Hogan told him, 'Raymond, we're going to be putting on roots.' It was Bermuda grass overseeded with rye but they cut it so short that from a 5-iron on down you can hear your ball land on the green. They probably hit 5-iron 170, 180 yards and the greens were so firm at Augusta that you could hear it land from where you played the shot. The guys would tend to try to fly the ball a little higher at Augusta.
>
> The U.S. Open is the same for firm greens and you try to hit a little higher there, but you've also got to try and hit it really straight off the tee. And then you go to the British Open and the ball rolls twice as far as at Augusta or Oakmont off the tee and you've got to deal with it. Totally different conditions, and of course you have British

Open weather, damp, with cold winds, and there's another variable he dealt with.

Hogan's strategy for conquering Carnoustie was developed in practice. Success off the tee would be paramount, that much was dictated by the course and the weather, the gorse and heather. His planning and calculations were dependent on how honed his game was. A lot of things would enter into this plan, including the type of course, the weather, places where there's a possible need for sacrifice, and places where chances may be taken. At the long sixth hole, Hogan sent Timms to the front of the green, took a two-iron and raked three shots—one to the right, one down the middle, and one to the left—and told Timms to chart which way the ball bounced on to the green.

Pat Ward-Thomas wrote that Hogan spent days "analyzing and dissecting the course with the cold detachment of a surgeon." Everything about Carnoustie—the undulations of the alien turf, the positioning of the bunkers, the effect of the winds—was studied and scrutinized by Hogan with extreme care. Hogan, said Ward-Thomas, planned the playing of Carnoustie with the "exactness of a modern military operation."

A Scottish golf writer watched Hogan coldly chart his way around Carnoustie and came away impressed. "Who else," he asked, "is going to win?" Still, Hogan came off the eighteenth green of his first practice tour of Carnoustie with misgivings. The 7,200-yard course, Gregston wrote, "did, indeed, loom as the 'monster' he had heard it called." Hogan must have sighed at the prospect of doing battle with yet another "monster." He had already slain golf's ultimate "monster"—the "Monster of Oakland Hills." Now he was being called on to defeat Scotland's scary course.

"Carnoustie's just a brute, especially with the rough around it," says Bruce Devlin, who has played the course several times. "It doesn't matter what time of the year or under what circumstances, it's still very difficult. You get a lot of up and down lies—uphill, downhill, sidehill—because of the contouring of the fairway. Then there's the wind, and there's been a time or two when it gets pretty chilly there. I played in the Open tournament a couple of times and was back in 2002 and it looked exactly the same. I don't think it's changed. I didn't see anything different in it."

Robert Stennett traveled to Scotland some sixty years after the 1953 Open and found himself facing the same Carnoustie beast Hogan dealt with. "I think Carnoustie has changed very little from 1953," Stennett states. "They don't take the same perspective that we take here in the States. I think they're very respectful of tradition and I don't know of the course changing at all. Carnoustie's so freaking hard you can't believe it. Especially the finishing holes. It is a heck of a test of golf."

Anderson wrote decades later that "the charm of Carnoustie is its treachery." He related the story of champion Horton Smith hitting what he believed to be a beautiful drive on the second hole. "You're in the 'boonker,'" Smith's Scottish caddie told him.

"That can't possibly be," an astounded Smith replied. "I never hit a better drive in my life." "You're in the boonker," his caddie repeated. "And so he was," Anderson wrote, "because the bunkers and the burns at Carnoustie, as on most Scottish links, are virtually invisible from the tees."

In his book *Sandy Lyle Takes You round Carnoustie*, written with Bob Ferrier, the Scottish pro takes the reader hole-by-hole through the famed course. The book was written in 1982 and from several firsthand accounts the course had not changed much from when Hogan played it in 1953. The first hole was a 406-yard par four called the Cup. It was so named because, as Lyle notes, "the cup is the hollow in which the green lies, the sunken effect enhanced by the ridge at the back." A player's initial impression on the opening hole was that they were, in Lyle's words, in "golfing purgatory."

The reason was a number of blind shots, hazards that were concealed, and an introduction to the Barry Burn, which snaked forty yards in front of the tee and then ran on the left side of the fairway to snare hooks off the tee. An opening shot off the tee that falls away to the right side produces a blind second shot; a drive into the high left side leaves an open view of a large green that's sunken in a hollow beyond a ridge that's engulfed in rough on the left and bunkered on the right. Lyle said that if played downwind, number one was not an unfavorable starting hole. But played in a sturdy southwest or west wind, it was a rugged start.

Number two, called Gulley because its fairway was shaped like a slender valley, was another par four and stretched 442 yards. Braid's Bunker, named for

Carnoustie architect James Braid, was one of the bunkers Hogan pointed out as sitting in the middle of the fairway. The valley angled to the right between large ridges. The green was long and narrow and presented a tough target as sand and rough guarded both flanks. Lyle considered this "a powerful hole to meet so early in the round, and calls for careful, accurate shots."

At 346 yards, number three was the shortest par four on the course. Called Jockie's Burn for the stream that ran across the front of the small green, ten yards shy of the putting surface, it's a classic links hole. Emphasis was placed on accuracy, as the fairway was tight and angled to the left and then to the right. Jockie's Burn and bunkers ran down the left side, and sizable sand dunes along the right side. Hogan could see the bank of the burn from the tee. Its impact was largely psychological, a hazard only for the player who mishits and fails to fly his ball over the burn. Lyle said positioning the drive was "the most important single task on this hole." He noted that golfers would be playing in "the opposite direction as they were on the other side of the ridge that runs down the right side of No. 2."

Distance returned on number four, a 430-yard par four titled Hillocks for the ground on the fairway's right side. The fourth hole featured a dogleg left, and clearing a corner bunker required a lengthy carry into the wind. Bunkers protected the front of a flat green. The putting surface of the course's only double green rose over a ridge.

Jockie's Burn came into play again on number five, a 388-yard par four called Brae, as it was uphill to a green that also sloped upward. The burn crossed 270–80 yards from the tee and would be a threat to long hitters playing with the wind at their backs. The hole had a left-to-right dogleg and an extremely long, two-tiered green.

Following five straight par fours to open play, number six offered the first par five. At 567 yards it was the longest hole at Carnoustie and was aptly named Long. It was considered by some the most difficult hole as well. A pair of bunkers in the middle of the fairway forced golfers to shoot for a thin strip to the left or an area to the right that led into the rough. Long hitters not facing a headwind could attempt to carry the bunkers. The angled green featured two-tier contours and was a tough target due to protective bunkers in the front and back.

Par four returned on number seven, a 389-yard hole called Plantation for the trees that ran for more than one hundred yards along the right side of the fairway and Lyle said helped "funnel" the view from the tee. The seventh was an uncomplicated driving hole. A compact green sloped away from golfers. Judgment could be impaired on the second shot if it was downwind, and the wind came from the east.

Carnoustie's first par three came on number eight, the shortest hole on the course at 162 yards and called Short for the obvious reason. Despite its lack of length, the eighth could be tricky if players were short with their shots and placed them in the deceptive hollow that fronted the green. Club selection was key on this hole, particularly if dealing with a left-to-right cross wind.

The front nine closed with a par-four hole called Railway for the line from Dundee to Aberdeen that ran along the back of the long, narrow green. Reaching 483 yards, it was the longest par four at Carnoustie. The driving area of the fairway was well bunkered, and one of the drainage ditches that concerned Hogan was close to the rough on the right.

Carnoustie measured 3,613 yards going out and was a par 36. It played shorter heading in, totaling 3,587 yards and par 36. The back nine began with the par-four, 446-yard number ten called South America for the area golfer who planned to emigrate to South America but advanced no further than the tenth hole. Barry Burn, the course's second water hazard, cut across the line of play thirty yards shy of the green and ran close to the putting surface's right side. The driving area was threatened by a trap on the left and bunkers on the right.

Number eleven was the second shortest par four on the course, a 368-yard hole titled Dyke for the dyke that once marked it. The demand for accuracy off the tee and approaching the green made up for the lack of length. The fairway was narrowed and bunkered on both sides to restrict the driving area. The combination of deep bunkers, hollows, and humps made a tight target of a green that angled away from golfers.

At 467 yards, number twelve was the second-longest par four on the course. The hole was known as Southward Ho because, as Lyle wrote, "from the west facing 11th green you turn almost through a right angle and head south." An unseen ditch on the right, combined with visible sand traps on that side, would cause the field to send their tee shots left. Approach shots would be aimed between bunkered mounds to a sunken green. A ridge split the wide, shallow putting surface into two levels, the higher side being the right side.

Number thirteen was the second of three par threes and, extending just 169 yards, was the second-shortest hole on the course. It was called Whins, which is how gorse is known in Scotland. In the old Celtic alphabet, Whin is the seventeenth letter, and in the ancient Celtic tradition it is associated with the Goddess of Winter, Cailleach. Whin was what Hogan and the field would see when they teed up on thirteen, and they would see more of it in the rear of a green that climbed steadily from front to back and was squeezed by bunkers right and left.

Fourteen was called Spectacles because, as Lyle wrote, "the famous bunkers stare at you from a fairway ridge," eclipsing the view of the green some fifty yards shy of the putting surface. The entrance to the double green was guarded by bunkers right and left. Number fourteen was the second of Carnoustie's three par fives. At 473 yards, it was the shortest par five on the course, yet that didn't make the scene from the tee any less formidable. The fairway swayed right to left, and beyond the sweep of heather, gorse, and rough, only a fragment of fairway could be seen.

That Hogan and his competitors wouldn't see the green on fifteen for a time gave credence to the hole's name, Luckyslap. A par four measuring 457 yards, the hole required planning and precision more than power. "Canny chartwork," said Lyle, "may be better than a random smash." From the fringe of the fairway the landscape plunged into rough. Shots were tossed to the right by a sloping fairway, and the approach to the green would have to clear a collection of bunkers and hillocks.

Number sixteen was called Barry Burn for the burn that ran along the left side. Yet the burn wasn't as threatening as it would be on numbers seventeen and eighteen. The final par three at Carnoustie measured a lengthy—for a par three—250 yards, and its long, thin green was guarded at times by a strong northeasterly wind. The green would become an easier target with a prevailing wind, yet out front there were still bracketing bunkers and a pronounced gulley.

The Island was the name for number seventeen, an apt description for the safe space across the looping Barry Burn that Hogan and company would want to reach with the initial shot. The burn coiled in front of the tee, veered up the left side, and sliced in diagonal fashion across the fairway some 240–80 yards out. This final par four covered 454 yards, and golfers not dealing with a headwind could be tempted to carry the burn and then take aim on a basin-shaped green that sloped down from the left and featured bunkers on the right.

Number eighteen was labeled Home for good reason. Lyle thought it "the classic name for the final hole on a Scottish course," and following an exhausting battle with the previous seventeen at Carnoustie, they would be glad to be heading home. Anyone expecting a letup would be disappointed. Carnoustie would be *Carnasty* to the bitter end. At 503 yards, this par-five finishing hole was the second longest distance on the course. The Barry Burn would again imperil the tee shots of Hogan and the field. So too would an easterly wind. The burn bordered the right side, slashed across the fairway, snaked out of sight up the left side, and then reappeared in front of the green. The drive line from the tee was tightened by a cluster of bunkers on the right.

A "beastly test" is how Carnoustie's head groundskeeper John Philip once described the course for Harrell. "Golf was never meant to be a fair game or an easy one," Philip said. "We've got the reputation of being a beastly test, but that's what golf is—it's a beastly test." Hogan had just bested a U.S. beast, the beast of Oakmont, and seeing Scotland for the first time had hard words for the beastly test that is Carnoustie. Scotland being the home of golf, the residents were proud of their historic course that sits hard by the North Sea. Hogan, however, was unimpressed by Carnoustie and stated so publicly.

"These greens are awful," he snapped. "It's like putting on glue. I've got a lawnmower back in Texas. I'll send it over to you." Hogan was said to have even offered to buy a mower "so they can cut them real close." Told that the green had already been cut twice that day, Hogan was unimpressed. "It would have helped," he snapped, "if they had put the blades in the mower."

Hogan remained unhappy with the slow-running greens, muttering, "You can't putt on putty." The Scots took offense. Carnoustie, with what *Time* then called "its jagged hillocks, fiendish traps and stubby greens" had been insulted, and not a wee bit either. The gauntlet had been thrown down, and one man described by *Time* as a "crusty old codger" spoke up in defense of Scotland. "Hogan talks a bloody lot about the greens and a bloody lot about his putter; he should put the two together and shut up."

Hogan was reportedly reprimanded by Valerie as well, as Stennett relates a story from golf pro and Hogan associate Mike Wright. "Mike tells a story that I think he heard from Mrs. Hogan," says Stennett. "They were still on rations over there [in Carnoustie] and Mr. Hogan went into a restaurant and ordered a steak, and they served him, I don't know, four ounces. Apparently, he got mad and said, 'Why the hell can't I get a decent piece of steak? I need the protein.' Mrs. Hogan, who was so respectful of him, put him in his place a little bit. She said, 'Ben, everybody here at this Inn threw in their rations so you could have that piece of beef.' I think it embarrassed Mr. Hogan."

Williamson recalls the controversy stirred up by Hogan. "He was a difficult person," he says. "He had a terrible upbringing, we know this. He saw things a child shouldn't see. He was small in size and was bullied by the other caddies, put in a barrel and rolled down a hill. So he had this hard upbringing, he had the accident, and it was natural he became what we call here a 'hard man.' People were frightened to approach him. He had that demeanor."

Williamson remembers another high-profile golfer visiting Carnoustie and jingling coins in his pocket on the course. That lack of decorum made the members in the crowd mad, and Williamson recalls them telling the golfer, "We don't like that sort of thing here."

The Scots, Williamson says, are a funny people. "Being one I can say that," he laughs. "When it comes to golf it doesn't matter if you're a cold individual, or if you don't like the course or the weather. At the end of the day the Scots will judge a person on his play, on how he golfs, and that's exactly what they did with Hogan. And that kind of threw him because I don't think he expected that. He did mention on several occasions how well he was treated by the crowd."

Williamson remembers occasions at Carnoustie in which Hogan mingled with autograph seekers. "Valerie, on seeing two wee boys nervously holding their books, said 'Ben, you have to give these wee mites your autograph!' He did. My Aunt Gertie Simpson cornered Ben. She said, 'My Uncle Jack

Simpson won the Open. I hope that you do.' He was intrigued and signed her book."

Hogan practiced at Panmure Golf Club, located ten miles from Dundee, where Ben and Valerie were staying, and just two miles west of Carnoustie. Golf has been played at Panmure for centuries.

Panmure Golf Club dates to 1845 and ranks as one of the oldest in the world. It also is one of twenty-four clubs that in 1885 helped purchase the trophy for the first British Amateur Championship. The course, influenced by Old Tom Morris and Braid, requires equal parts skill and strategy. Panmure GC's website states that its course "combines the best elements of links and heathland, with tight fairways, challenging carries, undulating greens and sandhills forged by nature. The touches of heather add a wonderful texture to the course and the moderately undulating hillocks add visual appeal as well as imparting their strategic influence."

The site states that Hogan "cemented his legendary reputation thanks to the help of Panmure Golf Club." Hogan and Timms spent two weeks on the course, whose design dated to Morris, one legend playing the terrain of links golf influenced by a legend of an earlier era. Number six was Hogan's favorite at Panmure. To the front right of the green is a hidden pot bunker that the club notes is "cleverly placed" and was suggested by Hogan. Some sixty years later, the bunker is still called "Hogan's Bunker" and remains a memorial to the man.

Williamson recalls Hogan's practice at Panmure. "There were about 50 people who had heard that he was coming to practice, so they turned up to watch," he says. "Unfortunately, so did a newsreel man. Ben was working his way through the clubs hitting balls to his caddie. The newsreel man asked if he could take some action shots. Hogan replied, 'I didn't come here to be photographed. I came to play in The Open.' After another spat, the newsman left. Hogan slammed his clubs in his bag and also left."

Contrary to the crowded practices at Carnoustie, Hogan was accompanied at Panmure by Timms alone. As it was said that the British ball prevented him from taking his traditional long divot, Hogan learned to dig the ball off the turf. As was his wont, he applied the diligent, searching shot-making to the British links course that he applied to American golf courses.

"Mr. Hogan wouldn't hit just one shot. He hit every shot—hit draws, fades, high, low, intermediate trajectory," remembers Randy Jacobs, who watched Hogan practice numerous times. "He was as accurate with the driver as he was with a 40-yard pitch. On the practice tee you're hitting balls every 30 or 45 seconds. On a golf course you're hitting a shot every six or seven or maybe 10 minutes. Once he developed that great golf swing and could repeat it, he could get into a rhythm and a feel on the practice tee. He was phenomenally accurate.

"Most great players play one way—either predominantly left-to-right or right-to-left," Jacobs continues. "Mr. Hogan hit the shot that was called for by the situation he was facing on a given hole. Ken Venturi said if the flag was on the right, Mr. Hogan brought it in left-to-right. If the flag was on the left, Mr. Hogan brought it in right-to-left. If it was on the back of the green, Mr. Hogan came in low. If it was in the front of the green, he came in high. It was fascinating to watch him." Jacobs says Hogan's intense preparation was inspiring: "He got there far in advance so he could prepare, and I'm not sure even Jack Nicklaus ever prepared for a major like Mr. Hogan prepared for that British Open. He went over there on a mission."

Williamson says Hogan "used the practice ground as a workshop, trying and perfecting many things. Hogan worked exceptionally hard at his game. As he played his practice rounds, he had the ability to memorize where to play and where to avoid. He would add to that by making notes." *Time* reported that as the days wore on, Hogan's orderly and well thought out practice routines slowly turned the Scots' displeasure to delight. They appreciated his analytic approach and warmed to his contemplative personality. *Time* noted that the natives began calling Hogan the "Wee Ice Mon."

Though he was an American there to take their treasured title, they filled his golf bag with good luck charms. Scots seeing Hogan up close for the first time might have thought of Braid, their native son and champion. Biographer Bernard Darwin wrote of Braid, "He was always dignified and respectful, he refused to allow his success to go to his head; and he demonstrated good natural manners on and off the course. All of this inspired affection for James."

As it did for Hogan. The Scots admired his studiousness, his drill-sergeant discipline. They saw the solitary silhouette of a little man walking the big course and watched with suspicion and then with sureness his superb shot-making. Sterling Slappey, covering the British Open for The United Press, overheard two golf-wizened Scots who watched Hogan place his approach shot eighteen inches from the cup. "Och, 'twas a great iron shot." "Aye, and he left himself only a wee putt adjacent." Still, many Scots were adamant that no American, not even Hogan, was going to burn up Carnoustie.

The effect of Hogan's entry in the British Open was spelled out in the Monday, July 6 issue of the *Glasgow Herald*. "The presence of Ben Hogan (U.S.A.) has made the Open championship which begins here tomorrow the most intriguing of modern times. The question this time is not 'Who will win?' but 'Can Hogan win?'"

The Associated Press agreed that the appearance of Hogan made this British Open an "Illustrious tournament—[the] most important in England or Scotland in a score of years." Oddsmakers believed Hogan would win and listed odds that the *Herald* wrote were "a seemingly absurd price in a field of 180." Yet considering Hogan's ability to overcome odds, the *Herald* wondered, "Is anything absurd where Hogan is concerned?" The *Herald* reviewed for readers Hogan's triumphant comeback from "dreadful injuries." American pro golfer "Big" Ed Dudley told the paper's golf correspondent that "any ordinary man would never have played golf again."

The measure of Hogan's will, and determination was such, the *Herald* wrote, that when he wanted to win a tournament, "the only question remaining is who will be second?" That Hogan had given himself a fortnight to acclimate himself to solving the problems of the Carnoustie course was enough evidence, said the *Herald*, that he was aiming to add the British Open to his lengthy list of titles. "We can assume," the *Herald* stated, "that he has concluded that to win the Open championship would set the seal upon his amazing career."

Victory in the world's oldest golf major would not come easy. Despite fifteen scratches, including 1932 champion Gene Sarazen and two-time runner-up Johnny Bulla, the field was "of the highest quality," said the *Herald*. The paper opined that any one of a dozen home players was talented enough to win, as were defending champion Bobby Locke of South Africa, who had won three of the previous four years; Argentinians Antonio Cerda, the 1951 runner-up, and Roberto de Vicenzo, who finished second in 1950; and Hogan's compatriot, Lloyd Mangrum.

The *Herald* stated that the Open champion would be the one who emerged from the tournament as the best putter. The paper sounded an alarm when it reported that Hogan "missed a few shortish putts" during his final practice on Saturday amid rain and a brisk westerly wind. Still, the *Herald* noted that the concentration was not the same for practice as it would be for the championship and that Hogan ranked with Locke, Mangrum, 1947 champion Fred Daly, and Flory Van Donck as the top putters in the field.

The qualifying rounds would be held Monday and Tuesday, July 6–7, at Carnoustie and Burnside, and The Open Championship proper would begin Wednesday. Hogan was scheduled to tee off Monday at Burnside at 2:03 p.m. When he walked to the tee for his first official shot in the Open, Hogan noticed there was no player announcement as there was in American golf and seemingly no one at all in charge of the proceedings.

Hogan saw in the distance a woman sitting in front of a small house. The pairing in front of Hogan and playing partner Bill Branch of England had played their second round, yet still not a word was said of Hogan teeing off. He walked onto the tee at what he thought was the appropriate time, placed his ball down, and noticed several fans shaking their heads in disapproving fashion.

A train rolled along the tracks that ran parallel to the first fairway. Three short blasts burst forth from the engineer's whistle and the train stopped. The engineer waved to Hogan, and some reports had Hogan negatively waving off the engineer. Instead, Hogan returned the wave. The woman at the house blew her horn. Fans lining the fairway nodded, and Hogan realized it was the signal to tee off. Valerie noticed it was all Ben could do to keep from laughing.

That Hogan had to qualify even though he had just won the Masters and U.S. Open still strikes some as ludicrous. "A big-name pro who's holding the trophy of the two preceding majors and he has to go over and qualify?" asks Stennett. "No big-name pro would do that today. Hogan had to go over and qualify and that wasn't easy for him. That takes a toll having to go over there and play extra rounds of golf and try to get his legs working for him."

Stories of Hogan's trip to Carnoustie continue to resonate with his family members, Lisa Scott says. "Traveling to the British Open was a big deal," says Scott. "When he first got there [to Carnoustie], he had to move out of his hotel because he needed a bath to be able to soak his legs. Then everybody put together their rations to give him steak to make sure he could eat. Aunt Valerie said something to him about it like, 'Don't say a word because everybody has done this. This is the best steak you've ever had.'"

Locke made the biggest news on the first day of qualifying, "Bad Boy" Bobby shooting a 33-32-65 course record at windswept Burnside to finish five strokes ahead of Hogan. Scotsman John Panton, playing amid equally windy conditions at Carnoustie, finished later than Locke but also shot a course record, a 35-34-69 that was the best to that point in official competition. The United Press reported that due to changing wind and weather conditions, there was no official par on the two courses that sit side-by-side along the Firth of Tay and North Sea. None of the field, noted the UP, managed the gusty winds better than Locke, Hogan, or Panton.

Hogan, Locke, and players who on Monday tested the 6,398-yard Burnside course, whose unofficial par was 71, would play Tuesday's qualifying round on the tougher Carnoustie course. Panton and those who played Carnoustie on Monday switched to the shorter Burnside layout on Tuesday. Though he set no course record in the first qualifying round and finished with a 70, Hogan was the star attraction. The UP stated that Hogan "had nearly all the gallery and got about 90 percent of the attention" as he played Burnside. A gallery reported at three thousand fans awaited the American champion on the first tee. "This is the place golf was invented," the UP wrote in noting the crowd size, "and these people take the game more seriously than almost anywhere else in the world."

Hogan had swapped words with a photographer the day before, but the AP described him "in a high humor—for Hogan. The usually dour little guy was actually smiling, posing for amateur and professional photographers and cracking enough jokes to keep the crowd smiling." He started strong, hitting his second shot, described by the UP as "a reported 70-yard high pitch," which the wind rattled but did not damage, to within two feet of the pin, then drained the putt for birdie.

Hogan went a stroke over par on number two following a short chip shot amid rough and high tiger grass. The remainder of the front nine saw him carding pars and birdies, and he shot two under par going out. Hogan got a birdie on the 363-yard number seven, the UP stating that he hit "a high, handsome shot up into the wind and let it blow his ball 250 to 260 yards down the center of the fairway." Hogan hammered his approach shot some one hundred yards to five feet from the pin. He sank the putt for a three. According to the UP, Hogan "was driving and putting excellently."

He was not as sharp on the back nine, posting a 38. Some of his putts missed by mere inches. "Coming home, Hogan's medium-long putts failed to drop as they did going out," the UP reported. "He missed four putts on the incoming nine holes and ten feet or less." Still, Hogan was smiling as he completed his round. The fact that he spent little time sighting his putts left writers with the impression that all Hogan wanted to do was achieve the needed qualifying score.

Locke led the news again the following day, Bobby shooting 71 on a wet and windy Carnoustie course to finish with a two-day qualifying total of 136. Hogan struggled a bit on the dampened greens and shot 75 for a 145. Mangrum dominated Burnside with a 67, the top score of the second qualifying day.

Hogan met for the first time the Carnoustie beast in full fury, the *Herald* stating that the course "showed its teeth." The battle was waged in grim conditions, "a strong north-west wind and occasional fierce showers of rain," wrote the *Herald*. The newspaper noted that all the competitors found Carnoustie's long front nine "an ordeal." Hogan hit solid shots, the *Herald* reported, but was betrayed by his putting and made the turn with a 41. "He did, however, give proof of his quality with an inward half of 34," wrote the *Herald*.

This was the Hogan the Scots braved bad weather to see—the little man in the flat cap, chain-smoking Chesterfields, his hawk-like stare sizing up a hole, then the discarding of the still smoldering butt, and the placing of another precise shot. Hogan closed with a strong 3-4-3 and on eighteen sank his lone putt of length, a twelve-footer. "One formed the impression that he was simply coasting to a comfortable qualifying position," the *Herald* opined, "and that tomorrow he will begin to give the answer to Carnoustie's problems." The *Herald* issued one more warning related to the weather for the championship rounds, stating that the rain and stiff wind in the previous Saturday's practice gave golfers "a foretaste of what this week's conditions are likely to be."

The British game was a rugged one. Henry Longhurst drew a comparison between British and American golf when he noted that while U.S. country club courses present players with similar golfing problems, golf in the UK offered four or five different species of the sport, "all presenting different problems," Longhurst wrote, "and demanding different degrees of golfing intelligence." Longhurst said Brits believed golf by the sea was "the real golf, and that everything else is a somewhat indifferent man-made substitute." Carnoustie, he added, was "a must for the golfing expert or connoisseur."

There had been dramatic occurrences in British Open history before— Old Tom Morris versus Willie Park Sr. in the 1860 inaugural at Prestwick; Harry Vardon's record-setting sixth Open win in 1914; Bobby Jones's "Impregnable Quadrilateral" at Royal Liverpool in 1930; Gene Sarazen's startling sand wedge at Prince's Golf Club in '32; Harry Bradshaw's bad lie on a broken bottle at Royal St. George's in '49. Hogan's first appearance, however, promised something new and different.

9

The Wee Ice Mon Cometh

Decades passed and the impression Ben Hogan made on Ben Wright at Carnoustie remained indelible. A twenty-year-old British golfer and future commentator in 1953, Wright was at Carnoustie when Hogan walked with his caddie, Cecil Timms, to the first tee early in the afternoon on July 8, the opening day of The Open Championship at Carnoustie. Along with what the *Glasgow Herald* reported to be a "remarkable gallery," Wright watched Hogan step from the chauffeured car. The American champion wore what Wright recalled as a "beautiful cashmere sweater," crisp white shirt, tan pants, black golf shoes, and a flat cap made of warm wool rather than the light linen he customarily wore in the spring and summer months in the states. One other difference was that Hogan's cap in Carnoustie was checkered, a departure from the plain white model he wore in the U.S.

Wright was among the thousands who watched the man who would be British Open king sign autographs for children and adults for a full ten minutes prior to teeing off in the first round of the British Open. Hogan glared at the course he was determined to conquer. Storm clouds gathered overhead. Hogan was in for a fight with these ancient grounds, the Associated Press at the time of the tournament calling Carnoustie "one of the most feared courses in the world." The ancient layout was "7,200 yard of tournament torture," stated the AP, reporting that this was a "mean Scottish course." It was also the longest golf course in Scotland.

Bantam Ben, the "Wee Ice Mon," would look to play David to Carnoustie's Goliath. British journalists saw in Hogan a quality, a grandeur, an overpowering personality to match "the Napoleons of Industry and of majesty in Leaders in Politics and Diplomacy." They acknowledged Hogan's monumental success in his own land, but believed he could not rank with countrymen Bobby Jones, Gene Sarazen, and Walter Hagen if he did not claim The Open Championship.

Wright remembers Hogan arriving for the first round of his epic confrontation dragging on his cigarette and looking elegant and almost regal in his appearance. Hogan, recalls Wright, looked like a king come to claim his land. Wright thought Hogan carried with him an air of invincibility and superiority.

Hogan's competitors noted the same. Ken Venturi, who would walk on the sun to win the 1964 U.S. Open at the dangerously overheated Congressional Country Club in Bethesda, Maryland, was a frequent playing partner of Hogan. Venturi was so enamored of Hogan that he copied his preference for muted colors—white shirts, gray pants, black golf shoes—and even wore a similar white linen cap. Venturi recalled Hogan telling him there were three ways to beat the competition: Outwork them, out-think them, intimidate them.

In Hogan's eyes, a champion has to know when he walks to the first tee that he's better than anyone else and he has to make sure his competitors know it too. British amateur golfer and sports journalist Frank Pennink was at Carnoustie and watched Hogan calmly puffing a Chesterfield as he waited his turn to hit on the first tee. Pennink had not been in Ganton, England, four years prior when Hogan captained the U.S. Ryder Cup team, so he would compare at Carnoustie the mental image he had of Hogan with an in-person view. Pennink found Hogan several inches taller than he had imagined and more broadly built. Pennink saw Hogan as being tanned by the summer sun, his face expressive and showing strong character. Pennink also discovered that Hogan was not the "ice box" he was made out to be but instead was given to issuing warm smiles.

Pennink thought Hogan's composed expression radiated confidence. The British amateur believed Hogan had the greatest golfing brain ever and that for every course he played, he prepared master plans that rarely failed. This Open Championship was all about Hogan, Pennink wrote. His presence made it a great event and was the primary reason for the doubling of the gate and the record number of fans. *Life* magazine noted in its coverage that while ninety-one players teed off in the championship, "the gallery had eyes for no one but Ben."

Also watching Hogan was Sir Guy Campbell, an amateur golfer and great-grandson of early British golf historian Robert Chambers, who was a co-designer of the original nine-hole course at Royal Liverpool and had seen firsthand many of the great golfers of the early and mid-twentieth century. Campbell had heard much about Hogan from authorities he had great confidence in and knew of Hogan's story: "the accident that plunged him into such desperate straits, his miraculous survival, his almost incredible recovery—a triumph of willpower and courage." Seeing Hogan in person at Carnoustie, Campbell thought Hogan showed himself to be in top form and confident in his understanding of the course.

Hogan stood on the first tee at Carnoustie, his cap pulled so low it nearly covered his penetrating stare. The Hawk felt the Scottish sea air. Wild was the wind, Hogan stating later that it was blowing hard and fierce. A hailstorm that day did not help matters. Sizing up the course, Hogan saw what writer Gwilym S. Brown later described as more than seven thousand yards of "torture and flagellation . . . a long, narrow, ugly, flat, knobby, wind-worn crusty stretch of wasteland that can probably be ranked as the hardest championship course in the world."

There are several reasons why Carnoustie is "Carnasty," the primary reason being, Brown wrote, that there is not a safe place to hit the ball. Deep rough, abundant bunkers, and greens that were nearly as fast as the fairways were further complicated by the Barry Burn, the watery, serpentine ditch that crosses the seventeenth and eighteenth holes three times. Add in gusting winds, said Brown, and the clubhouse was the only safe haven at Carnoustie.

Hogan knew length and accuracy would be in high demand to deal with the tight corridors from the tee. Precision and placement were required in approach shots to greens guarded by steep bunkers and winding burns. Carnoustie's finishing holes were arguably the most difficult of any in the world, and severe penalties awaited errant shots. Links golf would be far more rugged than the American game to which Hogan was accustomed.

At the same time, the beast that is Carnoustie may not have experienced a strategist the equal of Hogan. Here was a champion whom Venturi thought was the best course manager ever. Venturi believed Hogan's famous "secret" may have been his imagination. Hogan would tell him to study his shots when practicing so he could put them "in the computer." When people would tell Hogan he had great muscle memory, he replied that his muscles didn't have memory; he told them what to do.

The *Glasgow Herald* wrote that the "championship proper was given a fine send off, large crowds being drawn from all parts of Britain by the Hogan magnet." Tickets and programs were sold out early in the day, and caterers were unable to handle the many requests for lunch. Disliking British food— "awful," Hogan called it—he ate his tournament lunches in his car. The great gallery focused primarily on Hogan and Locke, and the crowd's sheer size slowed the pace of play. Still, fans would get what they came for—quality entertainment from star players. Trevor Williamson remembers,

Thousands watched Hogan, just to say they saw him. I was there, with my auntie and my mom. The crowds were far bigger; they came to see the stars. The ladies with prams, pushing them across the course. They were not giving a damn about the course. It was quite chaotic.

And it was not just Hogan they wanted to see at the Open. Lloyd Mangrum was a handsome hero, if he could act, would have been a film star. Frank Stranahan was a bodybuilder, a big chap with blond hair.

There's always been adoration in this country of American things—big cars, gangster films, things like that. We started to see more and more American-manufactured stuff coming on the golf shelfs, from MacGregor and Wilson. They eventually took over, a form of hero worship, and the British makers tended to disappear, sadly.

Fans weren't the only ones studying Hogan. Fellow pro Peter Alliss recalled his contemporaries looking in awe at the American import. "He was a total mystery," wrote Alliss, who would place ninth in the tournament. "He was from another planet. We were all in awe of him. He was like royalty—people would approach him deferentially."

To keep fans informed, Hogan would work with John Derr and broadcast radio reports from Carnoustie. Derr was an iconic personality. He reported on Hogan's first victory at Pinehurst in 1940 and was friends with Hogan, Sam

Snead, Byron Nelson, and Bobby Jones. Derr also associated with many of the leading figures of the twentieth century—Albert Einstein, U.S. president Dwight D. Eisenhower, Henry Ford, Mahatma Gandhi, Billy Graham, and numerous others.

A native of North Carolina, Derr served in the military and earned the Bronze Star. A pioneer in broadcast journalism, Derr was working for CBS when he negotiated the deal to broadcast the Kentucky Derby on TV for the first time. Over the course of his long career Derr broadcast on live TV more than 130 golf tournaments, as well as championship boxing and horse races, and college football bowl games.

Tee time for Hogan and playing partner Ugo Grappasonni of Italy was 1:16 p.m., and five minutes before Hogan began, defending champion Bobby Locke was finalizing his first-round 72 while fending off a severe west wind. The South African had opened the celebrated proceedings by teeing off at 9:40 a.m., and as he came off the course, the Bantam congratulated golf's "Bad Boy" for reaching par amid windswept conditions. The *Herald* reported that Locke "putted with his usual distinction but rather surprisingly missed from four feet at the long sixth." Locke carded a six on number six, but he saved strokes with an approach shot that was inches shy of the flag on fifteen after driving into a bunker. Far short of the green on seventeen, Locke holed a putt from thirty feet for a four.

Hogan thought Locke shot a wonderful round considering the conditions. An internal operation the previous autumn and a foot ailment that was treated in the Dundee Royal Infirmary on the eve of the British Open had slowed Bobby, but Alliss believed Locke's opening round showed that he wasn't going to surrender his title easily. Locke's iron play proved inaccurate, but he rescued his round with what Alliss described as "resolute chipping."

Locke led a field of four former British Open champions, the 1949, '50, and '52 winner joining Northern Ireland's Fred Daly (1947), England's Max Faulkner (1951), Dick Burton (1939), and Alf Padgham (1936). Notable past champions not in the tournament included Gene Sarazen (1932), Denny Shute (1933), three-time winner Henry Cotton (1934, '37, '48), Alf Perry (1935), Reg Whitcombe (1938), and Snead (1946). Despite the absentees, the '53 Open Championship brought together a strong and representative field at Carnoustie.

Lloyd Mangrum, one of the leading American contenders for the British crown, told reporters that if he couldn't win, he wished Hogan would. "This would be a great thing for Hogan," Mangrum said.

Bitter cold, strong wind, lashing rain, and hail greeted golfers in the opening round. The mixed Scottish weather added to the terrors of Carnoustie. Writer Malcolm Campbell thought that on such a day when the North Sea weather was against the golfers, the first hole required "a stinging blow" to reach the green. Carnoustie's difficulty would only increase from that point, with a demanding drive on the second hole and a deft pitch on number three to clear a stream and catch a green that was small and owning a severe slope. Then it's into the prevailing wind again, where the battle, Campbell wrote, "is well and truly joined."

Jockie's Burn factors into four of the first six holes, and then it's onto number nine, the lone downhill hole on one of the British Isles' flattest plains. Composure and a controlled nerve are needed to avoid the sand pits on thirteen, and a stiff, westerly wind can affect shots to the green on fourteen. Then come the famously fierce finishing holes, number sixteen being one of the toughest in the world. The meandering Barry Burn calls for a demanding tee shot on seventeen, and there's more water and bunkers on the eighteenth, where a carefully placed tee shot is once again required.

Pat Ward-Thomas of the *Manchester Guardian* joined the great crowd on Carnoustie's first tee. The wind blew strongly from the west, straining flags at their mast. Ward-Thomas thought there was tension and expectancy and a sense of history he had never known at the onset of any championship. He saw Hogan, a "slight grey figure," awaiting his call from the starter to tee off. Ward-Thomas knew Hogan the man had become a legend in the minds of many. British fans and golfers had hoped—perhaps even prayed, Ward-Thomas said—that Hogan would one day play in the British Open. It would not have been right, wrote Ward-Thomas, if among the great golfers in history Hogan alone had not competed for the Claret Jug.

The hopes and prayers of British golf fans would be answered at Carnoustie. A longing had been realized, Ward-Thomas thought, for here in the flesh was Hogan. Along with a compulsion to watch his every move and study his technique, there was a desire to see a man who had "achieved so much in the face of awful adversity," Ward-Thomas wrote.

The much-anticipated moment of Hogan teeing off arrived, and the thousands in attendance saw in person his famous mannerisms. Pennink took note of the shuffling of Hogan's feet into position, "the wristy address, and the long pause of the clubhead behind the ball, before his hands finally close firm on the grip, wrist arched high, a long, rather fast, upright and grooved swing sent the ball on the first of its many unerring flights to the spot marked X on the scheme in his mind."

Pennink saw that there was no obvious exertion of power on Hogan's part, and even when he delivered powerful shots, as he would on lengthy number six, there wasn't any sign of him swinging from his heels. Following Hogan around the course, Pennink was impressed that most of his drives were so exact that it was surprising if his shots landed more than five feet to the right or left of the flag. Pennink noticed that when Hogan putted, he did so off his left foot "whereon rests all his weight, and his stance is a fairly wide one." Pennink compared Hogan to Jones in his intention to "'die' the ball into the hole." Because he was putting on greens slower than he was accustomed to in the U.S., Hogan was almost always short of the hole.

Ward-Thomas considered Carnoustie "a fearsome challenge" for Hogan. The conditions of British golf were alien to him, as were the number of Brits eager to watch him win. He watched as Hogan's first drive off the tee was "lashed far up the slope of the fairway and then a two-iron rifled into the teeth of the wind, with that compelling searing flight. . . . It flew on towards the green in its deep bowl amongst the dunes and finished some twelve feet from the hole."

Hogan's putt stopped short, an omen of the difficulties he would experience on the heavy greens. Ward-Thomas, like Pennink and others, followed Hogan around the course on that foggy day. "Another two-iron shot cleaved the wind to the second," Ward-Thomas wrote, "a superb brassie found the fourth green, and yet another flew like a quail down the vast stretch of the sixth." Still, Hogan's putts consistently fell short, including what Ward-Thomas described as "distinctly holeable ones on each of the last three greens."

Buffeted by the salty gusts from the North Sea and battling a course whose challenges were relentless, Hogan grew increasingly fatigued in his first official round in The Open Championship. "Damn course," he was heard to mutter. "You just can't keep going on it." *Life* magazine reported that because the Carnoustie course is owned by the town, it takes an "unmerciful" beating from weekend hackers. They romped through the course's woolly rough and pockmarked its fairways with divots.

Rain and hail had Hogan handling an umbrella with almost as much frequency as he handled his clubs. Photographer Carl Mydans captured for *Life* magazine an image of Hogan beneath an umbrella as he headed toward his next shot. Spectators in heavy overcoats were photographed by Mydans crouching behind umbrellas as they sought shelter from the hailstorm. One man caught in the driving storm without an umbrella was shown popping the collar of his coat for protection. The scene was surreal. *Life* noted that smoke billowed from nearby factories, a freight train rumbled past the course, and explosions could be heard from mortar shells landing on a target range not far away.

Though they followed him around, many Scots were hoping on this first day to see, as *Life* said, "the Hogan legend come to a screeching halt." They considered his comments about Carnoustie rude; some Scots were outraged. By the time he teed off in his opening round, Hogan was reported by *Life* to have most of Scotland doing "a slow burn."

Hogan's first round resulted in a 73 that was topped by only six players. The Bantam deemed his play "satisfactory." His putting, however, was less so. Caught in the storm that burst forth from dark skies, Hogan sought to keep his hands warm with two cigarette holder sized heaters.

"We're a proper links course," Williamson says. "In the time that Hogan played the grass is green, but if you get a sunny spell in the summer for 10–12 days with a prevailing wind from the west, then the green grass will turn brown and dusty, and the ball will bounce all over the place. That's links golf. You took it as it was, it was nature, and it was you."

Hogan's physical fatigue could have been summed up by an old Scottish ballad:

Fight on, my men, says Sir Andrew Barton,
I am hurt, but I am not slain;
I'll lay me down and bleed a while,
And then I'll rise and fight again.

Departing the course, Hogan was tired, as he usually was following the first round of a tournament. He told Gene Gregston that the first round is always the most tiring for him. Hogan's physical condition was further complicated by his having lost twenty pounds since February, leaving him as low in poundage as he wanted to be.

Not helping Hogan's cause was the British diet, restricted as it was, since the UK was still dealing with the rations brought on by World War II. Hogan found fruit to be plentiful and ate it to maintain his strength. He carried as a supplement candy fruit drops and butterscotch candy in his golf bag and munched on them throughout his opening round to boost his energy. Hogan shared his candies with Timms at the start of their round together, Ben giving him a handful while telling him to save the rest. Soon, however, Hogan found Timms eating not only his share of candy but Ben's too. Hogan brought more fruit drops and told Timms not to eat them. "But Mr. Hogan, I could eat them all day they're so good." Two or three stern warnings from Hogan convinced Timms he'd better not consume any more of his boss's candies.

Timms had caddied for American golfers before, amateur champion Dick Chapman among them. Timms found Chapman to his liking, someone who enjoyed thinking over and talking over every shot. The involvement made Timms feel like a member of a team, a feeling the off-season soccer pro enjoyed. He preferred his golfer to be conversational, yet he knew that every player had their own personality.

Timms found Hogan the quietest of the Americans he'd worked with. Still, he thought that he and Hogan got along "quite nicely." Hogan's playing partner, Grappasonni, was also quiet, speaking in broken English when he did talk. Hogan's fatigue may have contributed to his slow pace of play, which proved disconcerting for competitors behind him, including C. H. Ward, whose best pro years were likely lost to World War II when he served in the RAF.

The *Herald* wrote that many of the day's better performances went unheralded as "the vast majority of the spectators spent the afternoon with Hogan." The Brits saw the Bantam score 36 on the front nine, the top total of the day. Hogan's achievement came despite, as the *Herald* noted, only one putt dropping for him—a seven-footer for a three on number seven. The *Herald* wrote that the American favorite "finished indifferently after playing 15 holes with all the distinction that one expects from a competitor of his stature."

Seeing Hogan play in person for the first time, his game was said by the *Herald* to be "so sound as to be unspectacular, and after 15 holes he needed the par 3, 4, 4, to tie with [Frank] Stranahan." Instead, Hogan failed on each hole, missing putts of six, three, and five feet. "Nevertheless, his form, even through a fierce hailstorm, was impressive enough to suggest that three strokes do not form for him an insurmountable obstacle," the *Herald* wrote.

Alliss noted that Hogan was pleased with the extra distance he was getting from the smaller ball and made a major adjustment to his iron play that had his clubhead skimming the turf rather than taking his customary deep divot. Due to Carnoustie's length, Hogan was said by Alliss to have figured out that long wooden club play was critical and tailored his strategy accordingly.

Alliss admitted to being "overawed by the presence of the great man," and he and British fans were seeing a golfer whose swing was such that Randy Jacobs remembers it as being almost hypnotic. "Mr. Hogan hit the ball hard," Jacobs says. "He generated a tremendous amount of speed and force. His rotation was tremendous. It was so technically sound it was a thing of beauty. Gardner Dickinson in his book made the point that Mr. Hogan was a 'shaft swinger.' Mr. Hogan wanted that shaft as stiff as he could handle because he felt like he could generate the speed to make it work and he didn't want any variables in there or any inconsistencies."

The American champion and Scottish fans took the measure of each other. Hogan noticed while he was playing through the harsh weather that the Brits were a hardy breed. Rain didn't bother them, he said later. Instead, they put on rain gear and kept watching.

When a wicked wind and rain whipped the course, Hogan watched as the Scots squatted beneath their umbrellas until the squall stopped. At that point, they would get up and go on, leaving Hogan shaking his head. Darndest sight he ever saw, he said later.

Alliss said the Scots were impressed with Hogan's length off the tee during this first round. His tendency to suffer cramps in his legs was worsened by the first day's hail, wind, and cold, yet he was still driving the ball as far as the more solidly built Roberto de Vicenzo. Alliss believed Hogan would have posted a below-par opening round but had let it slip away on the finishing holes. The greens had been cut to championship shortness, but Hogan still found them slow. Alliss remembered that when a birdie chance occurred, Hogan usually shot short. Still, his thirty-two putts were considered a respectable total.

Convinced as Hogan was that Locke would lead after the first round, the honor instead went to Stranahan, whom Hogan considered a fine player. Stranahan's 70 established an early tempo, and he was followed by Scotland's Eric Brown at 71 and Locke, de Vicenzo, Dai Rees, and Peter Thomson at 72. Hogan and Daly tied for seventh at 73.

In terms of physical fitness in golf, Stranahan was the Tiger Woods of his era. Stating that golfers "need length to be a winner," he traveled with weights in his suitcase, much to the chagrin of unknowing bellhops who attempted to carry his clanking bags in hotels. Known as the "Toledo Strongman," Stranahan was a powerlifter and ranked first in his weight class from 1945 to 1954. Stranahan wasn't very tall, but he was very muscular. He would win weight-lifting and bodybuilding competitions into his seventies. Close friend Arnold Palmer called him "Muscles," and Gary Player would cite him as his "fitness mentor." As inexhaustible as he was strong, Stranahan would later compete in 102 long-distance marathons.

Stranahan is also credited with helping salvage the British Open. Few American golfers competed in the tournament in the years immediately following World War II, yet Stranahan was a consistent competitor, playing in eight straight British Opens, including a runner-up finish to Daly in 1947 at Royal Liverpool Golf Club in Hoylake, England.

Stranahan's fifty-one amateur championships are part of an amateur career golf historians rank with Bobby Jones and Tiger Woods. Stranahan grew up in Toledo, Ohio playing famed Inverness, where he received golf instructions from the club's pro, Byron Nelson. He competed in more than two hundred tournaments spanning three continents and captured the 1948 and 1950 British Amateur titles—defeating England's Charles Stowe in the former and compatriot Chapman in the latter—six PGA Tour tournaments, and placed second in three majors. His tying Nelson as runner-up to Jimmy Demaret in the 1947 Masters helped the twenty-five-year-old Stranahan vault to prominence. He was also a member of the winning U.S. Walker Cup teams in 1947, '49, and '51.

Stranahan's start at Carnoustie saw him nail ten-foot putts on holes five and eight for a 37 on the front nine. He holed a twelve-foot putt on eleven and a six-footer on fifteen. Stranahan overclubbed his tee shot on sixteen and left a putt on eighteen agonizingly short, "half an inch" according to the *Herald*, and his 33 on the back nine missed by one stroke equaling the course record of 69 set the previous Monday.

Stranahan flexed on Carnoustie in the first round, and so did Brown. Like Stranahan, Brown believed might made right on the links, the Edinburgh native being nicknamed "Bomber" for a reason. He first played in The Open Championship in 1948 and would become known as a hero of the Ryder Cup, claiming a hotly contested singles match against Tommy Bolt. The two were famous for being contentious competitors, Bolt known for throwing his clubs in anger, real or feigned, and Brown for his intense play. Demaret joked that the last he saw of Brown and Bolt prior to their match they were heaving clubs at one another from fifty paces. The two showmen took turns trying to rile each other, and at the end of their match, claimed by Brown 4 and 3, they refused to shake hands.

Brown would win the Scottish PGA Championship eight times and was known as a speedy player. Fellow Scot John Panton thought Brown a great competitor. "He was very determined," Panton later told the *Herald*, "and a great holer-out and chipper." The Bomber was also known as a hard man with a volatile temperament. Alliss wrote that Brown excelled as a match player, the Bomber "thriving on the greater element of personal combat in that form of golf."

Bomber Brown warred not only with competitors but also with Carnoustie. He matched Daly's distinction of carding a 33 on the back nine, helped on number thirteen by his two-foot putt that "ran around the hole and dropped in at the front," according to the *Herald*. Suitably inspired, he landed an approach shot four feet from the flag on fifteen, found the center of the green on seventeen with a four-wood and sank an eight-foot putt for a third straight three.

Daly's 33 was built despite his sinking just one putt of length—from twelve feet on number ten—and missing from four feet on sixteen. De Vicenzo, Thomson, and Rees produced highlights as well. The former fashioned a streak of threes on numbers eleven through fourteen, his longest putt covering just three feet. He lost his chance to equal Stranahan's 70 when he slashed an errant tee shot on sixteen and blasted into a bunker on eighteen. Thomson's lone issue came on the tough number six, where he mishit his second shot en route to a six, and on number ten, his shot settling in the rough. He bounced back with a two on thirteen, courtesy of an eight-foot putt. Rees rode tremendous tee shots to twos on numbers eight and thirteen, offsetting an uneven start of 5-4-4-5-4-6.

Round Two on Thursday, July 9 promised more great theater, with weather conditions once again predicted to be unpredictable. The reports of ominous storms proved accurate, as for the second straight day the elements played a part in the events. The *Herald* reported that "a change in the direction of the wind from West to East about lunchtime brought frequent heavy showers in the afternoon." Despite the weather conditions the course played according to the *Herald* "at least four strokes easier than during yesterday's high wind."

As he had before Round One the previous day, Hogan spent ten minutes prior to teeing off for Round Two signing autographs for children and adults. He had become the Pied Piper of Carnoustie. Playing with Bill Branch, who like Grappasonni the day before was a nearly silent partner, Hogan felt he played well but couldn't get his putts to drop.

Timms didn't always help matters, dropping his head so as not to look whenever Hogan had a long putt. Ben saw the body language as Timms's lack of confidence in Hogan's putting. Timms would also fidget to the point that Hogan would tell him, "For goodness' sake, just stand still and shut up."

"Aye," the chastened Timms would answer. "Yes sir."

Struggling with his short game, Hogan said later that at times he shared Timms's feelings regarding his work on the greens and would have liked to refrain from watching. "I putted poorly over there," Hogan admitted, adding that part of his problem was that while the greens were hard, he couldn't reconcile the fact that they were slow when he expected them to be fast.

Despite his poor putting, Hogan's second-round 71 sliced two strokes from his previous day's total and kept him two strokes back of the lead, now shared by Brown and Rees, who were two under par at 142. The *Herald* reported that "no one had a better chance of getting down to the 60s than Hogan." The paper noted that he made an "ominous start" by carding 4-4-3-3 "then surprisingly showed that he too can have chinks in his armour."

Just as he had been in the opening round, Hogan was betrayed by his putting. He might have begun with four threes, but two midrange putts on the first two holes lipped out. He drained putts from six feet on holes three and four. With what the *Herald* reported as "another remarkable gallery" expecting peerless precision, Hogan played a shot on number seven from the bank of a bunker that the paper said "would have made even a handicap player hang his head in shame." Hogan bogeyed number nine, shot par through fifteen, then unsuccessfully tried in the words of the *Herald* "a Scotch run-up." Still, his 35 on the back nine was a stroke better than his 36 going out and put him at 144.

United Press International reported that Hogan's score "would have been even better had not some of his putts been amiss." Ward-Thomas thought Hogan might well have played the first six holes of the second round in nineteen strokes: "Shot after shot flew at the flag with such relentless precision that the senses trembled at their beauty and power." Hogan's 71, said Ward-Thomas, was "an absurd overstatement of the quality of his golf."

Ward-Thomas felt that for the second straight day, Hogan's putting had failed him. Of his dropping strokes at times, Hogan believed that many people built up in their minds a mythical Hogan who wins whenever he wants. "Well, it does not work out that way," he stated.

Covering the tournament for the London *Times*, Bernard Darwin believed Hogan in the first two rounds was "weighed down by his immense reputation." Darwin thought Hogan's putting unworthy of him, and that the slowness of the greens was getting on the champion's nerves, "so far as he has any nerves."

Darwin considered Hogan's putting the "least attractive part of his game." He noted that Hogan's stance when putting was stiff, that he would have the ball far forward, and nearly in front of, his left foot, and that his right foot would be back. Still, Darwin thought that when Hogan putted, he delivered a blow that was "wonderfully solid" and caused the ball not to trickle toward the cup but to head right for it.

Alliss said Brits studying Hogan up close noticed a critical difference between him and the field. Hogan's right hand and arm thrust through the ball, Alliss recalled, "and kept the clubhead low along the ground far beyond the time when others would have begun to lift up and away." What Alliss called the "long right arm through the ball" technique had arrived in the UK.

More than 2,300 fans crammed into Carnoustie for the tournament's second day, causing officials to use, for the first time, handheld ropes to control the crowd. Among those following Hogan that day was one of the more famous personalities of the twentieth century. Frank Sinatra was fighting a plunging career when he traveled to Scotland in July 1953. The "Chairman of the Board" was thirty-seven years old and pivoting away from the Bobbie Sox adulation he had received a decade before, though U.S. president Franklin Roosevelt was somewhat unimpressed after meeting the crooner in a 1944 White House meeting arranged by Toots Shor. FDR asked Sinatra how he made young women swoon, and after sizing up the skinny singer, Roosevelt jauntily told an aide, "He would never have made them swoon in *our* day."

Sinatra left Columbia Records in 1952 and then signed with Capitol Records. His public persona had taken a hit when he left his wife to marry actress Ava Gardner. Concerts were scheduled in the Scottish towns of Glasgow, Ayr, and Dundee, but the Chairman's pride took a hit when just five hundred people showed up in Dundee for a concert in a Caird Hall that seated 3,300.

The audience was so embarrassingly small that fans in the less expensive five-shilling seats were invited by Sinatra to "come down where I can see you" and fill in the fifteen-shilling seats close to the stage for the forty-five-minute performance. It was clear that "Ol' Blue Eyes," forever the saloon singer who craved close contact with his audience, didn't want fans to be "strangers in the night," as writer Graeme Strachan said in the *Courier Evening Telegraph*.

Sinatra's second show that night fared slightly better, his thirteen-song set containing hits like *Birth of the Blues* and *Ol' Man River* while he played to an audience of 1,189. A letter in the *Courier* explained the reason for the relatively low turnouts, stating that the teenagers who comprised the largest part of the fan following for the man sometimes called simply "The Voice" couldn't afford the ticket prices. More moderate prices "would have filled the hall easily with young people," the letter writer stated.

Sinatra thought Scottish fans "wonderfully enthusiastic," and they returned his affection, Strachan reporting that a pub on King Street was named in honor of Sinatra by Ian Hindmarsh. In 1990 Sinatra, aged seventy-five, returned to Scotland a final time for a concert at Glasgow's Ibrox Stadium.

By 1953, Sinatra had golf under his skin, and like fans on both sides of the Atlantic, he was intrigued by Hogan's attempt to win the British Open. Growing up in Hoboken in northern New Jersey, Sinatra had wanted to be a sportswriter, and he would later work as an office boy for the *Hudson Observer* (NJ).

Sinatra's love for sports and high drama took him to Carnoustie, and he followed Hogan throughout the second round. Sinatra told reporters, "All America is rooting for Hogan." Williamson recalls Sinatra's trip to Carnoustie and some controversy that went with it. "Sinatra was appearing in Glasgow and Dundee," he says. "My uncle ran the golf shop, and he was a very cantankerous old chap. He had no clue who Sinatra was, and Sinatra and my uncle fell out and got into a big fight, not a physical fight but an argument."

Sinatra had headed west to California in the 1940s and eventually gravitated toward golf, as it was a sport in which he could enjoy a glass of whiskey before, during, and after the match. Venturi, a friend of Sinatra and Hogan, told Jeff Rude of *Golfweek* that the two men shared similarities. If someone didn't like Hogan or Sinatra, it was only because they had never met them, Venturi said. He called Hogan the nicest person one ever wanted to meet. It wasn't wise to approach Hogan with a brusque, "Hi, Ben!" But if one went to Hogan and said, "I hate to bother you, but could I get your autograph?" Hogan would ask them to sit and talk.

Ol' Blue Eyes was fixated on the Hawk at Carnoustie, and to see Hogan in person, Sinatra would do it *his way*. The champion's success rubbed off on the Chairman. Three weeks after The Open Championship the film *From Here to Eternity* was released, and Sinatra won an Oscar for "Best Supporting Actor." His first album for Capitol, *Songs for Young Lovers*, was one of a series of concept records that earned critical acclaim.

Sinatra watching Hogan was a case of one American icon treading the same Scottish soil to cheer another American icon, one King of Swing paying tribute to another. Photos of Sinatra at Carnoustie show him fashionably attired in a tan blazer over a dark sweater, white shirt, and dark tie, dark slacks, and polished black shoes. A tournament program bulged his left jacket pocket and in two of the photos he is pulling on a pipe.

While Sinatra studied Hogan up close, it was Brown and Rees who took charge in Round Two. Brown carded a 71 for a second straight day and Rees recorded a birdie and eagle on seventeen and eighteen, respectively, for a 70 that was two strokes better than his first-round score.

A native of Font-y-Gary, Glamorgan, Wales, Rees remarked that he had been born with hickory in his hands. Perhaps it was due in part to his father being a pro at the Leys Club. Rees became friends with famed British Field Marshal Bernard Montgomery, one of the heroes of World War II. He was playing golf with Monty in Eindhoven when Eisenhower chose the field marshal to command Allied Forces in the Battle of the Bulge.

Rees would become known as "Mr. Ryder Cup," playing in nine matches and serving as captain in four of them. Rees won thirty-nine tournaments in Britain, Europe, and South Africa and would be appointed a Commander of the Order of the British Empire (CBE) following the GB&I's historic 1957 Ryder Cup victory over the U.S. at Lindrick, the first in the postwar era for the British and Irish team. Thirty-one years would pass before the Europeans would again defeat the United States.

Rees was proud of his Welsh heritage and stressed personal discipline. He emphasized physical fitness, never smoked, and was moderate in his use of alcohol. Rees was familiar with Hogan, the two squaring off in February 1947 in sunny San Diego. At the time Hogan was the PGA champion, Rees the leading British money winner from the previous year. Hogan claimed a five thousand dollar payoff by defeating Rees, 6 and 4, in a thirty-six-hole international duel. Black-and-white video of their match shows Rees, in rolled up white sleeves, and a sweatered Hogan teeing off, Hogan holing a putt from eighteen feet and Rees responding in kind.

At Carnoustie it was Rees, the experienced Ryder Cup player, and Brown, the former Scottish amateur champion, dueling for the lead. The *Herald* informed readers that the "Welshman started as he left off yesterday, holing an 8-yard putt on the first green for a 'birdie' 3." Rees lost a stroke on the second green for a five, then carded fours on numbers three through nine for a 36 on the front nine. He shot par coming back in until he found a bunker from the tee on sixteen. "Roused by that lapse," the *Herald* said, "he finished in a blaze of glory." Rees drained an eighteen-foot putt on seventeen for a three, then matched it on eighteen with an approach close to the pin for a back-nine 34.

Brown was likewise strong coming in. Overclubbing led to three consecutive fives on holes five, six, and seven and produced a 37 going out. It would've been worse, but the combative Bomber holed an eight-foot putt on number eight. He shot fours and threes on the back nine and impressed with his ability to save par. "He was bunkered at the tenth and seventeenth," the *Herald* wrote, "but recovered to the holeside and he almost holed a chip after having overshot the sixteenth green from the tee." The paper cited them as "fine recoveries," and Hogan agreed. He stated later that Rees, Brown, and the British golfers played with more confidence on their home course and with their own ball.

Hogan also believed that while the European game was technically the same as the American game when it came to swing, stroke, and method, the approach of British golfers to their game was more leisurely than that of Americans. The Hawk noticed one other thing. Most British pros, he said, used American-made clubs.

The *Herald* called it "a welcome experience to find two Britons heading such a representative field." One that was expected to lead the field was Locke, the reigning monarch who had won three of the previous four British Open crowns. He shot par in Round One and was expected by many to engage Hogan in a two-man duel for the title. The *Herald* wrote that Locke's second round was the "usual mixture of good and bad, emphasizing that he plays more indifferent strokes than the average top-class player, but is in a class apart when it comes to holing out."

Locke, whose many monikers included "Lantern Jowls," "Moon Face," "Muffin Face," and "Old Baggy Pants," lost a stroke from his first-round score and at 145 was tied for seventh, three shots back of Rees and Brown.

Like Locke, Stranahan struggled in the second round at Carnoustie. The first-round front-runner lost four strokes on the final four holes, opening the door for de Vicenzo to take third place. The *Herald* noted that the "long-hitting Argentinian is finding Carnoustie to his liking." De Vicenzo nearly gained a share of the second-round lead when he shot one over par over the first eight holes going out. On number nine he powered a prodigious but misdirected drive that sailed out of bounds and produced a six and front-nine 37. De Vicenzo rebounded on ten with an eight-foot putt for a three, then added threes on fifteen and sixteen. Poised to put himself in first place, he was foiled by a bad lie on the seventeenth fairway and posted a 71 for third place.

De Vicenzo's countryman, Cerda, also shot 71 but reversed his compatriot's totals, shooting 34 going out and 37 coming in. The latter was affected by constant rain and occasional wind. Mangrum and Panton made the thirty-six-hole cut despite inconsistent performances.

Friday, July 10, would feature thirty-six holes of championship golf, eighteen in Round Three in the morning and eighteen in the fourth and final round in the afternoon. A reporter had suggested to Hogan that he was in a good position to make a run at the title, even though he would have to negotiate thirty-six holes on tired legs. "Yeah, it's not a bad position," Hogan replied. "But you've really got to play."

Hogan found Hector Thomson, the Scottish champion and his playing partner this final day, to be like Grappasonni and Branch in that he was very soft-spoken. Suffering from exhaustion, wearied by the pressure that kept building as the tournament progressed, and battling influenza that hit him the night before, Hogan trudged to the first tee Friday morning feeling in his words "deathly tired." The Associated Press noted Hogan's alarming physical appearance. "The little Texan," the AP noted, looked "grim and greyish blue."

Alliss recalled Hogan's appearance on the tournament's final day as "unsmiling, intense, gaunt, and clad in somber greys." Turning to a tournament official, a weary Hogan looked ahead to the thirty-six-hole endurance test that lay before him. "Better have an oxygen tent ready on the 18th," Hogan told the official. "I'll need it." Robert Stennett says Hogan's legs would swell up so bad in Carnoustie he would "sit in the tub in his room apparently for hours just so he could walk the next day."

Hogan wore a dark sweater over a light-colored shirt to ward off the cold, wind, and intermittent rain, and Valerie carried medicine in case he needed it. He had taken a shot of penicillin prior to teeing off but opted not to take the additional medicine carried by Valerie so as not to upset his stomach. The *Herald* noted that Hogan in the morning round was occasionally behind Thomson from the tee.

Williamson states that on Carnoustie's course layout, "you can't take any chances because you won't get them back." Yet there was Hogan, launching a direct attack on a course that severely punished mishits. *Time* magazine noted that Hogan "began gunning out 300-yard drives in place of his usual, careful 250-yarders. Where his putts had been falling short, Ben changed style and stroked harder."

Digging deeper into his inner reservoir of resolve, Hogan for the third straight round lowered his score, shooting what the AP called a "spectacular 70" for a total of 214 that tied de Vicenzo for the fifty-four-hole lead. Hogan started his round with three straight pars, then dropped shots on numbers four and five. He birdied the sixth, carded a three on number seven and followed with more birdies to stand at four under after sixteen.

Hogan might have matched Cerda's course record 69 had he not found a bunker on number seventeen and carded a six. United Press International wrote that the 454-yard seventeenth hole "had buffaloed Hogan." He hung up what the UPI labeled "a horrible six." Hogan's drive was solid, but he buried his second shot in a bunker, short of the green.

"He pitched out weakly," wrote the UPI, "then took three putts to get down from 30 feet." Hogan needed two fours for a course record 68 and a two-stroke lead with one round to play. But as the *Herald* pointed out, Hogan "cut his second to the seventeenth, recovered indifferently, and then took three putts."

Alliss wrote that Hogan on seventeen "half-thinned" his four-wood second shot into a bunker, blasted out short of the pin, and three-putted. Ward-Thomas wrote that Hogan had spoiled his near flawless round with his six on number seventeen. He believed a 68 seemed certain after Hogan's drive found the island fairway, but his second shot, a four wood, "was cut and drifted into a bunker." Vexed, Hogan banged his club on the ground in frustration. Ben found balm with a birdie on eighteen, then headed for lunch. As he ate, Hogan thought of the task at hand and believed his original plan had to be changed.

Ward-Thomas thought it certain that Hogan would play a classic final round at Carnoustie. Energized by the excitement of being tied for the lead, Hogan headed out for his final eighteen holes feeling stronger than he had earlier in the day. It was common for him to become energized as tournaments rushed to their conclusion.

Aware that his extra strength allowed him to hit the ball for greater distance in the final round than he did in previous rounds led Hogan to knowingly underclub each shot. If he had taken a five-iron from Timms for a particular shot in earlier rounds, he would tell Cecil to hand him a six-iron in the final round.

Timms was never wrong when it came to club selection, according to Hogan. He said later that if he chose a five-iron and his shot was short, he would remark that he should have taken more club. "Yes," Timms would answer. "I had me hand on the 4-iron." Hogan said Timms always knew the correct club to use, "after the shot was taken."

The morning drizzle that marked the third round was replaced by a light wind and sunshine for the final round. The stage was set for drama, wrote the *Herald*: "No film scenario writer could have thought out a more dramatic story than that unfolding during this day."

Derr thought that hole after hole, "the crowd grew, the drama grew." Darwin felt the tension was "desperate" for the final round, the prospect of a tie not only looming but seeming to him to be almost inevitable. He checked his scores heading into the final round—Hogan and de Vicenzo tied atop the leaderboard at 214; Rees, Thomson, and Cerda at 215; Stranahan and Brown at 217; and Max Faulkner and Tommy Fairbairn at 218.

"Was there ever another championship like this?" a man in the crowd excitedly asked Darwin. A veteran writer who began covering golf in 1907, Darwin's first thought was that the agony of this final round was unique.

He then recalled Sandwich, England, in 1911, Harry Vardon earning his fifth Open Championship in a playoff against Arnaud Massy, the 1907 champion. Darwin considered that tournament at Royal St. George's Golf Club the only Open that matched what he and thousands more were witnessing at Carnoustie in 1953.

Scottish fans who had hoped to see Hogan fail were now cheering the tired champion, "ungrudgingly," *Life* remarked. They surged after him, with *Life* taking photos of fans romping though heather-strewn rough, leaping over ditches that sliced through the long grass, and hustling down fairways, all seeking a better vantage point of Hogan's next shot. One Scot was so determined to see Hogan that he followed him sans shoes, his feet covered only by socks on the cold, wet ground. Campbell wrote that the Scots' conversion to Hogan was based in part on his deportment, which was such that he thought any parent could point to Hogan and tell their children, "There's manners, copy 'em!"

"His manners were impeccable," Randy Jacobs recalls. "He might use a little salty language with his friends but never around a woman. He was very careful with his language around women. He was old school."

Derr approached Hogan and said that while he would not speak with him during the round, if Ben needed anything, he would be happy to help. *Time* wrote that Hogan's face was "pale with cold and exhaustion" as he teed off for his final round. The AP stated that "Hogan showed the effects of his steady golf diet when he walked to the tee for his second 18 holes." He was battling not only the "beastly test" that is Carnoustie but also flu, chills, and debilitating injuries from his auto accident.

Hogan had it in mind to change his tactical plan for Carnoustie, something he only did when he felt, as he said, "I'm in a corner and have to fight my way out." If he was leading, Hogan would let his competitors make mistakes. This time, however, he was tied with de Vicenzo and just a single stroke ahead of Thomson, Rees, and Cerda.

To accommodate the large crowds that milled around a scoreboard seeking updates, golfers' scores were posted via flashes from Bush Telephones. Beyond the leaderboard was a car park filled with nearly ten thousand automobiles.

Hogan sized up his competitors. He thought at the start of the tournament that de Vicenzo might run away with the title. As perhaps the strongest man in the tournament and a long-ball hitter, de Vicenzo could carry the traps in the fairways.

Rees, the tiny Welshman, was a physical opposite to the thickly built de Vicenzo, as was Cerda, who was roughly Hogan's size. The *Herald* praised Rees as a "perky little Welshman" with a "big golfing heart." The confident, smiling Rees was photographed pulling a driver from his bag to start his final round. Hogan saw Cerda as owning a solid swing and good all-around game. The top competitors were tightly bunched on the leaderboard for the final round, Cerda teeing off before de Vicenzo. By the time Hogan and Hector Thomson headed to the first tee they were several holes behind de Vicenzo, and Cerda would follow Hogan. Timms said later that while Mr. Hogan needed little assistance at Carnoustie, the caddie did think he helped somewhat, particularly on hole number two in the final round.

"On the second hole," Timms recalled, "we got home comfortably on the morning round with a six-iron on the second shot." But there was a measurable shift in the wind in the afternoon. Hogan smashed what Timms called "another beautiful drive." But he now encountered a wind that was blowing against him and was, according to Timms, "puffy in a very deceptive way." Timms examined the shot that was left to the green and thought it a two-iron. Hogan limped to the lie, studied it, and asked Timms, "What do you think?"

"It's a two."

Hogan disagreed, saying it couldn't be more than a four, since he had played a six that morning.

"I still think it's a two, a three at the least," Timms said.

Hogan took the two-iron and played what Timms called a "magnificent shot." It stuck eighteen feet from the hole. Timms thought it one of the hardest, and best, club calls he ever made. Hogan opened with three straight fours and was playing to par on number four when he learned that Cerda birdied number three. That tied him with Hogan, and the pressure being applied by Cerda made Hogan feel fortunate to chip in for birdie from a sand trap on number five. Fortunate, he explained later, because chipping out of the sand was the most difficult shot for him to execute. Hogan realized then that he had to get a couple of birdies and shoot a 70, or close to 70, to win.

Taking aim on Carnoustie's burned-out fairways and slow greens, Hogan's four consecutive fours prompted the AP to write, "The Texan was playing perfection golf." He was tired, however, and his drive on number five left him with what Alliss called "a poor fairway lie." Hogan's second shot on the fifth hole, which featured a slight dogleg right, found the green but rolled back and into the unforgiving deep grass on the lip of a sand trap on the left, an estimated thirty feet from the pin. Alliss thought it "a horrid sandy lie." Derr agreed and thought the hole could leave Hogan with a birdie three or bogey five. If it resulted in the latter, Derr believed Hogan would be forced to play the remaining holes "under 'catch-up' pressure."

On close inspection, the Hawk saw the ball hanging on the edge of the bunker, "held by two blades of grass," he said. He was unsure how much sand was beneath the ball or if it was possible to blast it out. Hogan was in trouble, and summer was running out. It was a bad angle, and he feared sending the ball over the green would result in a dangerous downhill shot to the hole. After studying the problem at length for several minutes, Hogan tossed his Chesterfield aside and grabbed the nine-iron from Timms and opted to try the chip-in. It was a shot he would not ordinarily attempt, since chipping out of sand was not his strength and he would usually send the ball too far or leave it in the trap.

"This time, as luck would have it, I hit it just right," he recalled to Gregston. "It was nipped just enough for backspin." What happened next was a sight Hogan would long remember. "The ball pitched against the bank of the green, skidded uphill to the pin, banged the back of the cup, bounced three or four inches in the air—then fell into the hole."

Derr considered it an "amazing shot, even for Hogan." The biggest crowd ever to attend the British Open had witnessed what Derr called "a miracle shot."

It was Hogan's first birdie in the final round and put him in front for the first time, leading by a shot. The AP referred to it as Hogan's greatest shot of the afternoon, "and one of the greatest in the history of the game in this Northland home of golf. . . . The ball, resting in the grass deep in a bunker beside the green, arched up after the master golfer swung his club . . . and fell into the hole with a happy 'plunk.'"

Time called it the "critical play," and wrote that a troubled Hogan "studied the difficult shot from all angles for fully five minutes" before swinging. "The ball bounced, rolled boldly toward the hole, struck the back lip, bounced a foot in the air and plunked into the cup for a birdie. From then on, the Wee Ice Mon was invincible."

The AP agreed, stating from that point on, Hogan "played old Carnoustie as an ordinary mortal plays a Tom Thumb course." UPI stated that "the champion's greatest shot came at the fifth in the final round. Deeply bunkered with a bad angle, he chipped into the hole from 30 feet for a birdie three. After that he really caught fire."

The *Herald* wrote that Hogan's "steady start was suddenly electrified when he ran down a chip from off the fifth green, and from that point, as if he knew he was sure of victory, he played more powerfully and purposefully than at any other time."

Darwin said that Hogan's magnificent iron play allowed him to begin taking chances, and once his putts began to drop, fans in the crowd remarked excitedly, "Now he's off!"

Derr believed Hogan had gained "a surge of strength" from the Scottish fans. Even being pressed for three rounds, sharing the lead with one player while several others were within striking distance, Hogan showed himself to be in one class while all other golfers were in another, Darwin wrote. It was enough to prompt Darwin to intently study Hogan's mannerisms. He noted that Hogan stood upright with his weight forward on his left foot and his right foot drawn back. Hogan held his hands high, Darwin wrote, the right hand far over and the right wrist nearly arched. He found Hogan's swing to be "rhythmic and easy" and not as long as Darwin had expected from seeing photographs. The impressive part of Hogan's swing, he thought, was that the clubhead traveled with such speed that it seemed to go through the ball.

Darwin was most impressed with Hogan's long-iron play, which he called "appallingly straight." When Hogan's drives to the green were eight or nine yards right or left of the pin, someone in the crowd would jokingly remark,

"He'd dreadfully crooked, isn't he?" Darwin smiled at the remark and said that yes, eight or nine yards was crooked—for Hogan.

Following his clutch birdie Hogan heard that de Vicenzo was one over par heading into the back nine. Hogan followed his tournament-turning birdie on number five with another birdie on six, this coming on what Williamson recalls as "an amazing 300-yard drive" down the thin strip of fairway now known as "Hogan's Alley." It is one of several "Hogan's Alleys" in golf, joining Riviera Country Club and Colonial Country Club. Brits claimed that Hogan's aggressive shot-making on number six was so accurate that his placements in the afternoon round landed in the same divots as they had in the morning. "To stand up on that par 5 and put the ball down between the out of bounds and the bunker was pretty remarkable," Bruce Devlin says.

Stennett has played Carnoustie and finds it amazing that Hogan was able in each of the four rounds to take the tight driving line between the bunkers and out of bounds left of the hole. "That hole on No. 6, the hole they named after him, the out of bounds on the left is so close to the fairway, it is *right there* against the fairway," says Stennett. "The fact that you're in a national championship and you've got a crosswind left to right and you have enough confidence in your swing to knock the ball out of bounds for four straight rounds knowing the wind was going to blow it back in, and to do that under pressure is pretty amazing. Nobody did that in that tournament but him."

The *Herald* reported that Hogan "cracked two mighty shots within 10 yards of the green at the 567-yard sixth and ran up to his 'dead' distance of a yard." Alliss remembered them as "two huge woods." Williamson recalls that Hogan skillfully "played his ball between the out of bounds fence on the left and the bunker right, a gap of about 20 yards."

Hogan shot par on numbers seven, eight, and nine, made the turn with a 34 and learned that Stranahan had shot 69 following an eagle on eighteen and was in at 286. Rees and Peter Thomson had good final rounds as well, each posting a 71 to forge a four-way tie at 286. De Vicenzo was in the process of negotiating the tough finishing holes.

Because golf is a sport without a clock, it is timeless. Drama and tension build slowly but inexorably, ratcheting up as shots are strategically placed to overcome odds and obstacles—bunkers, traps, and hazards—present on every hole.

Alliss recalled Hogan being followed by a "horde of thousands who wanted to seize the chance of watching the great American." He thought that as Hogan reached the turn, it was obvious that playing par the rest of the way was all he needed to do to win.

Eager to avoid a thirty-six-hole playoff that might have proved too much for him considering his condition, Hogan's concern was maintaining his steady play and following the progress of Cerda. Turning up his intensity, Hogan flashed the form that Brits had read about. He avoided potential disaster on number ten, his tunnel vision being momentarily distracted by a large black dog wandering ten yards in front of him as he teed off. He thought his drive missed the meandering mongrel by two inches. Had his ball not missed, Hogan feared it would have killed the dog.

Cigarette smoke swirled amid the salty sea breeze as Hogan scored a four on ten, then matched it on eleven and twelve. An indication of how much winning this British Open meant to Hogan can be found in AP photographs of the normally reserved American using body English to coax in his putts. The AP stated that Hogan "managed to sink a few of the putts which had failed to drop for him all week long. As usual, his game from tee to green was immaculate." Hogan hit a five-iron to the green on number thirteen and holed a twelve-foot putt for a birdie deuce and a two-shot lead. The UPI wrote that through the stretch drive Hogan "ignored chills, influenza, and aches from old injuries received in a 1949 auto accident" in his push to capture the coveted championship.

Ward-Thomas thought Hogan's "ruthless progression" was fully underway. Darwin agreed and believed Hogan to be in "an unstoppable mood."

Hogan's bold play prompted Nelson to state that he knew his old friend and rival had his heart set on winning at Carnoustie, and Hogan would tell Jim Trinkle of the *Fort Worth Star-Telegram* years later that his British Open performance provided the greatest pleasure of his long career. Other tournament victories were pleasurable, Hogan said then, but none gave him the will to excel that he had at Carnoustie.

Hogan's domination of Carnoustie stunned Scots who considered their course indomitable. British golf writer Henry Longhurst, however, recalled watching Hogan up close and being impressed by how he took apart a course. "In one tournament he stood pondering over a shot, cigarette midway between thin pursed lips," wrote Longhurst. "Then he flipped the cigarette to the ground, coldly drew out a club . . . and hit the ball a colossal clout to the middle of the green. He did the same at the next . . . and then, again flipping away the cigarette, whose smoke curled silently up beside him in the still summer afternoon, he hit the ball firmly at the hole. . . . I realized from the moment I set eyes on him it never occurred to me that he wouldn't win."

The *Herald* wrote that Hogan "set his seal on the championship by following a delicate run-up to the twelfth with a 5-yard putt for a 2 at the thirteenth." The report added that Hogan, now in machine-like mode, stumbled briefly "by being short with his second and then with his pitch to the fourteenth but made no repetition of his morning seventeenth-hole lapse."

De Vicenzo was in with a 73 and 287. Cerda stayed close to Hogan for much of the afternoon but went one over when his shot on number twelve found a spectator. An eight-time major winner, Hogan knew number nine was there for the taking.

"I felt for the first time," Hogan said later, "that I had the championship if I didn't do anything foolish." He didn't; the AP reported that "Hogan came home with nothing but pars and birdies." The *Herald* wrote that the championship "to all intents and purposes was Hogan's, and how majestically he finished."

Walking the fifteenth fairway, Hogan recalled Derr's offer to help if needed. He beckoned to Derr to join him inside the protective company of six Scottish policemen who were escorting him through the throng from greens to tees and down the fairway. Derr noticed that the Brits had taken the American champion to heart; some thought the moment of conversion for the Scots occurred as soon as it became clear that their champion, Brown, wasn't going to win. Hogan had willingly signed autographs prior to his first two rounds, but when the Scots began swarming him wherever he went, even if he was walking to his car, he and Derr devised a plan. Hogan would carry his putter in his right hand, his left hand would grip the back of Derr's belt.

Knowing there were way stations where Royal & Ancient officials manned the phones to update the scoring and that Derr had a press badge that allowed him access to the stations, Hogan asked the announcer for his competitors' scores.

"Where does Cerda stand?" Hogan asked. "See if you can find out."

Derr ventured into an R&A tent and relayed to Hogan that Rees, Stranahan, and Peter Thomson had each finished with a 286. Cerda was on thirteen and trailed Hogan by four shots.

"Is he on the tee or green?" Hogan asked.

Derr reported to Hogan that Cerda parred thirteen and remained three under. Hogan nodded, then played his tee shot on sixteen to what Derr estimated was twelve feet below the cup. Hogan sidled over to Derr, lit a cigarette, watched Hector Thomson hit his drive, and turned to Derr.

"John, you can go in and get ready for your broadcast. This tournament is over."

Derr noted that there was no bravado in Hogan's statement but recalled the intensity in Hogan's steel gray stare. Derr wrote years later that Hogan's appraisal of the situation was confident but also "unexpected, uncharacteristic, unmistakable." Derr theorized that the difficulty of the finishing holes, and the improbability of Cerda picking up enough shots to force a playoff, might have sparked Hogan's confident statement.

Punctuating his remark, Hogan birdied sixteen and saved par on seventeen, which was no small task, since as UPI wrote, the hole had "buffaloed" Hogan in the morning round. As was his wont, Hogan got his revenge. He placed his drive in the afternoon round short of the brook, and his approach, wrote UPI, "was dead on the line all the way." The ball rolled to a halt forty feet from the flag. "His bold first putt missed by a few feet," wrote the UPI, "but he got down in four."

Derr said that the stoic, unsmiling Hogan must have been satisfied by his birdie on sixteen but noted "there was no elation in Hogan's demeanor . . . no smile on his tight-lipped face."

Arthur Montford—a Scottish sports journalist who during his career would interview Hogan, Bobby Jones, Arnold Palmer, and Jack Nicklaus—wrote that Hogan was steering his way around the links in beautiful fashion. Montford thought Hogan was matching the occasion with "flawless golf" that reflected "courage and toughness." Montford called Hogan's final round a "shot-making masterclass."

Hogan walked slowly to the eighteenth where an estimated twenty thousand fans awaited him. The crowd was larger than any Hogan had experienced in the United States. Darwin called it "the greatest crowd of spectators" he had seen at a championship. The *Herald* described it as "massed down both sides" of the hole. "The welcome he received on the 18th green," the AP opined, "should be a cure for all his ills."

A weary Hogan acknowledged the great crowd with a smile. He hit poorly across the burn that winds its way through the eighteenth fairway but followed with what was said by an observer to be a perfect iron to the green. When his first putt stopped five feet shy of the hole, an audible gasp came from the crowd that lined both sides of the fairway and stretched far into the distance. Movietone News footage showed a disappointed Hogan put his right hand on his hip as he glared at the missed putt that would have given him a 67. With what one observer described as "meticulous care," Hogan holed his second putt.

Ward-Thomas remembered the scene on eighteen. There was "a great stillness" as Hogan approached the green. Victory was certain, and when Hogan holed his putt, Ward-Thomas wrote that the crowd "thundered its tribute to the evening skies."

Time noted that it wasn't until his final putt found the cup that Hogan relaxed. He doffed his cap and grinned at the gallery. Club in hand, Hector Thomson advanced to congratulate his playing partner. It was said that the great throng cheered so loudly it could be heard in the distant city of Dundee. Hogan acknowledged the cheers by bowing repeatedly to the encircling crowd. Ward-Thomas thought Hogan at that moment looked very much alone, and that even he seemed humbled at having won three major titles in the same summer. Hogan was indeed alone, wrote Ward-Thomas, "on that supreme peak of greatness where, in all the history of golf, only Bobby Jones had stood before him."

Hogan had played true to form, shooting a Carnoustie course record 68 that bettered the mark Cerda set in the morning round and posted a

73-71-70-68 = 282 total that was six under par for the 72 holes. He is one of just four Open champion golfers to better his score in each of his four rounds. One aged Scot who had caddied at Carnoustie for years shook his head in astonishment at Hogan's performance. "It's no' possible," he told Timms, "but it's a fact."

The final round of the British Open marked the third consecutive course record Hogan set in a major that season.

"I never had any thought of a record during the round," Hogan said later, "and I do not play to break records."

Cerda was still on the course, a couple of pairings behind Hogan and owning a slim chance of forging a tie and forcing a playoff.

"Don't even mention the possibility of a playoff," Hogan sighed to reporters. "I don't think I can make it."

He didn't have to. Cerda shot a 71 and tied for second place at 286. Hogan became the sixth man at that point to win the British Open in his first attempt, and he did so by collaring a strong field by four strokes, finishing ahead of an international foursome in Rees (Wales), Stranahan (U.S.), Peter Thomson (Australia), and Cerda (Argentina).

Movietone News called it "a thrilling finish" and showed footage of the "huge gallery" at Carnoustie. Movietone labeled it "Hogan's Open" in honor of "that miracle man, Ben Hogan, of the United States. . . . It certainly was Ben Hogan's Open, no doubt about it. The trophy went to the greatest golfer in the world today."

The awarding of the gleaming Claret Jug, made a century before by Edinburgh silversmiths Mackay, Cunningham & Co., was delayed due to the new champion preferring to appear respectful and properly attired in a jacket. Valerie agreed and believed it improper for Ben to accept the British trophy without wearing a jacket. Gregston wrote that there was another reason for Hogan's attire.

Due to the enormous gallery, Valerie had not been able to see Ben's final shots. What she did see when she got close to him was the fatigue etched deep into the face of her husband. Valerie called for their chauffeur to bring Ben a jacket to warm him. Her concern was not only for the proprieties but also for the health of her husband. He was ashen with exhaustion as he came off the course.

"I'm happy but so very, very tired," Hogan told reporters.

Clutching the coveted Claret Jug presented by Provost M'Laughlan at the direction of H. H. Turcan, chairman of the Royal and Ancient (R&A), Hogan said he didn't go to Carnoustie to take home a trophy. "Whether I won or lost was incidental," he stated. "I came over because a lot of people back home wanted me to, some people over here did, too."

Addressing his fatigue, flu, and old injuries, Hogan said, "I feel happy but not good." He said his return for the following year and Ryder Cup would depend on his health. He praised the British fans. "I think the galleries have been just terrific." He had admonished them earlier in the day when he waved his finger at a group to stop them from talking while he was preparing to putt. His shot fell short, but the incident was glossed over in his moment of triumph.

"Considering the mobs we have had here I cannot imagine their behaving any better," Hogan said. "After all, it is impossible to regiment 20,000 people. You always have rushes for the good positions to see strokes made."

Asked his opinion of Carnoustie, Hogan called the course "extremely tough." Remarking that many shots were blind or semiblind, he said golfers required "radar or something." He brushed off the question of impending retirement.

"I have just got where I started out to get at the age of five," he told reporters. "But I am now over 40 and have a lot of mileage behind me, and everybody has to quit sometime."

Alliss thought Hogan had won the championship in classic fashion, posting four good rounds with each better than the round before. He wrote years later that apart from Arnold Palmer in 1960, no golfer in the long history of the Open has made so great an impact on the British press and public in their initial appearance as Hogan.

Alliss recalled comments at the time stating that Hogan's game "has that stamp of inevitability which is only to be found among a handful of players"; that Hogan was in a class by himself, a "small colossus" who "bestrode and dominated the tournament" and left observers "overawed and abashed by the splendour of his game."

The AP lauded Hogan's triumph as one for the ages. "The final 68 was superb, sprinkled with perfection." It completed a career slam of the four majors and gave Hogan golf's "Triple Crown"—the Masters, U.S. Open, and British Open—to make him the first man to win those three championships in the same season.

"That is as close as a professional can get to the 'Impossible Quadruple' that Bobby Jones won in 1930—the U.S. Open and Amateur and the British Open the Amateur. The Masters was not in existence then," the AP stated.

The Hogan Slam, as it's now called, quieted his critics who said he couldn't adapt his game to win outside of the United States.

"This was Hogan's first British Open attempt," wrote the AP, "and his success ends abruptly the taunts and jeers that have followed the little man that 'you can't play that other kind of golf'—the Scottish kind in the wild-sea winds, sleet, and rain."

The UK media also heralded Hogan's victory. Pennink called the adage that "One cannot win without luck" an "obsolete observation" when Hogan was playing. Pennink said he would not call the chip shot Hogan holed in the final round or the much-needed two on thirteen "strokes of fortune." He could recall but one stroke of luck, occurring on the final hole of Round One.

Pennink thought the strangest aspects of Hogan's performance were the "weak" finishes of his first three rounds, and that Hogan found the 250-yard sixteenth hole "impossible to hit." Pennink thought the latter may have given Rees, Peter Thomson, Stranahan, and Cerda cause to hope that Hogan would again falter in the final round. Pennink, however, believed Hogan would make "quite certain not to fall into his previous errors, and so it proved."

Ward-Thomas called Hogan's final round on that gray afternoon "one of the finest ever played in an Open Championship." He noted that while much was made of Hogan's good fortune in holing a chip after missing the fifth green, it was the lone break he received in the entire tournament, which did not see him hole even one long putt over the four rounds. He carded nine fours and three threes on his first twelve holes of the final round.

London's *Daily Express* called it "The Hogan Open, the greatest open in modern times." The *Glasgow Herald* headed its report with the following:

"Timing is all important in golf. All good golfers have it in the execution of their strokes, but only the great can time their supreme effort with the same perfection. Ben Hogan, the greatest golfer who has played in this country since Bobby Jones himself, did just that here today when with final rounds of 70 and 68 he won the Open Championship at the first attempt."

The *Herald* stated that Hogan "more than lived up to his American reputations as 'Mr. Golf' and 'Little Ice Water' and he won the admiration and praise of the most educated golf audience in the world by his deportment and play." It added that the R&A "owe Hogan a hearty vote of thanks. His presence has attracted the largest crowds that one has seen at a championship."

"Hail the greatest golfer of our time," declared Morris Peden in the London *Daily Herald*. "And who," asked Leonard Crawley in London's *Daily Telegraph*, "shall say he's not the best of all time?"

10

Canyon of Heroes

Holding the Claret Jug and awarded a gold medal, the latter a tradition that began in 1872, Ben Hogan told the huge gathering of fans at The Open Championship that he hoped to return to the United Kingdom to defend his newly won title. United Press International quoted Hogan as stating, "I'll be back, perhaps next year. I have no thoughts of retiring."

As promised, he joined John Derr in the Starter's Box, a small building by the first tee that British technicians had converted into a studio. Hogan gave Derr's radio audience a hole-by-hole description of his final round, which clubs he used, the length of his putts, and so on. Derr noticed during their broadcast that Valerie was standing in the rain, so he left Hogan's side to invite her into their small studio. Not wanting special consideration, even if it meant getting out of the rain, Valerie politely declined. Derr then realized he had left Hogan alone in front of the microphone as he was describing his play. Rushing back inside the studio, he heard Hogan calmly continuing his recount. "Well, John, on the 8th, I put the ball down the right."

Derr wrote later that the British press fumed that Hogan, after signing his card, spent time with him before meeting with them. Hogan had one more gift for Derr. He told him that Cecil Timms had in his pocket the ball from the winning putt for Derr to give to Joe Dey for the USGA museum. When Derr found Timms, Cecil presented him with the ball and then took from his pocket another ball. "This is the ball we holed for a birdie deuce at the 13th hole," Timms told Derr. "Mr. Hogan told me to save it. He said Mr. Derr might want it for a souvenir. That was our only deuce the last round."

Studying the English-size Titleist No. 2, Derr was moved as he thought of the caring, sentimental side of Hogan that went largely unknown except to his inner circle. Hogan had one final task before departing Carnoustie. His legs had swelled up so badly during the tournament that he needed to soak in the tub in his room for hours just so he could compete in the next round. Grateful for the accommodation, he wanted to show his appreciation to the staff. "Mr. Hogan returned to the Inn where he stayed and met with each member of the staff and shook hands and thanked them," Robert Stennett says.

At the day's end, Pat Ward-Thomas returned to Carnoustie after dinner. The tournament was over, and he noted a gray, northern twilight settling over the links. The stations stood empty and silhouetted against the darkening skies, they looked to Ward-Thomas like "ghosts of a tumultuous day." He saw confetti carried by the night wind, and colored lights shining from the empty Starter's Box where Hogan and Derr had done their radio interview hours earlier.

In his mind's eye, Ward-Thomas could still see Hogan on the Carnoustie course. There was, he thought, "an unusual fascination about the man." Hogan, Derr wrote, "had a rare quality of stillness, and an impassivity which was almost oriental, as he studied his shots. One was aware of a cold force being generated within and also of an acute golfing brain."

There would always remain in the mind of Ward-Thomas an indelible image of Hogan, "standing motionless on a fairway, arms folded or resting lightly on his hips, the wide mouth drawn down into a thin line, with a cigarette often between his lips, and the eyes, bleak as an Arctic dawn, piercing the distance as if to shrivel the hole into submission."

Alone on the Carnoustie course in the dark of night, Ward-Thomas thought how Hogan earlier that day had joined the immortals of golf. He pondered Hogan's impact on golf history, and decades later, in 2023, Trevor Williamson spoke of Hogan's long-standing impact on the Scots. "It didn't matter how grumpy you were, or if you didn't chat with the crowd or sign autographs," Williamson says. "If you came to play golf that indeed might mean you are the best golfer ever, then you will win the hearts of this very critical audience. And that is exactly what Ben Hogan did."

Derr thought Hogan a colossal at Carnoustie. Bernard Darwin agreed and wrote that once Hogan became familiar with the erratic weather, small

British ball, and Carnoustie's slower greens, his scores improved with each round. Watching him play, Darwin got the feeling Hogan could score what was needed to take the title. "He had the game to do it," Darwin wrote.

As Ben and Valerie prepared for a well-earned week's vacation in Paris and then a leisurely return to the New World on the ss *United States*, plaudits poured in praising his historic accomplishment.

"Wonderful, simply wonderful," said Bobby Jones, the only man at the time to have achieved a Slam comparable to Hogan's. "I'm delighted that Ben won it." Noting the nefarious weather, the pressure of Hogan playing in his first British Open, and being an American playing on soil foreign to him, Jones stated that "under the conditions, it was a wonderful accomplishment."

Byron Nelson played up Hogan's course record at rugged Carnoustie. "He's eight strokes better than anyone else who ever played it over 72 holes," Nelson told reporters. "I knew he had his heart set on winning it and I'm glad he did." Former British Walker Cup star Leonard Crawley said Hogan's final round at Carnoustie proved that he had "the indefinable quality of being able to bring himself to his peak when the pressure is the greatest."

London *Daily Mail* writer Fred Pignon joined Crawley in placing Hogan's victory in historical context. Pignon had seen firsthand all of golf's greats dating back to Francis Ouimet and believed Hogan to be "the greatest golfer America has ever sent to our country. It's indisputable that he's the best. Not only does he possess skill to make a shot with a minimum of error, but he also has mental command, mental control, under stress where most golfers of equal skill do not." Pignon stated that while the odds against any golfer getting down from the fringe of the green in two might be ten to one, the odds were ten to one that Hogan would get down in "one-and-a-half, if he has to do it."

Like Pignon, Sir Guy Campbell followed each of Hogan's four rounds at Carnoustie and came away convinced that of all the great golfers he had seen firsthand, Hogan was the most accomplished and versatile. He thought Hogan's knowledge of the game encyclopedic and that there was not a single shot he could not master. The trajectory of his strokes, be it high, low, or in-between, was a matter of choice for Hogan, Campbell wrote. Hogan's judgment of topography was uncanny, said Campbell, leading to an unhurried glance and the correct club taken and the right shot played.

Only once did Campbell see Hogan err in his shot attempt, this coming on the seventeenth hole in Round Three when his second shot missed by inches and caught a sandy bunker. Otherwise, Campbell wrote, when Hogan needed an accurate shot, he could pinpoint his placement. He supplied power when needed, his drives rolling to a stop at what Campbell called "the strategic point from where the final attack can be launched and consummated." Vivid examples of this, he added, could be found on the second and sixth holes of the final round.

Campbell felt that only on Carnoustie's greens did Hogan's game fall short of expectations. Had Hogan not struggled with the slow greens, Campbell believed the champion's four rounds might have read 69, 68, 67, and 66. "Anyhow, and in all circumstances," Campbell finalized, "here is surely the bravest single adventure in the annals of our or any Open. So from one old golfer, at least, salute to that adventure and the man who made it."

Herbert Warren Wind saluted Hogan as well and said it was difficult to imagine a victory that could have been more complete. Wind wrote that Hogan's conquest had barely been over when it was already becoming legend. The facts surrounding Hogan's triumph—his first British Open, his arrival on soil strange to him, his cold completion of his task, and his sudden departure—seemed to Wind to be "sealed off from all other events, suspended as it were, in a separate and somehow unreal land of its own."

If one had not known there had been a British Open played in 1953, Wind wrote, one might have thought that the story was the "concoction of a garret-bound author of inspiration books for children who had dreamed up a golfing hero and a golfing tale which he hoped might catch on as had the exploits of Frank and Dick Merriwell in the days before golf was considered the proper vehicle for the dreams of glory of the red-blooded American boy."

There were several twists to the story involving the Hogans' departure. The day following his victory at Carnoustie, Hogan was driven to Leuchars airfield, where a U.S. Air Force plane was waiting to fly him to Paris to participate in a golf exhibition for the army. Williamson remembers the departure from Carnoustie being "a bit of a problem" for the Hogans.

"The plan was to travel by car to the ferry port in Dundee, take the ferry boat over the River Tay, travel on to the Leuchars Air Base, from there the Hogans would get a U.S. Air Force plane to Paris where Ben was to give a golf exhibition for U.S. soldiers stationed there," says Williamson. "When the car arrived at the ferry, they found themselves at the tail end of a long queue. This was due to the fact that the vessel, the *Abercraig*, had been withdrawn with engine failure. The attempts made to get the Hogans priority failed, there was to be priority for ambulances only. Hogan said, 'I don't want any priority. I just want to get on!' But to no avail. So the decision was made to take the long way round, going by Newburgh near Perth. One can only imagine what the reaction was when Mr. Henderson had to tell Ben that the ferry journey would have been six miles, but the round trip was to be 48 miles."

As Leuchars is but five miles from historic St. Andrews, it was thought by some that Hogan would travel the short distance to pay his respect to the legendary course. Instead, Hogan stayed away from St. Andrews, making him one of the few great golfers to have not seen his sport's ancestral home.

Nelson thought it "a strange decision" by Hogan but figured seeing St. Andrews just wasn't high on Hogan's priority list. Snead saw it as just a matter of Hogan being Hogan. Dave Anderson wrote that Hogan once explained his decision not to see St. Andrews.

"I didn't have time," Hogan said. "I was there for one purpose."

As it was, Hogan would return just once more to Britain to play, pairing with Snead at Wentworth Club in Surrey, England, to claim victory for the United States in the Canada Cup. Not surprisingly, Hogan won the individual title.

Hogan was gone from the UK, but his impact on Carnoustie continued. Williamson recalls the champion's famous flat cap starting a craze in Carnoustie. "Flat caps had been around for a long time, but this was a special one, and a lot of golfers wanted one," Williamson says. "I was witness to a great story regarding one of these hats. In my family's golf shop, Simpsons, my uncle had bought several of these caps in different sizes. They sold in the shop for 10/6d in old British money; today that would be 12.5p. The ones in the shop bore the Spalding Golf Company name. One of these caps never sold, it remained on the shelf where the headwear was. Years later in the late 1970s an American visitor spotted the single Hogan cap; he said he had been after one for years. He was told the story of how it had been there since the Open of 1953. He asked how much it was, we said we would sell it to him at the price shown on the original ticket. It was a fine moment."

Among the many congratulatory messages and telegrams Hogan received following the British Open, one stood out. It was from his friend and occasional golf student, U.S. president Dwight D. Eisenhower: "We are proud of you not only as a great competitor and as a master of your craft, but also as an envoy extraordinary in the business of building friendship for America," Eisenhower wrote. "Best wishes to you and Mrs. Hogan."

Planned for Hogan's return was a ticker-tape parade in New York City's "Canyon of Heroes." It would be the first such parade for a sports figure since 1930, when Jones was feted in similar fashion upon returning from England. Ben was worn thin from his high-stress competition and Valerie was tired as well from their long trip when the ss *United States* docked in New York Harbor at 5:30 a.m. on Tuesday, July 21.

Some fifty members of the media were waiting in the ship's salon, having been carried on a Coast Guard cutter from Pier Nine. Ben and Valerie engaged the reporters and photographers in small talk and were pleased to learn that their drought-ridden home area of Fort Worth had finally been receiving rain.

After the ocean liner was nudged by tugs into the harbor, Ben and Valerie posed for photos outside the salon on the sports deck and answered questions for print and newsreel reporters. As the ship passed the Statue of Liberty, boats and vessels, including those from the New York Police Department and Fire Department, sounded their horns. "I can't imagine people getting up so early to do this for us," Hogan told the press. "People are wonderful." Banners proclaiming "Welcome Hogan" adorned the West 46th Street pier.

Valerie told reporters her husband was "thoroughly exhausted." She said she preferred he not pursue more championships if it meant working as hard as he had to achieve his Triple Crown. "I would rather he started playing golf for fun," she said.

Hogan spoke of his plans to start his own company manufacturing golf clubs and that he would be active in its management. He emphasized that his new business would not interfere with his golf game. "I play golf because I like it and any time I enter a tournament I try to win," he told reporters. "But so far as trying to beat someone's record, I don't go for that. Sure, anyone would like to win five U.S. Opens, or one (British) Open. I'd like to win a fifth Open; I'd like to win 10 of them."

As the Hogans embarked on a twenty-five-mile ride around New York, fifty motorcycle policemen escorted their two open-top limousines. In back were Troop A and Troop B of the Mounted Squad of Police along with the fire department band and color guard. Thousands of fans lining the route greeted the conquering hero with cheers of "Hi, Champ!"

Sitting atop the rear seat, Hogan acknowledged them with alternate waves of his hands. The parade stretched from the Battery to the steps of City Hall and was estimated to include 150,000 fans, with thousands more leaning from office windows in high-rise buildings. Amid what lyricist Vernon Duke once referred to as New York City's "glittering crowds and shimmering clouds," confetti cascaded down from the canyons of steel.

At City Hall, Hogan received a citation from Mayor Vincent R. Impellitteri for being a champion whose "achievements as an outstanding sportsman are an inspiration to the youth of the nation." His Honor paraphrased former NYC mayor James J. Walker's remark to Jones: "Here you are, the greatest golfer in the world, being introduced by the worst one." To Hogan, Impellitteri said, "Here you are, the world's greatest golfer and I am probably the worst."

Impellitteri read a message from Ike, then stated that "More than the eyes of Texas were upon you in the British Open. We watched with devotion and excitement." The mayor said Hogan had set up three marks for others to take aim at—"a mark of ability, a mark of personality, and a mark of sportsmanship."

Gene Gregston thought the "Wee Ice Mon," as Hogan was called at Carnoustie, "melted visibly under the warmth of the welcome." The man Henry Longhurst called the hard case from Texas suddenly had his voice cracking and quivering with emotion. "This is the hardest course I've ever played," Hogan told New Yorkers. "I'm so grateful that I can't explain it in words. This sort of thing brings tears to my eyes. I have a tough skin but a soft spot in my heart and things like this find that soft spot. This tops anything I've ever received. I don't think anything can surpass what's happening now."

Anything almost did. It was announced that Hogan became the thirteenth player and first of his era to be selected for the PGA Hall of Fame. On
Wednesday, their second night in New York, Ben and Valerie told stories
of their experiences at Carnoustie. "Over there, the caddies drop the bags
on the greens when you get ready to putt and when the hole is finished the
people just walk right across the greens," Hogan told his audience. "Kids
and dogs, they let everybody and anything on the course; more dogs than
you ever saw."

Hogan saw women at Carnoustie carrying small children in their
arms for the length of the course, and ladies with babies would push bug-
gies for eighteen holes. People brought their lunch, he said later, and stayed
at the Carnoustie course the entire day. Ben and Valerie were impressed
by the friendliness and devotion to golf displayed by the Scottish people.
The galleries at Carnoustie were thought by the Hogans to be among the
most knowledgeable and polite they had ever known.

Hogan remembered that his mother, Clara, had not wanted him to go to
Scotland because she feared for his health. He did catch a cold and suffered
from influenza but said his health issues had something to do with having
turned forty the previous August. "I wake up every morning with a new ailment," he told acquaintances. He complained to Toots Shor about his aches
and pains, and the restaurateur remarked that only one word was needed to
explain Hogan's ailments. "Age," Shor said.

Advancing age, physical pain, extended travel, the fact that he had
won the tournament, and the lack of financial incentive—his purse for winning the British Open amounted to $1,400—were all contributing factors
to Hogan never returning to the UK to defend his title. In a large sense, it
didn't matter. His electric performance—shooting 73-71-70-68 in descending
order—silenced critics who said he could not win the British Open. He
remains just one of four Open champions to improve his score each round.
Longhurst said later that if there had been a fifth round, Hogan would have
shot 66, and if there had been a sixth round, he would have shot 64. As it
was, Longhurst wrote, Hogan won by four shots and then he was gone.

In Hogan's absence the following year, young Australian Peter Thomson,
who tied Antonio Cerda, Dai Rees, and Frank Stranahan for second place

four shots behind the winning score, won the British Open. Thomson's caddie in 1954 was none other than Timms. Thomson would win three straight British Opens and four of the next five.

Hogan's accomplishment in 1953 inspired a new generation of American golfers to make the trip to the UK to compete for the British title. It was an idea that had fallen out of favor, Sam Snead setting a trend when he declined to defend his title after winning at St. Andrews in 1946. Hogan's win was only the second for an American in the British Open since Snead a decade earlier, and just the third dating to Denny Shute in 1933 at St. Andrews. Shute's victory capped a run of eight straight victories by Americans in The Open Championship. From 1921 to 1933, U.S. golfers claimed eleven of thirteen British Open titles.

Hogan helped make American participation popular again, and in 1960 Arnold Palmer followed Hogan's example and headed across the Atlantic as an American champion looking to conquer the British Open. Palmer failed in his bid to bring back the British crown, losing by one stroke to Kell Nagle. One year later, Arnie was back in the UK and became the first American to win the Open since Hogan in 1953, outdueling Ben's old opponent, Rees, by one stroke at Royal Birkdale. Palmer returned in 1962 and beat Nagle by six strokes to become America's first repeat champion since Walter Hagen in 1928 and '29.

Jack Nicklaus won his first British Open in 1966 at Muirfield, and four years later his victory at St. Andrews began a new run of American dominance as U.S. golfers claimed four consecutive titles and eight of the next nine.

Hogan at Carnoustie became the first man in history to win three major championships in a single year, setting a standard that generations of golfers sought to match. It wasn't until 2000 that Tiger Woods tied Hogan by claiming his Triple Crown, and then in 2001 he created the "Tiger Slam" that saw Woods holding all four major trophies at the same time.

Since then, comparisons have been raised regarding the "Jones Slam," the "Hogan Slam," and the "Tiger Slam." Which of these ranks as the grandest slam remains open to debate.

Epilogue

The Grandest Slam: Jones vs. Hogan vs. Tiger

Asked once if he could have beaten Ben Hogan, Bobby Jones considered the question. "I don't know," he said. "I never played him." Jones and Hogan actually met in major competition eight times, all in the Masters, the only tournament Bobby played after retiring following his Grand Slam in 1930. Jones and Hogan played in the same Masters from 1938 to '42 and 1946 to '48.

That Hogan and Jones never met in competition in their respective primes didn't stop historians and writers from comparing two of golf's greatest legends following Hogan's "Triple Crown" campaign in 1953.

The Associated Press led its coverage by stating that the momentous victory allowed Hogan to "take his place forever beside Bobby Jones at the summit of all golf." United Press International stated that Hogan "proved to the British he belongs in the same class as the never-to-be-forgotten Jones." The *Glasgow Herald* noted in its coverage of Hogan's victory at Carnoustie, "There will be arguments about the respective merits of Hogan and Jones, but at least the Texan can claim that not even Jones won [the British Open] at the first time of asking."

The *Herald* stated that what captured the public's imagination regarding Hogan was the "amazing recovery he made from injuries which were thought to have ended his career just over four years ago." Not only did the debilitating injuries not end Hogan's career, but they also spurred him on to greater glory. "Since then," the *Herald* said, "he has won the American Open championship three times, the last time this year, and his victory here makes him without question the greatest golfer of his day and age."

Jack Allen, Jones's caddie in the 1926 British Open at Royal Lytham & St. Annes Golf Club, thought Hogan was better than Bobby. "Ben Hogan," the fifty-two-year-old Allen told the Associated Press at Carnoustie, "is the greatest golfer the world has ever seen."

Described by the AP as a man who had spent forty years staring down fairways, Allen watched Hogan do the unthinkable and dissect Carnoustie. It impressed Allen enough that he declared Hogan "almost too perfect—like a machine."

Allen himself had been described as "the perfect caddie," and while he did carry bags at Carnoustie in 1953, he was tasked with gathering scores from outlying greens. Past British Opens had seen Allen caddie for Jones, Walter Hagen, and Macdonald Smith, as well as serve as a personal caddie to the Duke of Windsor when he was Prince of Wales. "I've seen almost all of the great ones in my time," Allen told the AP. "I have formed the impression that Hogan is the greatest ever. While Jones and Hagen were golfers, this Ben Hogan is a golfing machine. . . . To win the British Open at the first attempt on a course like Carnoustie proves Hogan's greatness. I take my hat off to him as golfer Number One."

Frank Pennink said Hogan's feat was not of a generation or an age, but an Aeon. "Ben Hogan and Bobby Jones now sit together on twin thrones," Pennink wrote. "Thither they ascended by diverse achievements equivalent in scale. Who can say that they will not remain seated forever, inviolate, and unassailable?"

Jones showed respect for Hogan by flying to New York City for the United States Golf Association dinner, held in the banquet room of the Park Lane Hotel. Hogan appreciated Jones's gesture, particularly since Bobby by this time was suffering from syringomyelia, a degenerative spinal disease. He also appreciated Jones's comments to the large dinner crowd. "I am not one who believes my era was the greatest necessarily because I lived in it," Jones told the gathering. "People today run faster, jump higher, and run farther and it's only natural that they play golf better. Ben has proved pretty well that they can."

Jones remarked that precision play is not all that makes a champion. The person who works the hardest, he said, is the one who wins championships. "Ben, with the game he has, will keep winning championships as long as he wants to win badly enough," Jones remarked.

Jones was one of several former golf champions who made the trip to honor Hogan. The former U.S. Open champion, Francis Ouimet, who won the title in 1913, was in attendance, as was the 1908 champion Fred McLeod. Addressing the fact that the 140-pound Hogan was called "Bantam Ben," McLeod told attendees he weighed 108 pounds "soaking wet" when he won the U.S. Open. "How do you think I feel," he asked his audience, "when they call this guy Bantam Ben?"

Hogan laughed along with the rest of the crowd, sport's little big man enjoying the company of friends and fellow golfing greats at the celebratory dinner. He had earned the right to relax, having won a Triple Slam. His lone appearance in the world's oldest golf major was already taking on a mystique, providing as it did a fitting climax to a historic campaign and one of the most dominant years in the history of sport. He had played three majors on three of the most challenging courses in the world, won all three by a combined fifteen strokes, and set course records on each.

Had he been healthy enough to compete in the PGA Championship, which he won in 1946 and again in '48, and had the tournament not overlapped with the British Open, Hogan might have equaled Jones's historic achievement from the summer of 1930. In four months, Jones claimed the British Amateur Championship, British Open, U.S. Open, and U.S. Amateur Championship. Jones's accomplishment was unprecedented, and fans and media struggled mightily with a way to define it.

O. B. Keeler, called by the New York Times the dean of American golf writers and often referred to as Jones's "Boswell," borrowed a bridge term and called the four titles the "Grand Slam." George Trevor of the New York *Sun* said Jones crashed the "impregnable quadrilateral" of golf. "Atlanta's first citizen, like Napoleon before him, has stormed the supposedly impregnable 'quadrilateral,'" Trevor wrote. "Bob is the first golfer in all history to win the four major championships—American open, American amateur, British open and finally the British amateur."

Keeler wrote in a similar vein. "This victory, the fourth major title in the same season and in the space of four months, had now and for all time entrenched Bobby Jones safely within the 'Impregnable Quadrilateral of

Golf,' that granite fortress that he alone could take by escalade, and that others may attack in vain, forever," said Keeler.

Tiger Woods joined the conversation in August 2000, when he beat Bob May by one stroke in a three-hole playoff to win the PGA Championship at Valhalla Golf Club in Louisville, Kentucky. Tiger was just twenty-four years old when he equaled the Triple Slam the forty-year-old Hogan had achieved forty-seven summers earlier. Amid sun-streaked conditions and warm Kentucky climes, Woods worked overtime to win the playoff and become the only professional golfer other than Hogan to win three majors in the same year.

Woods's victory was historic for several reasons. Like Hogan, Tiger had won three straight majors and posted a tournament scoring mark each time. He recorded scores below par in his final fourteen rounds of major tournament competition, posting a scoring average of 67.7.

Woods forced the playoff with May with a pressure putt on the final hole from five feet out. It capped a round that saw Tiger fire five-under 67 with birdies on four of his final six holes. At round's end, Woods and May became the only golfers in the history of the PGA Championship to finish at eighteen under par. Tiger closed the show with a birdie and two pars in the three-hole playoff. By day's end, he held the scoring records in each of the four majors—Masters (eighteen-under 270), U.S. Open (twelve-under 272), and British Open (nineteen-under 269). By winning his fifth playoff in six attempts, Tiger denied May pulling off a stunning upset similar to Jack Fleck's shocker against Hogan in the 1955 U.S. Open at the Olympic Club in San Francisco.

Tom Watson said at the time that Woods's accomplishments were unprecedented and that Tiger was a phenomenon whose like had not been seen before and might not be seen again. Comparisons between Tiger and the Hawk at the time showed that Hogan's Triple Crown victories in '53 did not include a seventy-two-hole score lower than the 274 he posted at Augusta. At the same time, Hogan finished first in five of the six tournaments he competed in that year. Dave Anderson wrote in 2000 that fans were forgetting that Hogan had completed a Triple Crown and that his year "might have been even better than Tiger's year."

Dan Jenkins considered the Triple Crown years of Hogan and Woods equal. He said Jones's Grand Slam and Byron Nelson's eleven consecutive wins in 1945 were golf's two other legendary seasons. It's a toss-up among those four seasons as to which is the greatest, Jenkins stated then, adding that what Tiger accomplished in 2000 ranks "as one of the greatest four years in golf history."

Woods told reporters at the time that joining Hogan as a Triple Crown winner made for "a special day"—special since Woods and Hogan had spoken to one another by phone for the only time three years earlier just months prior to Hogan's passing. What also made it special was Tiger becoming the first golfer since Hogan in 1948 to win six straight PGA Tour events, and joining Hogan, Gene Sarazen, Jack Nicklaus, and Gary Player as golfers who completed a career Grand Slam. At the time of their career Slam victories, Woods was the youngest member of the group, Hogan the oldest. Nicklaus was twenty-six years old, Player twenty-nine, and Sarazen thirty-three.

"I have a lot of admiration for a lot of great champions that have played the game," Woods stated then. "Ben Hogan won so many tournaments, it's scary. He was incredible. He played at a level that not too many players could ever attain."

The following spring, Woods won his second Masters title. Following an opening-round 70, Tiger shot three straight rounds in the 60s and finished at sixteen under to become the first man to hold all four major trophies concurrently. Woods's achievement was called the Tiger Slam. "What it's called is irrelevant," Nicklaus said at the time. "What he's done is what matters most, and what he's done is unbelievable. I call it the most remarkable feat I have ever seen or heard of in golf."

Hogan supporters note that he remains the only man to win the Masters, U.S. Open, and British Open in the same calendar year, the first American-born golfer to win at Carnoustie, and that his accomplishments in '53 came in the wake of his crushing car crash. He was the miracle man of his era, even more so than Tiger would be following his comeback from an auto accident. That Hogan would win six of his eventual nine majors after his accident prompted Henry Longhurst to write how strange it was that the toughest person he ever met was "connected not with wartime deeds of violence and daring . . . but with the sedate, pedestrian game of golf."

Hogan's mental and physical toughness was revered by his contemporaries and by those who followed. When Woods battled back from his own auto accident in February 2021, he invoked the memory of Hogan's comeback. "Tiger keeps referring to Mr. Hogan whenever he's talking about his injury and his comeback," Robert Stennett says. "He's always referencing Hogan. Whenever they'd ask him when he came back initially if that was the greatest comeback, Tiger would say, 'No. It was Hogan.'" Stennett agrees, citing how much more serious Hogan's injuries were than Tiger's. "Hogan came back, really, with no legs," Stennett says.

Hogan's physical problems are a reason why some rank his Triple Slam season as a greater accomplishment than Jones's Grand Slam and the Tiger Slam. Randy Jacobs recalls how Hogan dealt with his challenges:

He would have to get up early to soak his legs and wrap them in elastic bandages. Those things would have to be very difficult to deal with and he's trying to play major championship golf. And then he has to go over to Scotland.

With all the balls he had in the air that year, all the physical problems, trying to start the Ben Hogan Golf Company, the travel involved, I'm biased but I have to give the nod to Mr. Hogan. Jones won two amateur events in his Slam. He wasn't playing all professionals, and not to shortchange that because it was a tremendous accomplishment. And of course, Tiger's Slam is over two seasons.

All three are great in their own right, but with all Mr. Hogan was juggling, physically and mentally, it's my favorite. Being a Fort Worth boy, my opinion is certainly prejudiced. In the singleness of purpose Mr. Hogan had to have to deal with all of that, and to be able to compartmentalize those things, it's pretty amazing.

Stennett states it's difficult to compare the three men without accounting for the circumstances that surround their achievements. "It's back to the story of perseverance," says Stennett. "Tiger was healthy when he did the Tiger Slam, and Bobby Jones was healthy [for the Grand Slam]. When Hogan did it, he didn't have legs to walk on. He had his body and legs destroyed and he had to rebuild his swing and he became the greatest ball-striker who ever lived.

"It's hard to compare and I wouldn't want to de-emphasize Tiger's [Slam] at all. It's amazing what he has accomplished and who he has brought to the game and how much he has influenced the game. Bobby Jones has his own legacy of what he did in such a short period of time. But in my mind, it's *how* Hogan did it."

What Hogan did in his Triple Slam season echoes in time. "He played in three majors and won three majors, and played in six tournaments and won five," says Stennett. "That's not a bad percentage."

Like Stennett, Bruce Devlin calls Hogan's Triple Slam "probably the most remarkable golf anyone has ever played. The fact that he was able to get back to the PGA Tour was astounding, really. I think it ranks higher than anyone who's ever played the game, from a year of play standpoint. You can certainly make an argument for them (Jones and Woods). It's hard to evaluate, particularly with what's happened to the game."

Devlin says Hogan's physical condition following his accident is "probably the most significant point when you try to separate his year away from everyone else. You look at Tiger trying to play now with his injury the last couple of years and it's nearly impossible for him."

John Boyette also notes the physical health of Hogan, Jones, and Woods in their Slam seasons. "Hogan was 41 in '53, Bobby Jones was 28 in 1930, and Tiger was 24, 25 in 2000, 2001," Boyette says. "Tiger was a healthy young man. Bobby Jones was a healthy young man, Hogan was a crippled old man, for lack of a better word. As great as Hogan was in '53, think of how much that accident took away from him."

Hogan's victories in the majors in 1953 came on three distinctly different courses, each presenting a challenge unique unto themselves. Stennett knows firsthand Augusta, Oakmont, and Carnoustie, and notes not only that the courses differed from one another but also that Augusta and Oakmont are much different today than when Hogan played them in 1953. "Augusta has changed dramatically," Stennett says. "When Hogan played it, they didn't have a rough. They mowed everything. They've probably added 1,000 yards to their course. I'm sure they've tried to do homage to what Bobby Jones did there, but they've added dramatic length to it. Today, they're trying to overpower Augusta, but in Hogan's day you couldn't."

I think Oakmont still has the same greens. I played it years ago and their claim to fame is that their greens are 80-something years old. In the south, greens have a 20-year life, but Oakmont's are very, very old greens.

Augusta and Oakmont have changed a lot, but Carnoustie hasn't. I went to Carnoustie, and my takeaway is that it was 65 years since Mr. Hogan won there and while they've had other great champions at Carnoustie, everything was all Hogan. He was a rock star.

The caddie master had Hogan's stuff he wanted to show me. They rebuilt the clubhouse and above the fireplace they have one of Mr. Hogan's clubs. They have plaques about Mr. Hogan, and my impression is that 65 years after the fact, how could he still be a rock star here? Shady Oaks and Colonial do a great job celebrating Hogan, as does Riviera and a lot of places, but Carnoustie's probably leading the pack.

Part of the reason for the Scots' long-held high regard for Hogan, Stennett says, has to do with his history-making appearance and performance. "I didn't realize that Carnoustie was kind of falling out of favor in the tournament rotation and probably not going to get another Open and they credit Hogan with putting Carnoustie on the map and keeping it in the rotation for The Open Championship," says Stennett.

Augusta, Oakmont, and Carnoustie share at least one important trait. "The common denominator of those three," states Stennett, "is they are ball-striker's courses that require intelligence and how you manage yourself around the course. They all challenged Mr. Hogan's ball-striking skill."

Challenged, too, the course management strategy that was as crucial to Hogan's success as his skilled shot-making. "Mr. Hogan said anyone can learn to hit a golf ball, but it's how you manage the course," Stennett recalls. "Course management, that's all Hogan."

That her great uncle was able to accomplish all that he did in '53 continues to impress Lisa Scott. "I didn't realize his golf company opened in 1953," she says. "I'm like, 'Are you insane? You had this big year and you open up a company.' His company opened in October, and it was after all the tournaments, but it was still a lot to do. There's the epic story of there being like $100,000 worth of clubs, and he said, 'These aren't right and we're not selling them.' He was always tinkering, trying stuff out. He really worked hard."

Hogan the champion golfer is impressive, and those who knew him are just as impressed with Hogan the person. "My personal opinion about the man is that you wouldn't meet a nicer gentleman," says Devlin.

He was always nice to me and my wife. I have nothing but great words about Ben Hogan as a person. His record as a player speaks for itself and as a man, he was a great guy.

When NBC and Liberty Mutual got together to do the original Legends of Golf Tournament, John Brodie did the play-by-play, and I was the color guy. The producer said to me, "I know you have a great relationship with Ben Hogan. Wouldn't it be nice to have him in the booth with you and John?" I said, "Yeah, that would be a great idea, but I can tell you what he's going to say."

He'd say, "That's wonderful of you to think that I would be a great asset. But this is about the golf tournament, not about me."

That's a perfect example of what Ben Hogan was like.

Scott says that when she was little, she didn't totally understand why so many people were in awe of her uncle. "When I got a little older, I learned some of that, but never from him," she says. "He never talked about himself. I always joke that the good news is, I had private golf lessons from Ben Hogan. The bad news is they were at dinnertime, and we were dressed up and in his study. He was a good person. That's the only side I saw. He was my uncle, but he was more grandfatherly. And he was funny, he had a great sense of humor. I loved visiting with him."

Hogan could be generous with his time and with his finances. Scott recalls him telling her not to worry about the price of her college education. He would pay for it. Jacobs remembers Mr. Hogan paying "very well" for someone to caddie for him or shag golf balls.

"At that time, it was $1.60 an hour to shag, and if you were lucky to shag for him, he would hit balls for 45 minutes to an hour and pay $7, which was well more than you would make on the clock," Jacobs recalls.

Jacobs was a teenager when he knew Hogan, and he recalls how he was around the country club. "A fascinating man in a lot of ways," Jacobs says. "We were acquaintances and I appreciate him more as I age and look back on being able to watch how he approached things. My experience with him was that he was a shy man and a humble man. He didn't try to explain himself, he just tried to do what he thought was right. He had strong opinions, but they were his opinions, and he didn't share them with just anyone who walked up to him. He shared them with his good friends." Jacobs says friends would ask Hogan how his golf game was, and Ben would grumble. "Terrible." Jacobs laughed at the memory.

"If his game wasn't ready to play a U.S. Open, it wasn't up to his standards, and he made no bones about it," he says. "He would have your mouth watering with the quality of his shots, but they weren't up to his standards. If they weren't in the trajectory he was looking for, it didn't matter where they finished in his opinion. He worked on controlling his trajectory because that's how he controlled distance and how you play in the wind. It was either ready to go or it was terrible, in his opinion. There were no in-betweens."

Hogan's dedication to excellence impressed Jacobs, who says he learned lessons from Hogan that extended far beyond golf. "He was a fascinating guy to observe," Jacobs says. "He analyzed something to figure out the best way to do it. Excellence was very much in his makeup; he didn't settle for mediocrity in anything he did. That was very impressive. It's a wonderful example to have when you need it."

Jacobs says there were great lessons to be learned from Hogan. "I feel like I benefitted greatly from seeing how Mr. Hogan did things," says Jacobs. "You don't realize the impact he had on you until you think back. You've watched a guy who wouldn't settle for mediocrity and later in your career you realize, 'You know what, I don't either.' I don't know how many times I've caught myself trying to cut corners because it was late in the day or something. Then I would stop and ask: 'What would that man in the little white cap think?'"

About.com. "1953 U.S. Open. Recap and Scores for the 1953 U.S. Open Golf Tournament." April 24, 2013.

Alliss, Peter. *My Life*. London: Hodder & Stoughton, 2004.

———. *The Open: The British Golf Open Championship since the War*. London: Collins, January 1, 1984.

———. *Peter Alliss's 100 Greatest Golfers*. London: Macdonald, December 31, 1989.

Anderson, Dave. "The Boonkers and Burns of Carnoustie." *New York Times*, July 10, 1975.

Anderson, Dave, with Valerie Hogan. "The Ben Hogan I Knew." *The Man behind the Mystique*. 2nd ed. Greenwich CT: American Golfer, 2002.

Arkush, Michael. "10 Memorable British Opens." *New York Times*, July 14, 2021.

Astor, Gerald. *The PGA World Golf Hall of Fame Book*. New York: Prentice Hall, 1991.

Augusta Chronicle. "Bobby Jones to Build His Ideal Golf Course on Berckmans' Place." July 15, 1931.

———. "It's the Field against Bobby." March 22, 1934.

———. "Year of Failures Led up to Ben Hogan's 1953 Masters Win." November 12, 2020.

Augusta.com. "1952 Masters Leaderboard and Scorecards." Accessed January 11, 2023.

Aultman, Dick, and Bowden, Ken. *The Methods of Golf Masters*. New York: Lyons, 2000.

Barkow, Al. *The Golden Era of Golf*. New York: Thomas Dunne, 2000.

———. *The History of the PGA Tour*. New York: Doubleday, 1989.

Bissell, Kathy. "Looking Back at Ben Hogan's Magical 1953 Run of Three Consecutive Majors." bleacherreport.com, July 13, 2015.

Bohn, Michael K. *Money Golf: 600 Years of Bettin' on Birdies*. Lincoln: University of Nebraska Press, 2008.

Bolt, Tommy. *The Hole Truth: Inside Big-Time, Big-Money Golf*. Lippincott, 1971.

Bonk, Thomas. "The One and Only." *Los Angeles Times*, July 15, 1999.

Boyette, John. "How the Masters Began: Bobby Jones, Cliff Roberts Build Augusta Dream Course, Start Tournament." *Augusta Chronicle*, March 24, 2022.

———. Interview with the author, May 2023.

———. "Jones' New Start Launched New Era." *Augusta Chronicle*, April 6, 2009.

———. "A Look at How the Masters Began." *Augusta Chronicle*, March 18, 2016.

———. "1925 U.S. Amateur: Jones Beats Clubmate for Second Straight Title." *Augusta Chronicle*, March 15, 2016.

Brown, Gwilym S. "A Sweet Win on a Sour Links." *Sports Illustrated*, July 22, 1968.

Brumby, Bob. "The Ben Hogan Story." *Sport Magazine*, December 1953.

Campbell, Guy. "St. Andrews to Carnoustie and Back." *Golf Monthly*, August 1953.

Campbell, Malcolm. *The Scottish Golf Book*. Champaign IL: Sports Publishing, 1999.

Campbell, Malcolm, and George Peper. *True Links: An Illustrated Guide to the Glories of the World's 246 Links Courses*. Artisan Division of Workman Publishing, October 15, 2010.

Carnoustie. "1999 Open Golf Championship Programme." Programme Publications Group, 1999.

Carroll, Steve. "This Club Is Famous for . . . Helping Ben Hogan Win the Open." nationalclubgolfer.com, December 12, 2019.

Carver, Lawton. "Wood Leads, Sam Byrd Second." *St. Petersburg (FL) Times*, April 6, 1941.

Cavagnaro, Bob. "Lloyd Mangrum Captures National Open, Beats Nelson, Ghezzi in 36-Hole Playoff." *Youngstown (OH) Vindicator*, June 17, 1946.

Clark, Michael S. "Frank Sinatra's Visit to Dundee and Carnoustie—an Alternate Mythology." instrumentali.wordpress.com, March 30, 2015.

Corcoran, Michael. "The Forgotten Soldier: Why This U.S. Open Champion Might Be the Best Player You've Never Heard Of." golf.com, June 13, 2021.

Daley, Arthur. "A Peek at the Mechanism." *New York Times*, June 17, 1953.

Darwin, Bernard. *Bernard Darwin on Golf*. UNKNO Publishing, January 1, 2004.

———. *Mostly Golf*. Islay, UK: Ailsa, 1986.

———. "Was There Ever One like It?" *Golf Monthly*, August 1953.

Derr, John. *My Place at the Table*. Old Sport Publishing, January 1, 2010.

Devlin, Bruce. Interview with the author, April 2023.

Diaz, Jaime. *Indomitable Enigma: Ben Hogan. Golf's Greatest Eighteen*. New York: McGraw-Hill, 2003.

Doak, Tom. "The Initiation." *The 1994 U.S. Open Official Magazine*. New York: Times Mirror Magazines, 1994.

———. "Universally Respected, but Not Often Loved." golfpass.com, June 13, 2016.

Dorson, Jill R. "Course at Oakmont Country Club Known for Being Tough—and Quirky." postgame.com, June 16, 2016.

Dulio, Tony. *The United States Open Golf Champions*. Stuart FL: Tony Dulio, 2014.

Earl, David. "The Reputation Maker." *The 1994 U.S. Open Official Magazine*. New York: Times Mirror Magazines, 1994.

Ellis, Havelock. "The War against War." *Atlantic*, June 1911.

Eugene (OR) Register-Guard. "150,000 Welcome Hogan in Ticker-Tape Parade." United Press, July 22, 1953.

———. "Picard Takes Augusta Title." Associated Press, April 5, 1938.

———. "Veteran Gene Sarazen Shoots 66 to Take Lead in Masters." United Press, April 2, 1939.

Fairholm, Sean. "Remembering Golf's Forgotten Man." globalgolfpost.com, November 3, 2020.

Ferguson, Doug. "See Oakmont's Storied U.S. Open History." pga.com, June 11, 2016.

Ferguson, Harry. "Golf's Mr. Cinderella Paces Masters Play." *Pittsburgh Press*, April 5, 1940.

———. "Jimmy Demaret Captures Masters Tournament." *Youngstown (OH) Vindicator*, April 8, 1940.

Fields, Bill. "A Fearsome Threesome." masters.com, April 9, 2022.

Finegan, James W. "Eternal Oakmont." *The 1994 U.S. Open Official Magazine.* New York: Times Mirror Magazines, 1994.

Fitzpatrick, Michael. "Is Bobby Jones' 1930 Grand Slam Season Overrated?" bleacherreport .com, July 24, 2015.

Ford, Bob. "Oakmont Country Club Hole-by-Hole." *The 1994 U.S. Open Official Magazine.* New York: Times Mirror Magazines, 1994.

Fraley, Oscar. "Boros Cops Open Title, Hogan 3rd." *Eugene (OR) Register-Guard*, June 15, 1952.

———. "Nelson, Mangrum, Ghezzi in Tie for National Open Title." *Eugene (OR) Register-Guard*, June 16, 1946.

———. "Steel Nerved Hogan Wins Open." *Victoria (TX) Advocate*, June 14, 1953.

Frost, Mark. *The Grand Slam: Bobby Jones, America, and the Story of Golf.* New York: Hyperion, 2004.

Fullerton, Hugh, Jr. "Clark Wins U.S. Open Qualifier with 138; Field of 157 Starts Play Today." *Youngstown (OH) Vindicator*, June 11, 1953.

Gaffney, Dennis. "Bernard 'Toots' Shor." American Experience, January 2, 2024. pbs.org.

Glasgow Herald Golf Correspondent. "Brown and Rees Leaders after Two Rounds of 'Open.'" *Glasgow Herald*, July 10, 1953.

———. "Hogan May Not Be Back Next Year." *Glasgow Herald*, July 11, 1953.

———. "Hogan Wins 'Open' by Four Strokes." *Glasgow Herald*, July 11, 1953.

———. "Effect of Hogan's Entry on Open." *Glasgow Herald*, July 5, 1953.

———. "Locke Leads Qualifiers for Open Title." *Glasgow Herald*, July 8, 1953.

———. "Open Golf Prize Increase." January 31, 1953.

———. "Stranahan's Great First Round in Open Championship." *Glasgow Herald*, July 9, 1953.

Glenn, Rhonda. "Fownes: The Oakmont Architect." usga.org, February 14, 2015.

Glick, Shav. "Cool Customer." *Los Angeles Times*, June 18, 1998.

Golf Bible. "Frank Stranahan." Golfbible.co.uk, April 28, 2019.

Golfcompendium.com. "Biography of Golfer, PGA Tour Winner Al Besselink." July 2019.

———. "Chick Harbert: PGA Championship Winner, Ryder Cup Captain." May 2022.

———. "Bob Hamilton: PGA Champion, Age-Shooter, Record-Holder." February 2019.

———. "Ky Laffoon Biography." October 2018.

———. "1953 British Open Winner and Scores."

———. "1953 U.S. Open Golf Tournament Winner and Scores." October 2018.

———. "1948 PGA Championship Winner and Scores." December 2018.

———. "Ted Kroll, Biography of the Pro Golfer." April 2020.

Golf Monthly. "Hogan, the Master—Come Over." May 1953.

Golfpass.com. "George Fazio." December 2019.

Goodwin, Stephen. "The Ultimate Darkhorse." *The 1994 U.S. Open Official Magazine.* New York: Times Mirror Magazines, 1994.

Gould, Alan. "Cooper Boosts Lead in Augusta National." *Spartanburg (SC) Herald,* April 5, 1936.

———. "Parks, 26-Year-Old Pittsburgher, New Open Champion." *(Montreal) Gazette,* June 10, 1935.

Greater Utica Sports Hall of Fame. "Ted Kroll." Accessed March 9, 2022. greateruticasports .com.

Gregston, Gene. *Hogan: The Man Who Played for Glory.* Grass Valley CA: Booklegger, 1978.

Grimsley, Will. "Hogan's 139 Leads Open by Two Strokes." *Youngstown (OH) Vindicator,* June 13, 1953.

———. "New York Welcome Thaws Ben Hogan." *Spokane (WA) Spokesman-Review,* July 22, 1953.

Gundelfinger, Phil. "Favorites Advance in PGA Play." *Pittsburgh Post-Gazette,* June 30, 1951.

———. "Harmon Wins Playoff to Capture PGA Medal." *Pittsburgh Post-Gazette,* June 29, 1951.

———. "140 to Tee Off Today in PGA Opening Round." *Pittsburgh Post-Gazette,* June 27, 1951.

———. "Sam Snead—1952 PGA Champion." 60th PGA Championship Tournament Program. Oakmont Country Club, 1978.

———. "Snead Gains Semi-finals in PGA Play." *Pittsburgh Post-Gazette,* July 2, 1951.

———. "Snead Routs Burkemo for Third PGA Title." *Pittsburgh Post-Gazette,* July 4, 1951.

Harrell, Eben. "Golf Is Hell." *Time,* July 11, 2007.

Hawkins, Fred. Interview with the author, June 2012.

Hogan, Jacqueline. Interview with the author, June 2020.

Holien, Ried. "Golf's Toughest Competitor: Lloyd Mangrum." golfnewsmag.com, December 30, 2014.

Huhn, Joe. "Sam Parks, Ted Luther Lead at Oakmont." *Pittsburgh Post-Gazette,* June 6, 1935.

Independent. "Tommy Bolt: Golf Champion Prone to Tantrums." independent.co.uk, September 9, 2008.

Jacobs, Randy. Interview with the author, April 2023.

Jemail, Jimmy. "Who Is the Greater Golfer, Ben Hogan or Sam Snead?" *Sports Illustrated,* April 27, 1959.

Jenkins, Dan. *Fairways and Greens: The Best Golf Writing of Dan Jenkins.* New York: Doubleday, 1994.

———. *Jenkins at the Majors: Sixty Years of the World's Best Golf Writing, from Hogan to Tiger.* New York: Doubleday, 2009.

Jones, Bobby. *Golf Is My Game. Bobby Jones' Own Story: A Dramatic Account of the Grand Slam Year; and a Look at Golf Then and Now.* New York: Doubleday, 1960.

Jones, Robert Trent, Jr., ed. *Great Golf Stories.* New York: Galahad Books, 1982.

Kaufmann, Martin. "A Relentless Beast—Raters Say 'Carnasty' Lives up to Nickname." golfweek.usatoday.com, July 16, 2018.

Kirshner, Alex. "How a Dang Interstate Highway Ended up in the Middle of the U.S. Open." sbnation.com, June 14, 2016.

———. "Oakmont May Be the Toughest U.S. Open Course Ever, but It's Still Fair." sbnation .com, June 15, 2016.

Leivenberg, Richard. "The 10 Most Thrilling Finishes in Masters History." bleacherreport .com, April 8, 2014.

Leominster (MA) Daily Enterprise. "Ben Hogan Wins Masters Golf Tournament." April 13, 1953.

Life Magazine. "Hogan in the Heather." July 20, 1953.

Livingston, Pat. "Oakmont—More Victims Than Winners." 60th PGA Championship Tournament Program. Oakmont Country Club, 1978.

Longhurst, Henry. *The Best of Henry Longhurst.* Golf Digest, 1978.

Lyle, Sandy. *Sandy Lyle Takes You round Carnoustie.* Kingswood UK: Worlds Work; Windmill Press, 1982.

Macklin, Tom. "Looking Back: 'Willie the Wedge' Wins 1938 U.S. Amateur." usga.org, March 22, 2016.

McEwan, Michael. "Hogan, Carnoustie, and the Most Unlikely Open Win of All." bunkered .co.uk, July 16, 2018.

McLemore, Henry. "Burke Shatters Par to Lead Masters." *Pittsburgh Press,* April 1, 1939.

———. "Cooper's Par-Smashing 68 Leads Classy Field in Masters' Golf Tourney." *Pittsburgh Press,* April 3, 1938.

Miamihistory.net. "Hometown Boy Makes Good: Ky Laffoon." December 29, 2017.

Michaux, Scott. "His Tournament." Greensboro.com, April 18, 1998.

Michigan Golf Hall of Fame. "Melvin 'Chick' Harbert." Accessed February 23, 2023. mghof.org.

———. "Walter Burkemo." Accessed March 25, 2023. mghof.org.

Michigan Sports Hall of Fame. "Melvin R. (Chick) Harbert." Accessed September 3, 2023. michigansportshof.org.

———. "Walter E. (Wally) Burkemo." Accessed October 23, 2023. michigansportshof.org.

(Montreal) Gazette. "Bobby Locke Has 32-33-65 in Qualifying for British Open." Associated Press, July 7, 1953.

———. "Cooper and Armour Playoff Today for U.S. Golf Laurels." Associated Press, June 17, 1927.

———. "Hogan Takes British Open with Final 68." Associated Press, July 11, 1953.

———. "Locke Paces British Qualifiers." Associated Press, July 8, 1953.

Moore, David. "The History of Oakmont Country Club." oakmontcc.org.

———. Interview with the author, October 2023.

Moss, Richard J. *The Kingdom of Golf in America.* Lincoln: University of Nebraska Press, 2013.

New York Times. "P.G.A. Tourney Will Open Today." Special to the New York Times, August 14, 1922.

———. "Pro Golfing Stars Beaten at Oakmont." Special to the New York Times, August 15, 1922.

———. "Sarazen Is Victor over Emmet French." Special to the New York Times, August 19, 1922.

———. "Sarazen Once More Defeats Hutchison." Special to the New York Times, August 17, 1922.

———. "Sarazen Wins from Bobby Cruickshank." Special to the New York Times, August 18, 1922.

———. "Tom Kerrigan Puts Out Farrell, 4–3." Special to the New York Times, August 16, 1922.

NJSports.com. "Al Besselink." Accessed February 10, 2023.

OakmontCC.org. "Henry & William Fownes." Accessed September 8, 2023.

Ohio Golf Association. "Frank Stranahan." Accessed April 12, 2023. ohiogolf.org.

O'Keefe, John. "Mike Souchak, Golfer." *Sports Illustrated*, January 16, 1956.

———. "Tommy Bolt, Tempestuous Golfer." *Sports Illustrated*, June 8, 1959.

Oklahoma Golf Hall of Fame. "Tommy Bolt." Accessed June 7, 2023.

TheOpen.com. "Ben Hogan at the Open in 1953." Accessed April 14, 2023.

———. "1953 Carnoustie." April 14, 2023.

The Open Championship Media Guide. U.S. Open tournament program, 2011.

Palm Beach Post. "Boros Rally Shatters Hogan's Golf Dynasty." United Press, June 15, 1952.

Panmure Golf Club. "The Great Hogan at Panmure." Accessed January 11, 2023. panmuregolfclub.co.uk.

Parascenzo, Marino. "Fownes and Oakmont: Stern Stewardship, Championship Mettle." usga.org, March 1, 2016.

———. "The Oakmont Reputation." 60th PGA Championship Tournament Program, Oakmont Country Club, 1978.

———. "A Player's Club." *The 1994 U.S. Open Official Magazine*. New York: Times Mirror Magazines, 1994.

Pennink, Frank. "They Sit on Twin Thrones." *Golf Monthly*, August 1953.

Peper, George. "Say a Prayer." *The 1994 U.S. Open Official Magazine*. New York: Times Mirror Magazines, 1994.

Pittsburgh Post-Gazette. "Alexander Wins PGA Qualifying Medal with 134." Associated Press, May 21, 1948.

———. "Ben Hogan's Hot Finish Wins Masters." Associated Press, April 11, 1951.

———. "Demaret Cards 69 for 283, Third Masters Title." Associated Press, April 11, 1950.

———. "'53 National Open at Oakmont Will Be Revised Sharply." Associated Press, June 13, 1952.

———. "Hogan Beats Oliver for PGA Title." United Press, August 26, 1946.

———. "Hogan's 138 Takes Open Lead." Associated Press, June 14, 1952.

———. "Hogan's Record 274 Wins Masters Golf." Associated Press, April 13, 1953.

———. "Hogan Takes Masters Golf Lead with 139." Associated Press, April 11, 1953.

———. "Horton Smith Wins Augusta Tourney." Associated Press, April 7, 1936.

———. "Horton Smith Wins; Jones Far Behind." Associated Press, March 26, 1934.

———. "Jim Ferrier Blasts Mark in P.G.A. Qualifying Round." United Press, August 21, 1946.

———. "Jones Continues Shaky at Augusta." Associated Press, March 24, 1934.

———. "Jones Off Form in Comeback Attempt." Associated Press, March 23, 1934.

———. "Jones Vies with Stars in Comeback." Associated Press, March 22, 1934.

———. "National Open Qualifiers." Associated Press, June 14, 1952.

———. "Nelson Beats Down 4 Stroke Lead on Last Nine to Win Augusta Tourney." Associated Press, April 5, 1937.

———. "Nelson Defeats Hogan in Playoff by One Stroke." Associated Press, April 14, 1942.

———. "Nelson Falters under Pressure, Hogan Ties for Masters Golf Lead." United Press, April 13, 1942.

———. "Oliver Edges Nelson, Winning 1-Up." United Press, August 24, 1946.

———. "Palmer, Gafford Fire 69s in Masters." Associated Press, April 4, 1952.

———. "Picard's 215 Nets Lead in Masters' Tournament." Associated Press, April 4, 1938.

———. "Sammy Snead Favored in Masters Golf Tourney." Associated Press, April 6, 1950.

———. "Sarazen Beats Wood in Golf Playoff." Associated Press, April 9, 1935.

———. "Sarazen Ties Wood in Augusta Golf." Associated Press, April 8, 1935.

———. "Snead's 286 Wins Masters Golf Title." Associated Press, April 7, 1952.

———. "Wood Retains Lead in Masters Tourney." Associated Press, April 5, 1941.

———. "Wood's 6-under 66 Leads in Masters." Associated Press, April 4, 1941.

———. "Wood's 280 Total Wins Masters Golf." Associated Press, April 7, 1941.

Price, Charles. *A Golf Story: Bobby Jones, Augusta National and the Masters Tournament.* Chicago: Triumph Books, 2001.

Rees, Dai, with John Ballantine. *Thirty Years of Championship Golf.* London: Stanley Paul, 1968.

Rice, Grantland. "Horton Smith Captures Masters Tourney, Jones outside Money." *Spokane (WA) Spokesman-Review*, March 26, 1934.

———. "Miracle Blow Wipes Out Lead." *Spokane (WA) Spokesman-Review*, April 7, 1935.

———. "Nelson Leads in Golf Play." *Spokane (WA) Spokesman-Review*, April 3, 1937.

———. "Via the Short Route." *American Golfer*, September 1934.

Roberts, Tony. *Golf's Magnificent Challenge.* New York: McGraw-Hill, 1989.

Robledo, Fred. "For the Record, Sam Snead Had No Fear of Hogan." *Los Angeles Times*, February 17, 1991.

Romine, Brentley. "The Toughest 18." *Golfweek Magazine*, July 2018.

Sarasota Herald-Tribune. "Oakmont, the Champ, the Man to Beat." June 10, 1953.

———. "PGA Tour Family Has Lost One of Its True Pioneers in Mike Souchak." September 4, 2008.

Sarazen, Gene, and Herbert Warren Wind. *Thirty Years of Championship Golf: The Life and Times of Gene Sarazen.* London: A&C Black, 1990.

Satterfield, Bill. "Oakmont Country Club." golfgurus.com.

Scott, Lisa. Interview with the author, April 2023.

Scott, Tim. *Ben Hogan: The Myths Everyone Knows, the Man No One Knew.* Chicago: Triumph Books, 2013.

Seitz, Nick. "How to Improve Your Golf Swing: Watch Snead." *New York Times*, May 5, 1974.

Snead, Sam, with George Mendoza. *Slammin' Sam: An Autobiography.* New York: Donald L. Fine, 1986.

Sommers, Robert. "I'll Always Remember." *The 1994 U.S. Open Official Magazine*. New York: Times Mirror Magazines, 1994.

———. *The U.S. Open: Golf's Ultimate Challenge*. Oxford: Oxford University Press, June 13, 1996.

Spartanburg (SC) Herald. "Bashful Byron Nelson's 66 Leads Golfers at Augusta." Associated Press, April 2, 1937.

———. "Guldahl Shoots 68 to Grab Lead in Augusta Golf Play." Associated Press, April 4, 1937.

Spokane Daily Chronicle. "Confident Boros Wins Open Title." United Press, June 16, 1952.

———. "Harrison Leads Pro Golf Field." Associated Press, August 20, 1946.

Spokane (WA) Spokesman-Review. "Bobby Jones Is Far down in Masters' Open Golf Tournament." Associated Press, April 2, 1939.

———. "Ferrier Blasts New Golf Mark." Associated Press, August 21, 1946.

———. "Guldahl Wins Augusta Cup." Associated Press, April 3, 1939.

———. "Lloyd Mangrum Catches Fire to Set Competitive Golf Scoring Record." Associated Press, April 5, 1940.

———. "Ward Shoots Sparkling 68 to Climb High among Pros in Golf Tourney." Associated Press, April 6, 1940.

TheSports.org. "The Open Championship 1953." Accessed January 26, 2023.

Sports Illustrated. "The Elegant Masters." April 4, 1960.

———. "The Masters." April 1, 1963.

———. "Spring Sets the Mood of the Masters." April 2, 1962.

Springfield Union. "Mighty Ben Hogan Wins Master Title with 274." April 13, 1953.

St. Petersburg (FL) Times. "Craig Wood's 66 Leads Masters by Five Strokes." United Press, April 4, 1941.

———. "Harmon Cards Blistering, Record-Tying 279 to Win Masters Golf Tourney." Associated Press, April 12, 1948.

———. "Nelson Holds Masters Lead, Ben Hogan Threatens." United Press, April 12, 1942.

Stennett, Robert. Interview with the author, May 2023.

Stollo, Lawrence M. "Ben Hogan Registers Par-Shattering 67 to Lead National Open by 3 Strokes." *Youngstown (OH) Vindicator*, June 12, 1953.

Strite, Dick. "Ben Hogan Stages Great Comeback to Take PGA Title from Ed Oliver." *Eugene (OR) Register-Guard*, August 26, 1946.

———. "Porky Oliver, Ben Hogan PGA Tourney Finalists." *Eugene (OR) Register-Guard*, August 25, 1946.

Student, Victoria. "The Outward Nine: Great Open Moments at Oakmont." usga.org, May 26, 2016.

Taggart, Bert. "Open Field Set to Tee Off at Oakmont Today." *Pittsburgh Post-Gazette*, June 6, 1935.

Tait, Alistair. "'Carnasty' Consensus." *Golfweek Magazine*, July 2018.

Talbot, Gayle. "Byron Nelson Beats Ben Hogan in Playoff to Win Second Masters Golf Title." *Youngstown (OH) Vindicator*, April 14, 1942.

———. "Nelson Battles Hogan in Playoff for Masters Title Today." *Youngstown (OH) Vindicator*, April 13, 1942.

Terrell, Roy. "A Golf Course for Men of Steel." *Sports Illustrated*, June 11, 1952.

Texas Golf Hall of Fame. "Lloyd Mangrum." texasgolfhof.org, 2023.

———. "Tommy Bolt." texasgolfhof.org, 2023.

Time Magazine. "At Oakmont." August 31, 1925.

———. "Augusta National." January 23, 1933.

———. "Down in Four." September 22, 1930.

———. "Masters in Augusta." April 2, 1934.

———. "Money Player." January 26, 1953.

———. "Prophetic Master." April 20, 1953.

———. "The Wee Ice Mon." July 20, 1953.

Toledo (OH) Blade. "Ben Hogan Wins British Open with 282." Associated Press, July 10, 1953.

———. "British Open Playoff Would Have Been Tough for Hogan." July 11, 1953.

———. "Stranahan and Hogan Trailing in Open." Associated Press, July 9, 1953.

Towle, Mike. *I Remember Ben Hogan*. Nashville: Cumberland House, 2000.

Triumph Books. *Tiger Woods: The Grandest Slam*. Chicago: Triumph Books, January 1, 2001.

United States Golf Association. "U.S. Open History 1953." June 18, 2013. golfcompendium .com, accessed January 11, 2022.

University of Miami Sports Hall of Fame. "Al Besselink." Accessed June 7, 2023. umsportshalloffame.com.

University of St. Andrews. "Open Championship 1953." Accessed April 14, 2023. collections .st-andrews.ac.uk.

Ward-Thomas, Pat. *The Lay of the Land: A Collection of the Golf Writings of Pat Ward-Thomas*. New York: Classics of Golf, 1990.

Ward-Thomas, Pat, Herbert Warren Wind, Charles Price, and Peter Thomson. *World Atlas of Golf*. San Diego: Thunder Bay Press, 2001.

Werden, Lincoln A. "Hogan Vanquishes Turnesa to Win His Second P.G.A. Championship." *New York Times*, May 26, 1948.

Williamson, Trevor. Interview with the author, March 2023.

Wind, Herbert Warren. "The Age of Hogan." *Sports Illustrated*, June 20, 1955.

———, ed. *The Complete Golfer*. New York: Simon & Schuster, 1991.

———. *Following Through*. New York: Harper Perennial, 1995.

———. *The Story of American Golf*. New York: Knopf, 1975.

———. "The Ways of a Perfect Caddy." *Sports Illustrated*, February 6, 1956.

Wright, Alfred. "Championship Trial on a U.S. Sahara." *Sports Illustrated*, June 11, 1952.

———. "Golf's First Summit." *Sports Illustrated*, April 3, 1961.

Wright, Ben. *Good Bounces & Bad Lies: The Autobiography of Ben Wright*. Chelsea MI: Sleeping Bear Press, 1999.

———. Interview with the author, April 2020.

Yocum, Guy. "It's Time to Remember Sam Snead." golfdigest.com, July 8, 2019.

———. "Ken Venturi on Rewind." golfdigest.com, June 30, 2013.

———. "My Shot: Tommy Bolt." golfdigest.com, August 26, 2008.

Youngstown (OH) Vindicator. "National Open Golf Scores." June 13, 1953.

———. "National Open Qualifying Scores." June 11, 1953.